Praise for *The Rhe*

"Black explores the rhetoric of the New Tes... ...y. He does not limit his treatment to the standard handbooks nor does he confine his insights to the most obvious places in the New Testament. He guides readers through a wide range of ancient theory—including the *Characters* of Theophrastus and *On the Sublime* by Longinus—and shows their relevance in unexpected places, such as the Lukan parables, the last supper discourses of the Fourth Gospel, and a mysterious narrative in Acts. With an eye to his audience, he finally focuses on the parabolic rhetoric appropriate to preaching, using the ancient masters Augustine and Quintilian. Any Christian orator, a.k.a. preacher, will find this work enormously helpful."
—Harold Attridge, Sterling Professor of Divinity, Yale Divinity School

"Here is a book for all who appreciate the power of language. Written for those charged to communicate the faith of the New Testament witnesses, it is also to be commended to those who may be suspicious of either rhetoric or the Bible. With understated grace, Clifton Black's updated 2001 collection of essays instructs and charms, and embodies what it is getting at."
—M. Eugene Boring, I. Wylie and Elizabeth M. Briscoe Professor of New Testament Emeritus, Brite Divinity School, Texas Christian University

"This revised, updated, and expanded edition of Clifton Black's book of incisive essays on rhetorical study of the Gospels and Acts illumines the rhetorical—and theological—artistry of these writings through a series of selective probes. Readers gain perspective on the diverse contemporary approaches to rhetorical analysis of the New Testament. Seven chapters refresh and update treatments in the 2001 edition. New chapters bring Luke's parables spinning into dialogue with Theophrastus's delightfully biting character sketches and then mine the wisdom of Quintilian, the first-century Roman jurist and teacher of rhetoric, with the aim of informing and inspiring the craft of preaching today. These are gems, alone worth the price of admission. Clifton Black, intrepid and astute biblical interpreter, is at his best here; while leading readers to renewed and deepened appreciation of the rhetorical, literary, and theological artistry of the Gospels and Acts, he never fails to entertain the reader with elegant word crafting, literary artistry, and theological acumen of his own. It's a very good read and a useful resource for preachers, theological students, and their teachers."
—John T. Carroll, Harriet Robertson Fitts Memorial Professor of New Testament, Union Presbyterian Seminary

"Is it possible for a volume on ancient rhetoric and the gospel to be scholarly, wise, pertinent, and witty all at once? When it's in the hands of Clifton Black, the answer is clearly yes. This welcome revised and expanded edition of Black's excellent *Rhetoric of the Gospel* is a magnificent resource for the student and the preacher alike. The chapter where Black brings the old lawyer and rhetorician Quintilian into the homiletics classroom, just to name but one of many delicious morsels in this volume, crackles with intellectual electricity, humor, and insight."

—Thomas G. Long, Bandy Professor of Preaching,
Candler School of Theology, Emory University

"Rhetorical criticism rarely penetrates New Testament narrative material in the Gospels and Acts, and C. Clifton Black's book is therefore somewhat of a rarity, and that is what makes his book both remarkable and valuable. Equipped with a complete rhetorical toolbox, Black uses the full range of classical and 'New Rhetorical' approaches to probe the theology that shapes the characters, orations, and sermons in this narrative world. In this book, a skilled rhetorician collects a colloquy of voices 'within a kind of New Rhetorical framework, "baptized" into the service of Christian theology and practice.' In this colloquy, history and rhetoric cooperate in the belief that in Jesus Christ, God 'was and remains personally at work for the redemption of all humanity and creation.' Like the pearl of great price, this gem of a book will enrich 'all those interested in the artistry and argument by which the Gospels and Acts attempt to convince readers of the truth of Christianity.' Highly recommended!"

—Troy W. Martin, Professor of Biblical Studies, Saint Xavier University

"This book is a delight. Clifton Black shares his unique capacities for wit and clarity in coherent theological appreciations of New Testament narratives, read through the eyes of classical rhetoric. His final chapters on preaching may shock—and educate."

—Francis J. Moloney, SDB, Senior Professorial Fellow,
Australian Catholic University, Melbourne, Australia

"C. Clifton Black enthralls us as our guide on a tour of the rhetoric of the Gospels and Acts. As we visit these works, Black helps us to appreciate their artistic and structural features. We get the inside scoop on the creation of these works, and their purpose and message. This tour is not given in isolation, for traditional questions and methods of interpretation are engaged all the way along. Black's own rhetorical flare, which is as skilled as the works he describes, makes for a delightful tour!"

—Duane F. Watson, Professor of New Testament Studies, Malone University

"Clifton Black has spent his academic life loving Scripture. In this book Black marvels at the creative artistry of these early Christian preachers who produced literature that changed the world. Something about the truth of Jesus Christ called for an unprecedented outburst of literary artistry. We could have no better guide through the art that is Scripture than Clifton Black."

—William H. Willimon, United Methodist Bishop and Professor
of the Practice of Christian Ministry, Duke Divinity School

The Rhetoric of the Gospel

SECOND EDITION

C. CLIFTON BLACK

The Rhetoric of the Gospel

Theological Artistry in the Gospels and Acts

SECOND EDITION

WESTMINSTER
JOHN KNOX PRESS
LOUISVILLE · KENTUCKY

© 2013 C. Clifton Black

Second edition
Published by Westminster John Knox Press
Louisville, Kentucky

First edition
Published by Chalice Press
St. Louis, Missouri

13 14 15 16 17 18 19 20 21 22—10 9 8 7 6 5 4 3 2 1

Unless otherwise identified, Scripture quotations are from the New Revised Standard Version of the Bible, copyright © 1989 by the Division of Christian Education of the National Council of the Churches of Christ in the U.S.A., and used by permission. See the list of abbreviations for other versions occasionally cited.

See acknowledgments, pp. xiii–xiv, for additional permission information.

Book design by Sharon Adams
Cover design by Dilu Nicholas
Cover illustration: abstract orange background © Attitude/shutterstock.com;
Paper on wood background or texture © Piotr Zajc/shutterstock.com

Library of Congress Cataloging-in-Publication Data

Black, C. Clifton (Carl Clifton), 1955–
    The rhetoric of the Gospel : theological artistry in the gospels and Acts / C. Clifton Black. — Second [edition].
        pages cm.
    Includes bibliographical references and indexes.
    ISBN 978-0-664-23822-3 (alk. paper)
    1. Bible. N.T.—Language, Style. 2. Rhetoric in the Bible. 3. Rhetorical criticism. I. Title.
    BS2575.2.B54 2013
    226'.066—dc23

                                                                            2013003070

For my brother
James Franklin Black, M.D.

Contents

Preface to the Second Edition

By dominical precept we know that new wine doesn't belong in old wineskins (Mark 2:22). What of old wine in new wineskins? Since Jesus does not directly address that question, the agents of Westminster John Knox Press have apparently reckoned it seemly to reissue this book, first published in 2001. For that kindness, and particularly for the conscientious counsel of my editors, Marianne Blickenstaff and Daniel Braden, I am grateful. Like its predecessor this volume gathers kindred studies undertaken across many years, updated to take account of recent research. Chapters 4 and 9 are fresh additions, written for this edition. Though grounded in the classical tradition of rhetoric, where I feel most at home, this book persists in adopting a broad approach, embracing an audience of scholars and pastors, graduate and theological students. Everyone is welcome to this sideboard; nosh as you please.

In addition to the many creditors acknowledged in the first edition's preface, I am indebted to Melanie A. Howard, a candidate for the PhD in New Testament at Princeton Theological Seminary, who provided invaluable bibliographical assistance in bringing my thoughts up to date. I also thank Professor John T. Carroll, of Union Presbyterian Seminary, and Professor George L. Parsenios, of Princeton Seminary, for their critique and encouragement of my work.

C. C. B.

THE NATIVITY OF ST JOHN THE BAPTIST, JUNE 24, 2012
PRINCETON, NEW JERSEY

Preface to the First Edition

Some years ago my friend and editor Jon Berquist invited me to write a primer on rhetorical analysis of the New Testament for students in seminaries. Since by then several fine introductions to the field had already appeared in print, my heart didn't leap at the thrill of opportunity.

As the days thence were melting away, I did notice, however, two curiosities. To me it seemed, first, that the lion's portion of New Testament rhetorical inquiry was being awarded the Epistles and even the Revelation to John. Meanwhile, a number of folk expressed to me appreciation for some literary studies, scattered in places far off the beaten path. For those reasons I am emboldened to gather these pieces on the Gospels and Acts between more convenient covers, belatedly accepting while modifying Dr. Berquist's kind invitation. Some who have encouraged me in this venture are pastors. Along with theological students and other scholarly colleagues, preachers are among those for whom I have prepared this book. I hope it may find its way into their hands. Even more, I hope it may help them, despite its refusal of pretense to offer practical guidance in the art of sermon preparation.

The chapters assembled here originally appeared in various books and journals across a dozen years. I am indeed grateful to all the publishers who have graciously permitted me use of those essays for this fresh purpose. All the contents have been revised, lightly or heavily, to fit the need. Throughout I have made a good-faith attempt to update notes and bibliography. Rhetorical criticism has become so voluminous that I cannot hope to have succeeded; where I have failed, I can only beg my reader's pardon.

I just spoke of my debt to Jon L. Berquist, Academic Editor of Chalice Press. There are others to whom I am debtor. Several chapters were immediately stimulated by the findings of scholars who have taught me much about the New Testament, even when I have been unable to agree with all their conclusions. For introducing me to the study of rhetoric, I thank George A. Kennedy, Paddison Professor of Classics, Emeritus, at the University of North Carolina at Chapel Hill, and Visiting Professor of Speech Communication at Colorado State University. Earlier versions of this material received critical readings by many learned friends: Jouette M. Bassler, R. Alan Culpepper, Beverly Roberts Gaventa, James B. Glasscock, Joel B. Green, Amy-Jill Levine, John R. Levison, Vickie E. Pittard, Frank Thielman, Duane F. Watson, Lawrence M. Wills, and Patrick J. Willson. For the blemishes and howlers that remain, they are not to be faulted: them I heard but didn't always heed. For technological and bibliographical assistance, I am grateful to Justin Mitchell and Callie Plunket, students matriculating for the PhD at, respectively, Southern Methodist University and Princeton Theological Seminary. As always, my debts to Harriet and Caroline are as inexpressible as they are profound, and affectionate.

C. CLIFTON BLACK

THE FEAST DAY OF SAINT PETER AND SAINT PAUL

JUNE 29, 2000

Acknowledgments

These credits are a continuation of the copyright page. Grateful acknowledgment is made to the following for permission to quote from copyrighted material and in most cases develop it further:

Chapter 1: Alfred Publishing, for kind permission to reprint lyrics from "Show Me" (from *My Fair Lady*). Words by Alan Jay Lerner. Music by Frederick Loewe. © 1956 (Renewed) Alan Jay Lerner and Frederick Loewe. Publication and Allied Rights Assigned to Chappell & Co., Inc. All rights reserved. Used by permission.

Chapter 1: William B. Eerdmans Publishing Company, for kind permission to reprint, in revised form, the original version of chapter 1, "Rhetorical Criticism," pp. 256–77, in Joel B. Green, ed., *Hearing the New Testament: Strategies for Interpretation* (Grand Rapids: Mich.; and Carlisle: William B. Eerdmans/Paternoster Press, 1995); revised, pp. 166–88 in Joel B. Green, ed., *Hearing the New Testament: Strategies for Interpretation* (2nd ed.; Grand Rapids, Mich., and Carlisle: William B. Eerdmans/Paternoster Press, 2010).

Chapter 2: An earlier version of chapter 2 first appeared under the title "Depth of Characterization and Degrees of Faith in Matthew," in *Society of Biblical Literature 1989 Seminar Papers*, edited by David J. Lull, Society of Biblical Literature Seminar Papers Series (Atlanta: Society of Biblical Literature, 1989), 604–23.

Chapter 3: T&T Clark, an imprint of Bloomsbury Publishing PLC, for kind permission to reprint, in revised form, the original version of chapter 3, "An Oration at Olivet: Some Rhetorical Dimensions of Mark 13," in Duane F. Watson, editor, *Persuasive Artistry: Studies in New Testament Rhetoric in Honor of George A. Kennedy*, Journal for the Study of the New Testament Supplement Series 50 (Sheffield: JSOT Press, 1991), pp. 66–92. Copyright © 1991 Sheffield Academic Press.

Abbreviations

GENERAL

//	and parallel(s), parallel to
alt.	altered (adapted)
AT	author's translation
b.	born
BCE	before the common era (= BC, before Christ)
ca.	circa, around
CE	common era (= AD, anno Domini)
chap.	chapter
contra	against
d.	died
ed(s).	editor(s), edited by
e.g.	*exempli gratia*, for example
esp.	especially, location of a quote
ET	English translation
et al.	*et alii*, and others
(et) passim	(and) here and there, throughout
ibid.	*ibidem*, in the same place (as immediately preceding)
idem	the same author (as immediately preceding)
i.e.	*id est*, that is
L	Hypothetical Lukan Tradition or Source
lit.	literally
M	Hypothetical Matthean Tradition or Source
n.	(foot)note

N.B.	*note bene*, note carefully
NF	*neue Folge*, new series
no./#	number
NT	New Testament
OT	Old Testament
pace	contrary to the opinion of, yet with all due respect to
pr.	prologue
Q	Hypothetical tradition or source for both Matthew and Luke
repr.	reprinted
rev.	revised
trans.	translator(s), translated by
v., vv.	verse, verses
vol.	volume
vs.	versus

ANCIENT TEXTS

Greek and Roman Rhetoricians

De or.	Cicero, *De oratore* = *On the Orator*
Eloc.	Demetrius, *De elocutione* = *On Style*
Inst.	Quintilian, *Institutio oratoria* = *Education of the Orator*
Inv.	Cicero, *De inventione rhetorica* = *Invention of Rhetoric*
Opt. gen.	Cicero, *De optimo genere oratorum* = *The Best Kind of Orator*
Or.	Cicero, *Orator* = *Orator*
Part. or.	Cicero, *Partitiones oratoriae* = *The Parts of Oratory*
Per. id.	Hermogenes of Tarsus, *Peri ideōn* = *On Types of Style*
Poet.	Aristotle, *Poetica* = *Poetics*
Rhet.	Aristotle, *Ars rhetorica* = *The Art of Rhetoric*
Rhet. ad Alex.	Anaximenes of Lampsacus (?), *Rhetorica ad Alexandrum* = *Rhetoric for Alexander*
Rhet. ad Her.	Cornificius (?), *Rhetorica ad Herennium* = *Rhetoric for Herennius*
Subl.	Longinus, *On Sublimity*

Other Greek and Latin Authors

Eth. Nic.	Aristotle, *Ethica Nicomachea* = *Nicomachean Ethics*
Hist.	Thucydides, *History of the Peloponnesian War*
Mem.	Xenophon, *Memorabilia*
Phaedr.	Plato, *Phaedrus*
Polit.	Plato, *Politicus* = *Politics*

Resp.	Plato, *Respublica* = *The Republic*
Soph.	Plato, *Sophista* = *Sophist*
Wars	Herodotus, *Persian Wars*

Old Testament Apocrypha

2 Esd.	2 Esdras (= *4 Ezra*)
1–4 Macc.	1–4 Maccabees
Sir.	Sirach (= Ecclesiasticus)
Tob.	Tobit

Old Testament Pseudepigrapha

2 Apoc. Bar.	*2 Baruch (Syriac Apocalypse)*
1 En.	*1 Enoch*
Ep. Arist.	*Epistle of Aristeas*
4 Ezra	*4 Ezra* = 2 Esdras
Jub.	*Jubilees*
Sib. Or.	*Sibylline Oracles*
T. Benj.	*Testament of Benjamin*
T. Jos.	*Testament of Joseph*
T. Levi	*Testament of Levi*
T. Naph.	*Testament of Naphtali*
T. Reu.	*Testament of Reuben*

Other Jewish Authors

Ant.	Josephus, *Jewish Antiquities*
J.W.	Josephus, *Jewish War*
LXX	Septuagint

Rabbinic Literature

b.	Babylonian Talmud (before a tractate)
m.	Mishnah (before a tractate)
t.	Tosefta (before a tractate)

Apostolic Fathers

Barn.	*Barnabas*
1 Clem.	*1 Clement*

Herm. *Sim.*   Shepherd of Hermas, *Similitudes*
Ign. *Eph.*   Ignatius, *To the Ephesians*

Patristic Authors

Adv. haer.   Irenaeus, *Adversus (omnes) haereses = Against (All) Heresies*
1 Apol.   Justin Martyr, *First Apology*
Ap. Const.   *Apostolic Constitutions*
Conf.   Augustine, *Confessiones = Confessions*
Doctr. chr.   Augustine, *De doctrina christiana = Christian Instruction*
Gos. Thom.   *Gospel of Thomas*
Hist. eccl.   Eusebius, *Historia ecclesiastica = Church History*
Serm.   Augustine, *Sermones = Sermons*
Trin.   Augustine, *De trinitate = The Trinity*
Util. cred.   Augustine, *De utilitate credendi = The Usefulness of Believing*

MODERN SOURCES

Dictionaries, Encyclopedias, and Other Reference Works

ABD   *Anchor Bible Dictionary.* Edited by D. N. Freedman. 6 vols. New York: Doubleday, 1992.

ANRW   *Aufstieg und Niedergang der römischen Welt: Geschichte und Kultur Roms im Spiegel der neueren Forschung.* Edited by H. Temporini and W. Haase. Berlin: W. de Gruyter, 1972–.

IB   *The Interpreter's Bible.* Edited by G. A. Buttrick et al. 12 vols. New York: Abingdon Press, 1951–57.

IDB   *The Interpreter's Dictionary of the Bible.* Edited by G. A. Buttrick et al. 4 vols. Nashville: Abingdon Press, 1962. Supplementary volume, 1976.

LSJ   *A Greek-English Lexicon.* Compiled by H. G. Liddell and R. Scott. Revised by H. S. Jones and R. McKenzie. 9th ed. with rev. supplement. Oxford: Oxford University Press, 1996.

NIB   *The New Interpreter's Bible.* Edited by L. E. Keck. 12 vols. Nashville: Abingdon Press, 1994–2004.

RAC   *Reallexikon für Antike und Christentum.* Edited by T. Klauser et al. Stuttgart: Hiersemann,1950–.

TDNT   *Theological Dictionary of the New Testament.* Edited by G. Kittel and G. Friedrich. Translated by G. W. Bromiley. 10 vols. Grand Rapids: Wm. B. Eerdmans Publishing Co., 1964–76.

Journals

AfER	African Ecclesial Review
AsJT	Asia Journal of Theology
AThR	Anglican Theological Review
Bib	Biblica
BibInt	Biblical Interpretation
BJRL	Bulletin of the John Rylands University Library of Manchester
BMCR	The Bryn Mawr Classical Review
BR	Biblical Research
BSac	Bibliotheca sacra
BTB	Biblical Theology Bulletin
CBQ	Catholic Biblical Quarterly
ChrMin	The Christian Ministry
CritInq	Critical Inquiry
Di	Dialog
EstBib	Estudios bíblicos
ExpTim	Expository Times
Greg	Gregorianum
HSCP	Harvard Studies in Classical Philology
HTR	Harvard Theological Review
HUCA	Hebrew Union College Annual
Int	Interpretation
JBL	Journal of Biblical Literature
JBPR	Journal of Biblical and Phenomenological Research
JLT	Journal of Literature and Theology
JR	Journal of Religion
JSJ	Journal for the Study of Judaism in the Persian, Hellenistic, and Roman Periods
JSNT	Journal for the Study of the New Testament
Neot	Neotestamentica
NTS	New Testament Studies
PR	Philosophy and Rhetoric
ProEcc	Pro ecclesia
PRSt	Perspectives in Religious Studies
PSB	Princeton Seminary Bulletin
QJS	Quarterly Journal of Speech
RelSRev	Religious Studies Review
ResQ	Restoration Quarterly
RevExp	Review and Expositor
SBLSP	Society of Biblical Literature Seminar Papers

Sem	Semeia
SJT	Scottish Journal of Theology
SM	Speech Monographs
SR	Studies in Religion / Sciences religieuses
ZNW	Zeitschrift für die neutestamentliche Wissenschaft und die Kunde der älteren Kirche

Commentary and Monograph Series

AB	Anchor Bible
ABG	Arbeiten zur Bibel und ihrer Geschichte
ACNT	Augsburg Commentary on the New Testament
AnBib	Analecta biblica
ANTC	Abingdon New Testament Commentaries
AnVlad	Analecta Vladaton
BETL	Bibliotheca ephemeridum theologicarum lovaniensium
BPC	Biblical Performance Criticism
BZNW	Beihefte zur Zeitschrift für die neutestamentliche Wissenschaft und die Kunde der älteren Kirche
CCJSV	Cambridge Classical Journal Supplementary Volume
CHS	Center for Hermeneutical Studies
ConBNT	Coniectanea biblica: New Testament Series
CWS	Classics of Western Spirituality
ÉC	Études et commentaires
ECC	Eerdmans Critical Commentary
ESEC	Emory Studies in Early Christianity
FBBS	Facet Books: Biblical Studies
FF	Foundations and Facets: Literary Facets
FRLANT	Forschungen zur Religion und Literatur des Alten und Neuen Testaments
GBSOT	Guides to Biblical Scholarship: Old Testament
HCP	A History of Christian Preaching
HTKNT	Herders theologischer Kommentar zum Neuen Testament
HUT	Hermeneutische Untersuchungen zur Theologie
IBC	Interpretation: A Bible Commentary for Teaching and Preaching
JSNTSup	Journal for the Study of the New Testament: Supplement Series
KBANT	Kommentare und Beiträge zum Alten und Neuen Testament
LCL	Loeb Classical Library
LLA	Library of Liberal Arts
LNTS	Library of New Testament Studies

NCB	New Century Bible
NCE	Norton Critical Edition
NHS	A New History of the Sermon
NICNT	New International Commentary on the New Testament
NIGTC	New International Greek Testament Commentary
NovTSup	Novum Testamentum Supplements
NTH	New Testament Handbooks
NTL	New Testament Library
NTM	New Testament Message
NTT	New Testament Theology
NTTS	New Testament Tools and Studies
OBT	Overtures to Biblical Theology
OWC	Oxford World's Classics
PC	Proclamation Commentaries
PGC	Pelican Gospel Commentaries
PS	Pauline Studies
PSBSup	Princeton Seminary Bulletin Supplements
PTMS	Pittsburgh Theological Monograph Series
SAC	Studies in Antiquity and Christianity
SBLDS	Society of Biblical Literature Dissertation Series
SBLSymS	Society of Biblical Literature Symposium Series
SemeiaSt	Semeia Studies
SNTSMS	Society for New Testament Studies Monograph Series
SP	Sacra pagina
SPNT	Studies on Personalities in the New Testament
SRR	Studies in Rhetoric and Religion
TBS	Tools for Biblical Study
TWAS	Twayne's World Authors Series
VCSup	Vigiliae christianae Supplements
WGRW	Writings from the Greco-Roman World
WSA	Works of Saint Augustine
WUNT	Wissenschaftliche Untersuchungen zum Neuen Testament
WWSup	Word and World Supplement Series

Modern Versions of the Bible

GOODSPEED	*The Complete Bible: An American Translation*, E. J. Goodspeed
KJV	King James Version
NEB	New English Bible
NIV	New International Version

NJB	New Jerusalem Bible
NJPS	*Tanakh: The Holy Scriptures; The New JPS Translation according to the Traditional Hebrew Text*
NKJV	New King James Version
NRSV	New Revised Standard Version
RSV	Revised Standard Version

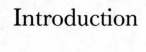

Introduction

Chapter One

Rhetorical Questions
in New Testament Study

Words!
Words! Words! I'm so sick of words!
I get words all day through;
First from him, now from you!
Is that all you blighters can do?

Eliza Doolittle[1]

As Wilhelm Wuellner once prophesied, a tidal wave of rhetorical analysis continues to pound NT conferences, journals, and bibliographies.[2] Its force is tsunamic, with no signs of ebbing. For the uninitiated this must seem bizarre, since the "rhetoric" to which our news media alert us is, in the lead entry of *The Random House Dictionary of the English Language*, "the undue use of exaggeration or display; bombast."[3] If this is what NT interpreters are now expected to study, most of us would gladly lie down until the urge passes.

The problem, as one might guess, lies less with rhetoric than with its cheap connotation in our vernacular. For wherever someone attempts to persuade others—whether from the pulpit or the Op-Ed page, in a term paper or around the kitchen table—there you find rhetoric employed. As I shall use the term in this book, rhetoric bears on those distinctive properties of human discourse, especially its artistry and argument, by which early Christian authors endeavored to convince others of the truth of their beliefs.

---

1. Lerner and Loewe, *My Fair Lady*, 146.
2. Wuellner, "Rhetorical Criticism." Watson tabulates thousands of investigations in *Rhetoric* (2006).
3. Flexner, *Random House Dictionary*, 1650.

THE TRADITION OF RHETORICAL PRACTICE AND STUDY

If the study of rhetoric appears innovative to modern biblical interpreters, then that bespeaks their philosophical amnesia. The practice of oratory is as old as Homer (ninth or eighth century BCE), whose epics are not only punctuated with heroic speeches but also are themselves exquisite testimonies of the bard's own oratorical craft.[4] By the fifth century BCE the Sicilian teacher Corax, also known as Tisias,[5] had compiled technical handbooks on rhetoric for the use of ordinary Greek citizens in political assemblies and courts of law.[6] Gorgias (ca. 480–375 BCE) and Isocrates (ca. 436–338 BCE) refined the sophistic approach to rhetoric: the orator's skillful deployment of rhythm, rhyme, and other poetic embellishments to move or to entertain an audience. A backlash against the morally vacuous exploitation of sophistic rhetoric appears in some dialogues of Plato (ca. 429–347 BCE; see esp. his works *Gorgias* and *Phaedrus*).[7] Yet it was Plato's own pupil Aristotle (384–322 BCE) who systematized the theoretical substructure of classical rhetoric and related its practice to the arts, sciences, and dialectical logic in particular.[8]

With the hellenization of the Mediterranean world, first by Alexander the Great (356–323 BCE) and later by imperial Rome (27 BCE–476 CE), technical rhetoric became essential in secondary education and its preparation of Roman citizens for advancement in public life.[9] Although it is impossible (and needless) to demonstrate that Jesus, the earliest apostles, or the authors of the Gospels received formal education in rhetoric, indisputably they lived in a culture whose everyday modes of oral and written discourse were saturated with a rhetorical tradition, mediated by such practitioners and theoreticians as Caecilius (a Sicilian Jew of the late first century BCE), Cicero (106–43 BCE), and Quintilian (ca. 40–95 CE). The influence of technical and sophistic rhetoric on Christian preaching, teaching, and apologetics is manifest throughout the patristic period, conspicuously in the Greek sermons of John Chrysostom (ca. 347–407) and of the three great Cappadocians: Gregory of Nazianzus (ca. 329–389), Basil of Caesarea (ca. 330–379), and Gregory of Nyssa (ca. 330–395).[10] Of the eight most notable Latin fathers

---

4. Toohey, "Epic and Rhetoric," articulates the structure and its elaboration in Nestor's four speeches of the *Iliad* (1.254–84; 7.124–60; 11.656–803; 23.626–50)—an unexpected level of development, since Homer wrote years before the formulation of rhetoric as a discipline.

5. Classicists debate whether Tisias was Corax's pupil or the two names refer to the same person ("Tisias the Crow"). Recent scholarship leans toward the second possibility: see Kennedy, *A New History*, 11, 18, 32–34.

6. Consult Harris, "Law and Oratory."

7. See Herrick, *History and Theory of Rhetoric*, 52–72.

8. Consult Rorty, *Essays on Aristotle's Rhetoric*.

9. Clark's *Rhetoric in Greco-Roman Education* (1957) and S. Bonner's *Education in Ancient Rome* (1977) are standard histories of the subject.

10. See Kennedy, *Greek Rhetoric*, 180–264; Pelikan, *Divine Rhetoric*; Mitchell, *Heavenly Trumpet*.

of the church, three were schooled in rhetoric: Hilary of Poitiers (ca. 315–367), Ambrose (ca. 337–397), and Jerome (ca. 345–420). The remaining five had been professional rhetoricians before their conversion to Christianity: Tertullian (ca. 160–225), Cyprian (d. ca. 258), Arnobius (d. ca. 330), Lactantius (ca. 240–320), and Augustine (354–430).[11] In his celebrated *De doctrina Christiana*, Augustine first educed the implications of rhetorical theory for Christian belief and practice, hermeneutics and homiletics.[12]

Not only did rhetorical study pervade the early Christian tradition; it also enriched the medieval, Renaissance, and Enlightenment academic legacy of which modern theological students are beneficiaries. As barbarism descended on Italy, Cassiodorus Senator (ca. 487–585) kept aflame the study of rhetoric and the other six liberal arts (grammar, dialectic, geometry, arithmetic, astronomy, and music) from his monastery at Vivarium.[13] During the European Renaissance and Reformation, the renewal of biblical criticism and the recovery of Ciceronian rhetoric fit hand in glove in the scholarship of such humanists as Lorenzo Valla (ca. 1406–57), Desiderius Erasmus (1469–1536), Philipp Melanchthon (1497–1560), and John Calvin (1509–64). Buoyed by the neoclassical revival of the arts in Europe and North America during the eighteenth and nineteenth centuries, rhetorical modes of NT analysis persisted into the early twentieth century, as illustrated by the dissertation of the young Rudolf Bultmann (1884–1976)[14] and the still-standard grammar of NT Greek by Friedrich Wilhelm Blass (1843–1907).[15] The exercise and conceptualization of classical rhetoric have exerted profound impact, not only on the NT writings, but also on successive centuries of its study. Viewed in that light, rhetorical criticism is one of the oldest approaches to NT interpretation.

MAJOR CURRENTS IN RHETORICAL CRITICISM

As suggested by the preceding differentiation of its technical, sophistic, and philosophical varieties, orators and their analysts have never agreed on how rhetoric should be conceptualized. Similar disagreement, if not confusion, characterizes contemporary rhetorical analyses of the Bible. Much as "literary criticism" has been applied to so broad a field of interpretive strategies[16] that

---

11. Kennedy, *Classical Rhetoric*, 132–60.
12. R. Green, *Augustine*, is the current critical edition.
13. See Jones, *Cassiodorus Senator*; Murphy, *Rhetoric in the Middle Ages*.
14. Bultmann, *Der Stil*; refined by Stowers, *The Diatribe*.
15. Blass and Debrunner, *Greek Grammar* (first German edition, 1896).
16. During the past sixty years, "literary criticism" has been used with reference to source reconstruction; analysis of poetic structure; study of a narrative's genre, plot, or characters; psychoanthropological decoding of a text's "deep structure"; postmodernist deconstruction of a text by an individual or community of readers; and a great many things besides. For a good overview, see Aune, *Blackwell Companion*, 116–39.

the label probably deserves retirement from overwork, "rhetorical criticism" is a portmanteau that carries kindred yet distinguishable approaches to biblical exegesis.

Rhetorical Analysis as Study of the Bible's Literary Artistry

Among both OT and NT scholars the term "rhetorical criticism" is intimately associated with James Muilenburg (1896–1974), whose 1968 presidential address to the Society of Biblical Literature summed up his career-long interest in biblical poetics while issuing a programmatic call for the study of Hebrew literary composition. Muilenburg conceived rhetorical criticism as a supplement to the work of form critics, among whom he sympathetically numbered himself, and as a corrective to some of that earlier method's exaggerated tendencies. In an era that had stressed a literary genre's typical and representative aspects, abstracted from their settings in Israel's social and religious life, Muilenburg argued for recovery of the particularities of any given pericope—"the many and various devices by which the predications [in a literary unit] are formulated and ordered into a unified whole"—with attention to the author's intention, historical context, and distinctive blending of form and content.[17]

In NT research the writings of Amos Niven Wilder (1895–1993) approximate Muilenburg's understanding of biblical rhetoric. Like Muilenburg's, Wilder's approach was historically grounded, regarding the study of modes of NT discourse as a complement to historical criticism of biblical traditions. Also like Muilenburg, Wilder rejected the separation of form and content: biblical genres like dialogue, story, parable, and poem are "deeply determined by the faith or life-orientation that produced them," which themselves were governed by specific social and religious patterns.[18] More so than Muilenburg, Wilder probed biblical rhetoric's phenomenological dimensions, the ways in which human existence is experienced and interpreted through religious discourse.[19]

Whether Muilenburg and Wilder founded a definable school of rhetorical criticism is debatable. Easier to assess is the degree to which they reopened convergent avenues of research into biblical rhetoric that have ended up veering appreciably from their own approaches. Typical of much interpretation that takes its bearings from Wilder and Muilenburg is an understanding of rhetoric that concentrates on the aesthetic or inherently literary properties of biblical discourse, with

---

17. Muilenburg, "Form Criticism," 4–8. Muilenburg's challenge amounted to proof of a pudding he had tasted a dozen years previously ("Book of Isaiah," in *IB* 5 [1956]). Esp. in Deutero-Isaiah (ibid., 386–93, 415–18), Muilenburg discerned hallmarks of strophic structure and poetic style: parallelism, meter, assonance, triads, and repetitions of key words.

18. Wilder, *Early Christian Rhetoric*, 25–26.

19. See Wilder, *The New Voice* and *Jesus' Parables*; with his approach compare Hyde and Smith, "Hermeneutics and Rhetoric"; and Funk, *Language, Hermeneutic, and Word of God.*

attention paid to its metaphorical, stylistic, and structural features.[20] This mode of rhetorical analysis often melts into so-called New Criticism, adopted by many Anglo-American literary critics of the mid-twentieth century.[21] At the point where it prescinds from considering the historical and social location of biblical texts and their authors' intent, rhetorical criticism of this sort diverges from Muilenburg's or Wilder's own exegetical inclinations.[22]

Analysis of the New Testament according to the Canons of Classical Rhetoric

Muilenburg's and Wilder's historical interests are deliberately fulfilled in the work of the North American classicist George A. Kennedy (b. 1928). For Kennedy, rhetoric refers less to "literary artistry" than to the disciplined art of persuasion, as practiced and theorized by Greeks and Romans of the classical and Hellenistic periods. "What we need to do is to try to hear [early Christian authors'] words as a Greek-speaking audience would have heard them, and that involves some understanding of classical rhetoric," particularly the norms of persuasive discourse that suffused the culture of Mediterranean antiquity. While Kennedy is not the first scholar to have reclaimed technical rhetoric for biblical exegesis,[23] his accessible presentation of classical concepts has been the most influential among English-speaking scholars.[24]

Kennedy's method of rhetorical criticism may be summarized in six steps, the first of which is determining the rhetorical unit to be analyzed. As form critics (like Muilenburg) identify discrete pericopes, so also rhetorical critics like Kennedy search for evidence of inclusio, opening and closure, in a unit of discourse with some magnitude. Second, an attempt is made to define the rhetorical situation: the complex of persons, events, and relations that generates pressure for a verbal response. With this one might compare the form critic's discovery of a genre's *Sitz im Leben*, or setting in life. Third is to identify the primary rhetorical problem addressed by the discourse. Kennedy suggests two classical frameworks within

20. Thus Lund, *Chiasmus in the New Testament*; J. Jackson and Kessler, *Rhetorical Criticism*; Dewey, *Markan Public Debate*.

21. Frye, *The Great Code*; Booth, *Rhetoric of Fiction*; Rhoads, Michie, and Dewey, *Mark as Story*, 2nd ed. (1999).

22. In *Rhetorical Criticism* (1994), Muilenburg's student Trible offers an account of his work and its aftermath.

23. Thus the Venerable Bede (672/73–735), *De schematibus et tropis*: ET, "Concerning Figures and Tropes"; Leon, *The Book of the Honeycomb's Flow* (originating in ca. 1420–75 CE). In the early twentieth century Norden was an important exponent of the Bible's rhetorical artistry, particularly in Paul's Letters: see *Die antike Kunstprosa* and also *Agnostos Theos*.

24. Kennedy, *New Testament Interpretation*, esp. 10. This approach is based on ancient rhetorical handbooks that are all available, with English translation, in the LCL: Aristotle, *Ars rhetorica*; Cicero, *De inventione rhetorica*; Cornificius, *Rhetorica ad Herennium*; and Quintilian, *Institutio oratoria*. See also Wooten, *Hermogenes' "On Types of Style"*; and Kennedy, *Invention and Method*. Critical assessments of Kennedy's scholarship may be found in Black and Watson, *Words Well Spoken*.

which this identification can be made: one may pinpoint the *stasis*, or specific question, at issue (which can be crucial for interpreting Paul's Letters, the speeches in Acts, or Jesus' controversies with Pharisees). Alternatively, the critic can ascertain the kind of judgment that an audience is asked to render: whether it is a *judicial* assessment of past circumstances (e.g., the character of Paul's ministry in Corinth, to which much of 2 Corinthians refers), a *deliberative* reckoning of actions expedient or beneficial for the listeners' future performance (thus the Sermon on the Mount in Matt. 5–7), or the *epideictic* instillation and enhancement of beliefs or values in the present (for instance, Jesus' farewell address to his disciples in John 14–16).[25]

Considering the arrangement (*taxis*) of the parts into a unified discourse is the fourth of Kennedy's critical steps. Compared with the structure of deliberative and epideictic address, judicial oratory displays the most elaborate arrangement: an introductory *proem*, followed by a *narration* of background information, the *proposition* to be proved, the *proof* itself, *refutation* of contrary views, and a concluding *epilogue*. The fifth step is analysis of the discourse's invention and style. Invention (*heuresis*) is the crafting of arguments based on proofs: *ēthos*, the persuasive power of the speaker's authoritative character (see Mark 1:22); *pathos*, the emotional responses generated among listeners (cf. Acts 2:37); and *logos*, the deductive or inductive arguments of the discourse itself (e.g., Heb. 1:1–2:14). Style (*lexis*) refers to the text's choice of words and their formulation in "figures" of speech and of thought. Sixth, reviewing the whole analysis, the critic assesses the unit's rhetorical effectiveness.

In this classical mode rhetorical criticism has stimulated so much NT research that it defies easy summary; nevertheless, some basic trends are discernible. (1) Application of Kennedy's six-stage method to various canonical documents (usually Epistles) is notable in the works by Robert Jewett[26] and Duane Watson.[27] (2) Perhaps most fruitful to date for interpreting the Gospels is the study of *chreiai*, didactic anecdotes developed by Hermogenes of Tarsus (late second century CE) and other rhetoricians for training pupils in composition and orations.[28] (3) As exemplified by Margaret Mitchell's constructive argument for the

---

25. Connor (*Greek Orations*) collects examples of all three major genres of ancient oratory. Great speeches in modern history also conform to these basic genres. Lincoln's Gettysburg Address (November 19, 1863) is an unforgettable instance of epideictic: "that government of the people, by the people, for the people, shall not perish from the earth." Zola's demand that Dreyfus be exonerated of treason (February 22, 1898) lodges a judicial plea: "[He] is innocent: I swear it; I stake my life on it—my honor!" Churchill's appeal to Parliament for approval of Britain's war against Germany (May 13, 1940) is essentially deliberative, most memorable for his alliterative offer of "nothing . . . but blood, toil, tears and sweat."

26. Jewett, *Thessalonian Correspondence*; idem, *Romans*.

27. Representative of Watson's many investigations is *Invention, Arrangement, and Style*.

28. Primary texts are available in Hock and O'Neil, *Chreia and Ancient Rhetoric*; and Kennedy, *Progymnasmata*. On chreia in the Gospels, see Mack and Robbins, *Patterns of Persuasion*. Generations of North American children have been schooled in honesty through an apocryphal *chreia* popularized by Mason Locke Weems (1759–1825): young Washington's confession of chopping down a cherry tree (*The Life and Memorable Actions of George Washington* [1801]).

unity of 1 Corinthians,[29] ancient rhetoric has been employed to throw fresh light on long-standing questions of NT exegesis. (4) Theorists have adopted classical rhetoric in reformulating traditio-historical forms of interpretation like form criticism.[30] (5) Most provocatively, some scholars use ancient rhetorical precepts and practices as a springboard for revising the concepts of rhetoric and rhetorical analysis themselves. With that, we dive into yet another wave of rhetorical criticism.

Cohesion within Reading Communities: Rhetoric for the Consolidation of Power

Some NT interpretation concentrates neither on ancient poetics nor on classical modes of persuasion. Indeed, for those engaged in "the reinvention of rhetoric," diachronic pursuit of biblical authors' intentions is regarded as evidence of "the devastating grip of [historical-critical] positivism in our discipline," which should yield to the text's argumentative function for any reader in any age.[31] Likewise, preoccupation with biblical stylistics is viewed as "the [academic] ghetto," "the Babylonian captivity" from which rhetorical study must be liberated.[32] So what, properly understood, is the role of rhetoric and its criticism? Elisabeth Schüssler Fiorenza has proposed one answer:

> Whereas the poetic work attempts to create and to organize imaginative experience, rhetoric seeks to persuade and to motivate people to *act rightly*. Rhetoric seeks to instigate a change of attitudes and motivations, and it strives to persuade, to teach, and to engage the hearer/reader by eliciting reactions, emotions, convictions, and identifications. The evaluative criterion for rhetoric is not aesthetics, but praxis.[33]

For proponents of so-called New Rhetoric, the seminal work is that of Chaïm Perelman (1912–84) and Lucie Olbrechts-Tyteca (1899–1988). In the view of these two theorists, ancient rhetoric offers the modern critic, not so much interpretive norms for repristination, as a foundational if flawed theory to be revised, accenting the inducement or enhancement of an audience's adherence to particular values by means of various strategies of practical reasoning. For Perelman and Olbrechts-Tyteca the key to rhetoric lies in "the social aspect of language,

---

29. Mitchell, *Paul and the Rhetoric of Reconciliation*. Mitchell's *Doktorvater* at the University of Chicago, Hans Dieter Betz, has written the most influential Pauline commentary that appropriates the tradition of classical rhetoric: *Galatians* (1979).

30. Thus Berger, *Formgeschichte des Neuen Testaments*; and esp. Robbins, *New Boundaries*; idem, *Exploring the Texture*; idem, *Tapestry*. In "Rhetoric, Culture, and Ideology," Bloomquist appraises Robbins's approach.

31. Botha, esp. 27; see also Thurén, *Rhetorical Strategy*.

32. Wuellner, "Rhetorical Criticism," 457, 462.

33. Schüssler Fiorenza, *Rhetoric and Ethic*, 108.

which is an instrument of communication and influence on others."[34] Thus there is an irreducibly *social* and *practical* thrust to rhetorical criticism: a text's arguments invite evaluation less in terms of their persuasive intent or logical validity and more with respect to the implied values of their social context and the capacity of those arguments to secure commitment and to motivate action. Similarly, in treatises less systematic and more allusive,[35] Kenneth Burke (1897–1993) stresses the capacity of oral and written discourse to induce social cohesion or transformation by projecting comprehensive, symbolic visions of reality.

Of all the currents in rhetorical analysis, the New Rhetoric of Burke, Perelman, and others is most difficult to classify. Among practitioners within the biblical guild, its center of gravity resides in the text's power to move an audience or community of readers, whether ancient or modern. Grounded in the social experience of reading, the New Rhetoric usually moves beyond aesthetic or historical analysis, deliberately and often eclectically expanding the classical tradition of rhetoric into twentieth-century social psychology, hermeneutics, and semiotics (the study of sign-using behavior). When a rhetorical critic of this stripe explores the intricate creation and subversion of a reader's expectations by a biblical text, the outcome resembles an ahistorical, reader-response interpretation.[36] Nevertheless, other New Rhetorical analyses of the NT exhibit a greater measure of historical interest.[37]

One such example is Vernon Robbins's "socio-rhetorical" interpretation of the Second Gospel. Adopting Burke's perspective and terminology, Robbins explores three stylistic identifications used by Mark in cementing a rapport between the evangelist and his readers: a "conventional form," portraying the emerging relationship between a teacher and his disciples; "repetitive forms," which replicate that convention in cycles of relationships within the Gospel narrative; and "progressive forms," through which the teacher's character is unfolded in usually logical though sometimes unexpected (or "qualitative") progression. Robbins deems the Second Gospel a rhetorical success because it perpetuates an image of Jesus and an understanding of discipleship compatible with the ideology of the ancient Mediterranean world.[38]

---

34. Perelman and Olbrechts-Tyteca, *The New Rhetoric*, 513. Perelman's interest in rhetoric evolved from his studies of philosophy and jurisprudence; he subsequently pruned and developed his magnum opus in *The Realm of Rhetoric*. By investigating how modern societies publicly reason about values, Perelman returned rhetorical interpretation to its roots in Greco-Roman law.

35. Burke, *Rhetoric of Motives*; idem, *Rhetoric of Religion*. Crafton ("Dancing of an Attitude") inquires into Burke's brilliant yet recondite scholarship. "With a little more help from Burke," Wudel ("Enticements to Community," 282) argues, "rhetorical analysis can show how [Matthew's] Sermon on the Mount employs strategies not only for constituting a community, but [also] for perpetually destabilizing it from within."

36. E.g., Staley, *The Print's First Kiss*.

37. To date, Pauline scholars have most ambitiously adopted Perelman's approach: Siegert, *Argumentation bei Paulus*; Wire, *Corinthian Women Prophets*.

38. Robbins, *Jesus the Teacher*, 209–13. In "Rhetorical Questions" I assess Robbins's argument.

Known for a body of work produced over many years, Wilhelm Wuellner (1927–2004) is an exponent of the New Rhetorical approach. While his analyses of NT texts sometimes intersect with the classical tradition, Wuellner's musings on rhetoric became increasingly impatient with historical questions, instead emphasizing the intrinsically rhetorical constitution of human beings and discourse as a practical exercise of power.[39] "Rhetorical criticism," Wuellner once claimed, "is taking us beyond hermeneutics and structuralism to poststructuralism and posthermeneutics."[40] And yet "the verdict is still out on just how successful and profitable the application of rhetorical theory has become in the rebirth of rhetorical criticism in today's practices of biblical interpretation."[41]

RHETORICAL CRITICISM APPLIED:
THREE TRIPS TO A SAMARITAN WELL

By now the attentive reader is probably suffering a methodological migraine. Let's get down to cases by testing this variegated rhetorical criticism in reading a specific text. A full-blown exegesis of John 4:1–42 is out of the question and for our purposes unnecessary. All that need be proffered here are some appreciative sips of the current vintage and different varieties of rhetorical analysis.

In a Manner of Speaking

Jesus' comments in John 4 are exchanges in a dialogue with the Samaritan woman, not an uninterrupted oration. Still, for illustrative purposes we can touch on some aspects of a classical approach to rhetorical analysis.

Kennedy's understanding of "*the rhetorical situation*" (which is not an ancient notion but a modern abstraction)[42] offers us a useful way of positioning John 4:1–42 in its literary context. If we ask what conditions have created pressure for Jesus' declarations at this point in the Fourth Gospel, we might recall such things as his departure from Judea and return to Galilee in the wake of controversy (2:13–21) and incomprehension (3:1–21); the (divine?) necessity of his passing through Samaria (4:4; cf. 3:14); attestations of Jesus' importance from John

---

39. See Wuellner, "Hermeneutics and Rhetorics."

40. Wuellner, "Rhetorical Criticism," 449. Illustrating Wuellner's assessment are Schüssler Fiorenza, "Challenging the Rhetorical Half-Turn"; and Goosen, "Rhetoric of the Scapegoat." Those essays arrive at conclusions almost diametrically opposed to each other, which would doubtless elicit a smile from Jacques Derrida.

41. Wuellner, "Biblical Exegesis," 512. Important engagements with Wuellner's scholarship are collected in Hester and Hester (Amador), *Rhetorics and Hermeneutics*.

42. For this concept Kennedy (*New Testament Interpretation*, 34) is indebted to Bitzer, "Rhetorical Situation" (1968), whose proposal has predictably come under fire: among others, see Vatz, "Myth of the Rhetorical Situation" (1973); and Brinton, "Situation in the Theory of Rhetoric" (1981).

the baptizer (1:19–35; 3:25–36), from Jesus' own disciples (1:36–51), and from the Gospel's narrator (1:1–18); and the evangelist's reminder that Jesus is prescient in his dealings with people (2:23–25). Within this framework Jesus and the woman's responses to one another are striking. Forthcoming about his identity (4:26), Jesus initiates and sustains with her a theologically serious, educational dialogue (4:7–26). This woman proves to be a quick study: markedly responsive to "the gift of God" (4:10; cf. 3:3–4), she advances so far in her understanding of Jesus' significance (4:9, 11, 19, 29) that by the story's end she bears witness of it to others (4:28–30, 39).

Following Kennedy's lead, one may inquire about *the overriding rhetorical problem* implied by John 4. Most of Jesus' remarks to the woman seem intended, neither to elicit her judgment about past events nor to spur her future action, but rather to clarify her present understanding of some important religious matters (see 4:10, 21–24, 26). The force of Jesus' discourse therefore is primarily epideictic, which admittedly entails for this woman a judicial reconsideration of previously held beliefs as well as a deliberative decision, by the pericope's end, to missionize on the strength of her encounter with Jesus.

The distinctive *style* of Jesus' discourse in John 4 invites exploration by means of classical canons. Once readers have cultivated an ear for it, Jesus' manner of speech in the Fourth Gospel presents one of the most striking differences between John and the Synoptics. Even in English translation the Johannine Jesus' remarks are less terse and conversational, more exalted and almost operatic: "But the hour is coming, and now is here, when the true worshipers will worship the Father in spirit and truth, for the Father seeks such as these to worship him. God is spirit, and those who worship him must worship in spirit and truth" (John 4:23–24; see also 4:13–14, 21–22).[43] On Jesus' lips seemingly innocent turns of phrase in John can be galvanized with double entendre: for instance, ὕδωρ ζῶν (*hydōr zōn*, 4:10) can mean "running water" (as the woman takes Jesus' comment, v. 11) but is surely intended by him to suggest "living water" (see also 6:35; cf. Jer. 2:13; Zech. 14:8; Sir. 24:21).[44] From the Johannine Jesus' utterances flows a heavenly force that rolls over the heads of his earthbound interlocutors (John 4:7–10, 16–18, 31–34). In John 4, as throughout this Gospel, Jesus' speech displays the otherworldly discernment of one who does not originate from this world but transcends it (3:31–32; 6:31–59; 7:35, 46; 8:22–23).[45]

---

43. Scripture translations are NRSV unless otherwise indicated. My rendering is identified as author translation (AT). First appearances of Greek words are immediately followed by English transliterations.

44. Another example of turbocharged double meaning occurs in John 4:26 with Jesus' acknowledgment of his messiahship: ἐγώ εἰμι, (*egō eimi*), "I am," functions in John's Gospel as an expression of Jesus' oneness with God (see also 6:20; 8:24, 28, 58; 13:19; cf. Exod. 3:14; Isa. 43:10–11, 25; 51:12).

45. Of this I shall say more in chap. 5.

Several stylistic traits are peculiarly associated with religious themes in antiquity: sublimity (ὕψος, *hypsos*), solemnity (σεμνότης, *semnotēs*), and obscurity (ἀσάφεια, *asapheia*).[46] In the writings of "Longinus" (first century CE) and others, *sublimity* refers to an inspired form of human utterance that "contains much food for reflection" (*Subl.* 7.3; see also 13.2; 36.1). For Hermogenes of Tarsus (*Per id.* 242.1–246.1) *solemnity* is especially appropriate for expressing general thoughts about the gods and aspects of humanity that intersect with divinity, such as righteousness and the soul's immortality. Whereas *obscurity* could be regarded as a stylistic fault (Aristotle, *Rhet.* 3.3.3.1406a), in other contexts (such as pronouncements by the Delphic oracle) ἀσάφεια could be considered appropriate to religion's mysterious character (thus Demetrius, *Eloc.* 2.101). Since *sublimity* and *solemnity* could be characteristic of the merely wise or noble, these stylistic properties were potentially but not necessarily indicative of proximity to the divine (Philo, *The Worse Attacks the Better* 43–44, 79; Hermogenes, *Per. id.* 246.1–9).

The relationship between these considerations and John's depiction of Jesus should be obvious. In the Fourth Gospel, Jesus is recognizably human (1:14; 4:6–7) yet speaks in a way that suggests divinity, according to classical conventions of style. Interlocutors like the Samaritan woman and the disciples are attuned to only the lower level of Jesus' polyvalent discourse, whose divine nuances are pitched at a frequency inaudible without a boost from God. The exalted tenor of Jesus' remarks are happily intelligible, however, to one who has read the Gospel's stylistically similar prologue: John 1:1–18 affords the reader information about Jesus' transcendent origin, to which the story's characters (save God and Jesus himself) are not privy. Johannine style attempts to portray "the dialogue between heaven and earth," and "it is the feature of distortion, perhaps only slight, which is the sign of genuine religious immediacy and creativeness."[47]

Poetics at Noonday

Considering the rhetoric of John 4 in Muilenburg's manner invites scrutiny of the text's bonds and bounds, its internal arrangement and repetitive features. Viewed under this magnifying glass, John's account of Jesus and the woman at the well exhibits a fugal entwining of (A) request, (B) resistance, (C) explanation, and (D) belief:

A Structural Analysis of John 4:7–42

<u>First Movement: Jesus and an unexpected disciple (4:7–26)</u>
First theme: A taste of eschatological water (4:7–15)
First interchange: Requests for a drink (4:7–10)
   A. Jesus' request of water from the Samaritan woman (4:7–8)
   B. The woman's rejection of his request, in the form of a guarded question (4:9)

---

46. For much of what follows I am indebted to Thielman, "Style of the Fourth Gospel."
47. Wilder, *Early Christian Rhetoric*, 50–51.

C. Jesus' response to her rejection (4:10)
    i. If she were to recognize her interlocutor's identity, (4:10a)
    ii. she would ask him for a drink (4:10b)

Second interchange: Confusion over "water" (4:11–15)
    B. The woman's misunderstanding of the water mentioned by Jesus (4:11–12)
    C. Jesus' explanation: He speaks of spiritual, not mundane, water (4:13–14)
    A. The woman's request of water from Jesus (4:15; fulfilling 4:10b)

Second theme: A taste of eschatological worship (4:16–26)
Third interchange: Request for the woman's husband (4:16–18)
    A. Jesus' request that the woman call her husband (4:16)
    B. The woman's oblique rejection of this request (4:17a)
    C. Jesus' discerning affirmation of her response (4:17b–18)

Fourth interchange: Confusion over Jesus' identity (4:19–26)
    D. The woman's partial perception of Jesus' identity (4:19–20)
    C. Jesus' explanation: Genuine worship is spiritual (4:21–24)
    D. The woman's leaning toward an accurate identification of Jesus (4:25), which he accepts (4:26; fulfilling 4:10a)

Second Movement: Jesus and his other followers (4:27–42)
Third theme: A taste of eschatological food (4:27–38)
Fifth interchange: Invitations to leave (4:27–30)
    B. Arriving, Jesus' disciples implicitly question the woman's presence (4:27)
    D. Leaving, the woman explicitly invites the city to witness Jesus (4:28–29)
    D. Accepting the woman's invitation, the city leaves in search of Jesus (4:30)

Sixth interchange: An imminent harvest (4:31–38)
    A. The disciples' request that Jesus eat (4:31)
    C. Jesus' explanation: he has food unknown to them (4:32)
    B. The disciples misunderstand the food mentioned by Jesus (4:33; cf. 4:11–12)
    C. Jesus' explanation: He speaks of spiritual, not mundane, food (4:34–38)
        i. First proverb: No interval between sowing and harvest (4:35–36)
        ii. Second proverb: The sower's end-time dispatch of the reapers (4:37–38)
Fourth theme: A taste of eschatological knowledge (4:39–42)
    D. The city believes the woman about Jesus (4:39; cf. 4:29)
    C. Accepting the citizens' invitation, Jesus stays in the city (4:40; cf. 4:30)
    D. Because of Jesus' word the city believes "the Savior of the world" (4:41–42)

For all the distortion generated by any outline, the elegant architecture of John 4:7–42 is clear. Obviously, this story oscillates between the themes of drink and worship (in 4:4–26), of food and missionary acclamation (in 4:27–42; cf. 6:1–59). The woman's and the disciples' requests, misunderstandings, and partial realizations repeatedly crack open larger theological issues. These, in turn, stimulate an apparent escalation of belief about Jesus, who is addressed as "a Jew" (4:9), "Sir" (4:11, 15, 19), "greater than our ancestor Jacob" (4:12), "a prophet" (4:19), "Messiah" or "Christ" (4:25, 29), "Rabbi" (4:31), and ultimately as "the Savior of the world" (4:42). The text's internal unity is tightly stitched with many verbal threads: "drink" (πινεῖν [pinein] and its cognates: 4:7, 9, 10a, 12, 13, 14); "water" (ὕδωρ [hydōr]: 4:7, 13, 14, 15), which soon shades into "living water" (ὕδωρ ζῶν [hydōr zōn]: 4:10, 11) and "eternal life" (ζωὴν αἰώνιον [zōēn aiōnion]: 4:14; cf. also 7:37–38); "worship" (προσκυνεῖν [proskynein] and its cognates: 4:20, 21, 22, 23, 24); "seek" (ζητεῖν [zētein]: 4:23, 27); "harvest" (θερισμός [therismos] and its cognates: 4:35, 36, 37, 38); "believe" (πιστεύειν [pisteuein]: 4:21, 39, 41, 42); "truth" (ἀλήθεια [alētheia] and its cognates: 4:18, 23, 24, 37, 42).

Muilenburg's brand of rhetorical criticism is intended to recover a text's unique features, which have been clothed in a traditional form. John 4 reminds us of a familiar OT type-scene: the betrothal. Whether its characters are Isaac's servant and Rebekah (Gen. 24:10–20), Jacob and Rachel (Gen. 29:1–14), or Moses and Zipporah (Exod. 2:15b–21), the betrothal scene unfolds in a predictable though mutable way. Upon leaving his family circle and journeying to a foreign land, a prospective bridegroom encounters a marriageable woman at a well. After water has been drawn and news of his arrival has been hurriedly reported back home, the stranger is invited to dinner. Soon thereafter, the betrothal is consummated. Robert Alter has argued that contemporary audiences of these ancient stories— who were as familiar with their conventions as we are with those of detective mysteries or westerns—would have enjoyed their skillful adaptation: "As is true of all original art, what is really interesting is not the schema of convention but what is done in each individual application of the schema to give it a sudden tilt of innovation or even to refashion it radically for the imaginative purposes at hand."[48]

In this light John 4:4–42 dances recognizably and mischievously. Indeed, it is a tour de force. All the familiar elements of the betrothal-scene are in play: on leaving his "family circle" ("the Jews" of John 2:13–25; 4:1–3) and journeying to a foreign land (Samaria: 4:4), a "bridegroom" named Jesus (3:29; see also 2:1–11) encounters a woman at a well (4:6–7a). After a request to draw water (4:7b), news of the stranger's arrival is hurriedly reported back home (4:28–29), and he is invited to stay (4:40). John's adoption of this ancient *form* intimates the *content* of Jesus' forthright announcement in 4:22–23: the same God who established the

---

48. Alter, *Art of Biblical Narrative*, 47–62, esp. 52.

rhythm of Israel's history is the Father of Jesus and the Samaritan woman. Yet the Fourth Evangelist has twisted the type-scene to potent theological effect: now it is *Jesus* who gives to those who believe in him "living water, gushing up to eternal life" (4:14 AT). The result is a very different betrothal—not in marriage, but in worship (4:21–24) and in mission (4:35–42).

What Is a Reader to Do?

Since the New Rhetoricians have not yet arrived at a procedural consensus, any attempt to offer a fully representative interpretation of some portion of John 4 from this point of view is hopeless. It is on *general outcome* that the New Rhetoricians tend to concur: because the experience of reading is tethered to the reader's socially situated experience, the fundamental criterion for rhetorical analysis is not aesthetic but practical.

Following Perelman and Wuellner's lead, we begin with the proposition that the story of Jesus and the Samaritan woman is presented in John for the same purpose as the Gospel's other components: "so that you may come to believe [or "continue to believe"] that Jesus is the Messiah, the Son of God, and that through believing you may have life in his name" (20:31). John 4:4–42 induces or enhances belief in these values. Just here in the Fourth Gospel, Jesus does what the Jews will demand of him in 10:24: he plainly acknowledges that he is the Messiah (4:26). Trust that Jesus is the Christ, the agent of indestructible life for the world, is the final destination to which Jesus' discourse is intended to lead, not only for the Samaritan woman and her fellow citizens (4:10, 14, 26, 36, 41–42), but also for the audience of John's narrative.[49]

Perelman and Olbrechts-Tyteca categorize four general techniques of argumentation: (1) quasi-logical arguments, which operate in the domain of common sense; (2) arguments that, by appealing to customary relationships of cause and effect, derive from assumptions about the structure of reality; (3) arguments that seek to establish the structure of reality by extrapolating general principles from particular cases; and (4) arguments that, by dissociating concepts, attempt to reformulate reality and to provoke new understanding.[50] If we view the conversation presented in John 4:7–26 through this analytical prism, two things become clear. First, *both* Jesus *and* the woman are engaged in rhetorical performance. She is no mute pupil, nor is he the imperious lecturer who entertains no questions from the audience. Here we have *two* interlocutors, the one attempting to persuade the other.[51]

---

49. Okure (*Johannine Approach to Mission*) probes the conjunction of John's rhetoric and missionary interests.

50. Perelman and Olbrechts-Tyteca, *The New Rhetoric*, 187–92.

51. So also Schneiders, *Revelatory Text*, 189, 191, 194.

Second, the woman is inclined toward the first and more deductive set of strategies: use of common sense and cause and effect; Jesus tends toward the second and more inductive pair of techniques: use of general principles and conceptual dissociation. Her comments tend to move in the realm of the obvious (AT: "Mister, you haven't got a bucket and the well's deep" [4:11]) and long-standing custom ("You're a Jew, I'm a Samaritan" [4:9]; "Our ancestors worshiped on Gerizim, you people on Zion" [4:20]). Through the use of oblique metaphors ("the gift of God" [4:10], "running/living water" [4:10], "eternal life" [4:14]), Jesus, by contrast, is making a case for the structure of reality. More than that, Jesus' argument to the woman—and by implication to the reader—proceeds from and instantiates, as Perelman and Olbrechts-Tyteca put it, "another outlook and another criterion of reality,"[52] namely, the tolling of an hour when God is worshiped "in spirit and in truth" (4:23–24). Ultimately, worship is dissociated from the practice of both Samaritans and Jews (4:21) and is reconceived as praise of God that participates in the transforming energy, mediated by Jesus, that offers access to authentic reality.

The transaction that mysteriously propels the encounter at Jacob's well beyond rhetorical stalemate involves Jesus' request for the woman's husband (John 4:16), her response (4:17), and his rejoinder (4:18). Commentators have fulminated over this exchange and whether it should be taken literally or metaphorically (e.g., as a veiled reference to Samaria's "adulterous" idolatry [2 Kgs. 17:13–34]). One could as easily ask the same about Jesus' initial request for a drink (4:7): in both cases the question is a red herring. The central issue is no more the woman's sexual history than the Samaritans' alleged apostasy, neither of which the conversation develops. As this story unfolds, the crux is whether Jesus may be trusted as the revealer of the truth about human life and the life of God. That is the concern intimated by the woman's common-sense and therefore truncated acknowledgment of Jesus as a prophet (4:19), perhaps the Messiah (4:29), "who told me everything I have ever done!" (4:29, 39). The same concern is indicated by the city's more expansive response to Jesus (4:39–40) and by their conviction, based on unmediated access to his word, "that this is truly the Savior of the world" (4:41–42).

If we accept Wuellner's proposition that rhetorical analysis entails the critic's personal and social identification, even transformation, in what such directions does the rhetoric of John 4 lead us? Clearly Jesus is no more disqualified from interaction with the woman because he is a Jew (contrary to her assumption in 4:9) than she is disqualified from conversation with him because she is a woman (contrary to the disciples' prejudice in 4:27). The egalitarian force of this analysis is inadequately realized by those who have seized Jesus' statements in John 4:17–18 to castigate the woman's moral turpitude—about which the text says nothing. And the christological force of this analysis is insufficiently appreciated by others,

52. Perelman and Olbrechts-Tyteca, The New Rhetoric, 436.

who have claimed the woman's evangelism (4:28–29) to extol her womanhood as such—about which the text is equally silent. If rhetorical interpretation of John 4 exposes our foreshortened presuppositions about race or sex and instead invites us as readers to faith in Jesus Christ as "the Savior of the world," then such analysis is not only political but also theological in its critical bearing.

SOME RHETORICAL QUESTIONS

Is There a Rhetorical-Critical Method?

As described and illustrated here, *how coherent are the different expressions of rhetorical criticism?* Are we dealing with a unified method or with three disparate approaches, each of which styles itself as "rhetorically critical"? No unanimity exists among rhetorical critics themselves. Although the various forms of rhetorical study are reconcilable for some, for others the attempt to blend, say, the classical tradition with a modern, praxis-oriented understanding of rhetoric courts hermeneutical confusion.[53]

While granting that particular formulations of rhetorical criticism may be philo- sophically at odds with others, we can conceive the enterprise in a way that coordi- nates the several approaches we have observed. Heuristically drawing on classical theory, one may consider rhetorical interpretation as a three-legged stool on which many different critics may sit, with each applying more weight to one leg than to the others. Muilenburg's approach leans on *logos*, the structure and style of a biblical text. Kennedy's version, emphasizing authorial intent and technique, inclines toward the text's underlying *ēthos*. Perelman's stress on a text's reception by its audience recalls the rhetorical dimension that the ancients characterized as *pathos*. I see no reason, in principle, why biblical interpreters may not tilt the critical stool in whichever direc- tion their interests dispose them. One could radically theorize the stool's redesign by sawing off any two of its legs that seem nonsupportive of one's particular interests. The result would then be a wobbly stool, on which a reader would find it hard to maintain interpretive balance. For that reason the current multiformity of NT rhe- torical criticism is a healthy development, whose effect overall is to equilibrate its various tendencies, restraining the potential of each for exegetical distortion.

The rest of this book evinces comparable variety. Chapters 2 and 6 veer in the direction I have associated with Wilder and Booth, adopting a formal- ist approach for studying literary characterization in the Gospel of Matthew and the Acts of the Apostles. Chapters 4, 5, and 7 address particular questions

---

53. Contrast, e.g., the procedures of Jewett, *Thessalonian Correspondence*, 63–87; and Mitchell, *Paul and the Rhetoric of Reconciliation*, 1–19.

prompted by Luke, John, and Acts that classical rhetoric seems to me best equipped to answer. Adhering to Kennedy's method, a full-dress analysis of a speech in Mark's Gospel is offered in chapter 3. Four very different voices—those of Jonah, Paul, Luke, and Augustine of Hippo—are assembled in chapter 8 for a conversation on homiletics. Chapter 9 inquires of an ancient theorist, Quintilian, for suggestions in contemporary preaching. In effect, this volume constitutes a colloquy within a kind of New Rhetorical framework, "baptized" into the service of Christian theology and practice. A modus operandi so wide ranging may stimulate methodological purists to weep and gnash their teeth. Others, I hope, may find pleasure in rhetorical criticism's flexibility and canonical purview.

Is Rhetorical Criticism Compatible with Historical Criticism?

Theorists also dispute this question. For some, rhetorical criticism complements traditional analyses of the NT. For others, historical research and rhetorical study are impassably divided by a big ugly ditch.[54]

Some expressions of rhetorical criticism may be impossible to harmonize with a historical frame of reference. Nevertheless, I regard historical and rhetorical inquiries as fundamentally cooperative, not contesting. Philosophically, most forms of historical and rhetorical criticism presuppose a shared model of communication that attempts to triangulate (1) the intent of an author (2) in formulating a text (3) that forms or informs a reader.[55] It should be recognized, moreover, that all interpretive approaches to the Bible are by-products of intellectual traditions and other cultural influences; even the most adamantly ahistorical brands of rhetorical criticism are *themselves* historically conditioned. I cannot imagine a well-rounded rhetorical analysis of a NT text that could altogether ignore its historical characteristics and assumptions. Much of the rhetorical force of John 4 turns on awareness of ancient aversions—of some rabbis toward protracted conversation with women (cf. v. 27) and of Jews and Samaritans toward one another (cf. v. 9)—that are irrecoverable apart from historical reconstruction.[56]

54. Contrast the assessments of Kennedy, *New Testament Interpretation*, 3–12, 157–60; and Stamps, "Rhetorical Criticism." Controversy now rages over the degree to which rhetorical study of the Bible ought to be historical or ideological in orientation. See Porter and Stamps, *Rhetorical Interpretation of Scripture*, 27–151.

55. Compare the analogous conclusion drawn by de Boer, "Narrative Criticism, Historical Criticism."

56. Relevant primary texts are considered in Barrett, *Gospel according to St. John*, 232–33, 240.

What Are the Drawbacks of Rhetorical Criticism?

Each type of rhetorical study has its peculiar liabilities. Common to all forms of rhetorical criticism—to all interpretive strategies, for that matter—is a tendency among some practitioners to absolutize the insights of their favored approach and to lose clear sight of the text itself. For rhetorical critics this danger typically manifests itself in the imposition of some ideal construct—be it a chiastic structure, or classical taxonomies of invention, or a theory of the irreducibly rhetorical character of human behavior—on a particular biblical passage or book that resists such preset patterns. Sensitivity to the multiple dimensions of NT texts and their interpretation, which this volume intends to encourage, remains the best safeguard against all sorts of "cookie-cutter criticism," rhetorical or otherwise.[57]

What Is Gained by Rhetorical Criticism?

In the academic marketplace of ideas, the study of rhetoric is a proven site for exchange among biblical interpreters of many methodological allegiances: historical critics and literary analysts, linguists and social scientists, philosophers and theologians.[58] For biblical teachers and preachers, rhetorical criticism offers a lively forum in which the complex dynamics of religious discourse may be considered. From its beginnings Christian proclamation has necessarily availed itself of reasoned argument and stylistic conventions; yet preaching has indulged neither in logic nor in aesthetics for its own sake. The prime movers of the early church were the *ēthos* of Christ and the *pathos* of a Spirit-imbued life. Creatively fusing form and content, the church's *kerygma* was designed to construe Christian experience, to express its power, and to persuade others of its truth. When rhetorical criticism assists in clarifying these aspects of the NT, it illumines the text to be interpreted as well as the challenge of its modern interpreters.

---

57. This warning is sounded in Meyer's trenchant review (1981) of Betz, *Galatians*. In *Ancient Rhetorical Theory* R. D. Anderson argues that Galatians, Romans, and 1 Corinthians do not exhibit, nor do they intend to execute, the kind of argumentation that a hypothetical professor of rhetoric, contemporaneous with Paul, would have reckoned as convincing. Because the apostle's arguments do not measure up to ancient canons, application of rhetorical theory to his letters is severely limited and in some cases irrelevant (see esp. 28, 144, 166, 205, 238). It seems to me that Anderson is generally correct in what he affirms (a too-hasty assumption, by some, of Paul's reliance on rhetorical theory) and often wrong in what he denies (a fair degree of rhetorical effectiveness in Paul's Letters, which ironically surfaces from Anderson's own treatment). See my review (1997) of Anderson's study.

58. Beyond biblical studies, rhetorical research continues to stimulate philosophers and theorists of communication: see Herrick, *History and Theory of Rhetoric*, 194–266; S. Foss, K. Foss, and Trapp, *Contemporary Perspectives on Rhetoric*.

The Gospels

Chapter Two

Matthew's Characterization of Faith

I want the character to do his job. If someone is raking leaves in the background while the hero and heroine are having their tragic conversation in the autumn park, I am content that he should be simply someone raking leaves. People do after all rake leaves, and so long as he looks like someone raking leaves, that is enough for me. I positively do not want him "round"; in fact, I do not even want him "flat." More than that: unless his raking those leaves adds something to what is going on, I want him to quit raking them and just disappear. He should never have existed in the first place.

Elder Olson[1]

Aristotle's analysis of tragedy is remembered for its emphasis on plot, with characters (τὰ ἤθη [*ta ēthē*]) serving mainly to propagate the action (*Poet.* 6.19.1450b). Perhaps less well known is his observation, in *The Art of Rhetoric* (1.2.3–6.1356a), that *to ēthos* ([τὸ ἦθος] the orator's own character) may almost be called the most effective means of persuasion.[2] If it be true that authors cannot avoid making persuasive appeals to their readers,[3] then those who are interested in narrative rhetoric would do well to attend carefully to characterization. The scant investigation of this subject by biblical critics is scarcely surprising: because of its conceptual difficulty, the study of character has been slighted even among secular literary theorists.[4]

---

1. Olson, *Tragedy and the Theory of Drama*, 85.
2. Given Aristotle's stress on the persuasive power of *logos*, this admission is all the more impressive (see *Rhet.* 2.18.1.1391b–2.26.5.1403ab; 3.19.10.1417b–3.19.6.1420a).
3. Thus Booth, *Rhetoric of Fiction*, 67–209.
4. Some scholars are ameliorating this state of affairs: Spilka, "Character as a Lost Cause"; R. Wilson, "The Bright Chimera"; Malbon and Berlin, *Characterization in Biblical Literature*.

This chapter explores some aspects of characterization in the First Gospel.[5] My principal partner in conversation is Jack Dean Kingsbury, whose literary-critical scholarship set Matthean interpretation on some new paths.[6] My procedure: first, a review of Kingsbury's assessment of the characters in Matthew's story; second, a reconsideration of that subject in the light of recent examinations of character among literary theorists; third, some concluding reflections on this critical perspective and its exegetical implications.

KINGSBURY'S APPRAISAL REVISITED

Theoretical Assumptions

Considering characterization within Matthew's narrative, Kingsbury acknowledges his indebtedness to four literary critics. From M. H. Abrams he draws his definition of "characters": "the persons who appear in a narrative work such as Matthew's Gospel."[7] Following Abrams and David Rhoads, Kingsbury associates "'characterization' . . . with the way in which an author brings character to life in a narrative," either by "showing" to a reader the characters in speech or in action, or by "telling" the reader about them.[8] Beyond these basic premises, Kingsbury derives his fundamental conception of character from Seymour Chatman and E. M. Forster. With Chatman, Kingsbury proposes that characters can be differentiated on the basis of "traits," those distinctive and persistent qualities exhibited by the character.[9] Moreover (as Forster suggests), one may distinguish characters by their number and variety of traits. Round characters possess an abundance or diversity of traits, creating the impression of "real people"; characters that display only a few traits are flat, or highly predictable in their behavior.[10] Based on these assumptions, Kingsbury sketches five principal characters in Matthew's narrative.[11]

Exegetical Assessments

1. For Kingsbury, *Jesus* is the protagonist of Matthew's story, the focal character around whom all action revolves and by whom the qualities of all other characters

---

5. My focus is narrow; plot, atmosphere, tone, "quality of mind," and other narrative components are considered only tangentially. For a helpful guide to this broader range of elements in both the OT and NT, consult Kort, *Story, Text, and Scripture*.

6. Kingsbury's *Matthew as Story* is the principal study that my own engages.

7. Ibid., 9; Abrams, *Glossary of Literary Terms*, 21.

8. Kingsbury, *Matthew as Story*, 9–10; cf. Rhoads and Michie, *Mark as Story*, 101–3.

9. Kingsbury, *Matthew as Story*, 10; cf. Chatman, *Story and Discourse*, 119–34.

10. Kingsbury, *Matthew as Story* 10; cf. Forster, *Aspects of the Novel*, 65–82.

11. Kingsbury, *Matthew as Story*, 11–28.

are evaluated. Two features of the Matthean Jesus are noteworthy. First, from beginning to end, the First Gospel presents Jesus as "the supreme arbiter of the will of God," "God's supreme agent who is in complete accord with God's system of values. Other than God himself, therefore, Jesus is the one major character whom Matthew always puts in the right."[12] Second, Jesus in the First Gospel evinces a multiplicity of positive and indeed "righteous" traits. For this reason, in Kingsbury's judgment, "[Jesus] is in Forster's terms a 'round' character."[13]

2. Collectively, *the disciples* may be evaluated as a single character. "Like Jesus [reasons Kingsbury] they are 'round,' but whereas this is the case with Jesus because of the great number of traits he possesses, this is the case with the disciples because they possess not only numerous traits but also traits that conflict."[14] As the story of Matthew progresses, the position of the disciples unevenly regresses from loyal obedience to ignominious apostasy.[15] Nevertheless, reconciliation rather than failure is the note on which Matthew concludes (28:16–20): albeit subject to bouts of "little faith," the disciples confidently undertake the worldwide mission for which the risen Lord has commissioned and empowered them.[16] Through encounter with the disciples' vacillation, and by identifying with or distancing herself from their conflicting traits, Matthew's reader may plumb Jesus' dictum in Matthew 10:25a: "It is sufficient for a disciple to be like his teacher" (AT).[17]

3. Like the disciples, *Israel's religious leaders* can be treated as a single character within the Matthean narrative. However, in literary terms, those who occupy positions of religious authority are unlike the disciples in at least three ways. First, whereas the disciples do not sway the Matthean plot, the religious authorities are second only to Jesus in their exertion of influence on the flow of Matthew's story.[18] Second, the Pharisees, Sadducees, chief priests, elders, and scribes constitute a united front that is opposed to Jesus. Third, while Jesus and the disciples are round characters, the religious leaders in Matthew coalesce into a flat character. "The many traits ascribed to them are in essence manifestations of a single 'root trait' ['evilness' (*sic*)], and they give no evidence of undergoing change in the course of the story."[19] On the contrary, "Matthew's characterization of them [is] uniformly, even monotonously, negative."[20] Indeed, the religious leaders assume "a singularly villainous role"; they "think the things of men" and are thereby quintessentially opposed to Jesus, who "thinks the things of God" (cf. Matt. 16:23b).[21]

---

12. Ibid., 11, 64; see also 52–55.
13. Ibid., 12.
14. Ibid., 13.
15. Ibid., 13–17, 129–45.
16. Ibid., 17, 144.
17. Ibid., 14, 17.
18. Ibid., 116.
19. Ibid., 18; cf. 19.
20. Ibid., 19.
21. Ibid., 115.

As the account of their growing enmity unfolds, "Matthew makes it exceedingly plain that, whether directly or indirectly, the issue of authority underlies all the controversies Jesus has with the religious leaders and that it is therefore pivotal to his entire conflict with them."[22]

4. Like his depictions of the disciples and the religious authorities, Matthew's characterization of *the Jewish crowds* evolves through their interaction with Jesus; moreover, the crowds exhibit traits similar to those of the other two groups. Like the disciples, yet unlike the religious leaders, the crowds are generally well disposed toward Jesus. Amazed and astonished, harassed and helpless, leaderless and famished, the crowds are objects of Jesus' compassion (see Matt. 9:33–36; 14:14; 15:32). Like their leaders, yet unlike the disciples, the crowds are "blind, deaf, and without understanding" of the one whose crucifixion they ultimately ratify (13:1–2, 10–13; 27:25). In Kingsbury's assessment, the crowds, like their leaders, also constitute a single, flat character. "They are not rich in traits, and the ones they possess tend not to change until the end of Matthew's story, when they suddenly appear with Judas to arrest Jesus (26:47, 55)."[23]

5. Almost without exception, the minor characters that proliferate within Matthew's narrative are, to use Kingsbury's term, "*stock*" *characters* that possess a single trait. Although these "persons" sometimes do little more than blend into the setting, they serve principally as foils for the story's major characters. Their occasionally perceptive faith in Jesus contrasts with the blind unbelief of Israel's leaders and populace at large (see Matt. 2:1–12; 8:5–13). More frequently, these minor characters' faith in and service to Jesus are foils for the disciples' "little faith" and defection (cf. 14:28–36; 27:55–28:1). Thus the minor characters exemplify values advocated by the protagonist (Jesus) and the implied author of Matthew's story.[24]

MATTHEAN CHARACTERIZATION REVISITED

Theoretical Assumptions

With Kingsbury I agree on this point: studying Matthew as a story involves taking seriously the narrative form adopted by an ancient author to convey certain religious beliefs. To discern Matthew's theological commitments requires that attention be paid to his characterization of figures within that narrative. Considering characterization is not an anachronistic exercise, since literary theorists and

22. Ibid., 125.
23. Ibid., 24–25, esp. 24.
24. Ibid., 25–28. The "implied author" refers to the inferred core of norms that informs a narrative, shapes its style and construction, and thereby influences what the reader reads (Booth, *Rhetoric of Fiction*, 66–77). I use the traditional appellation "Matthew" in reference to the First Gospel's implied author.

biblical scholars have long turned to the classical world for help in conceptualizing characters within Greco-Roman narrative and drama.[25]

My questions arise, not from Kingsbury's approach, but from what I regard as lacunae in his assumptions about literary figures and their characterization. I begin with an observation: *Kingsbury's working definition of "character" is inadequate to describe the complexity of that phenomenon in the First Gospel.* In accordance with his prior decision to concentrate on Matthew as a unified narrative, apart from other methods' historical, traditional, or theological concerns, Kingsbury settles for a cautious—I think overly restrictive—definition of character as the "persons" brought to life in a narrative.[26] Such a definition is insufficient: it fails to offer adequate foundation for Kingsbury's inquiry into characterization and its disclosure of the implied author's evaluative point of view. By contrast, Mary Doyle Springer proposes an alternative definition of "character" that is more conceptually serviceable for the kind of endeavor to which Kingsbury invites us:

> A literary character is an artificial construct drawn from, and relatively imitative of, people in the real world. The identity of a character becomes known primarily from a continuity of his or her own choices, speeches, and acts, consistent with the kind of person to be presented. Secondarily, identity is reinforced by description, diction, and in incidents of apposition to other characters. The choices, acts, and habits that constitute a character are limited by, consistent with, and suitable to the governing principle of the whole work of which the character is a part.[27]

Springer's formulation incorporates important aspects of Kingsbury's definition (literary characters as relatively imitative of "real persons"; characterization as developed through action, speech, and interaction with other characters).[28] Moreover, it articulates two concepts that are tacit in his assumptions but writ large throughout his analysis: (a) in narrative, a shaping principle governs characters and their acts; (b) the values attending this governing principle are implied by those characters' choices. I shall argue that both of these ideas enrich our understanding of characterization in Matthew.

A second observation: even on literary-critical premises, *Matthean characterization and Matthean theology are intricately interwoven* and need not be heuristically separated. For Springer, an author's evaluative beliefs and creation of characters are virtually impossible to segregate: "characters will be as lifelike, or as fleshless and stylized,

---

25. Burnett, "Characterization," is a temperate comparison of ancient and modern literary theories that neither minimizes nor exaggerates the distance between them. Chapter 4 (below) approaches characterization from a classical frame of reference.

26. Kingsbury, *Matthew as Story*, 9.

27. Springer, *Rhetoric of Literary Character*, 14, italicized in the original.

28. Thus, too, Harvey: "The [narrative's] human context, then, is primarily a web of relationships; the characters do not develop along single and linear roads of destiny but are, so to speak, human cross-roads" (*Character and the Novel*, 69).

as they have to be to do their job, provided that the artist knows his job. . . . [All] characters have a discoverable formal job—to serve under 'the governing principle of the whole work.'"[29]

Of course, such an idea moves critical inquiry back by one step: how might we conceptualize the shaping principle of Matthew's Gospel? Here we receive assistance from Martin Price, who has identified three principal functions that a novel may serve: a *formulaic* function, whereby the reader's enjoyment arises from the work's pure form (as in a detective mystery); an *expressive* function, whereby the feelings of the author and reader are engaged and molded; and a *cognitive* function, through which, by precept or example, fresh insight into the world or into ourselves is communicated.[30] Insofar as Price's observations are pertinent to ancient narratives, not only modern novels, Matthew's Gospel functions to some degree in all of these ways. Nevertheless, the third aspect predominates: the First Gospel purports to be a source of knowledge about matters of ultimate importance, couched in a biographical narrative and colored by religious beliefs. The characters within that story are governed by, and evocative of, those religious confessions. Entering the world of Matthew's narrative as readers, we risk being challenged and even molded by the evangelist's convictions.

Although Kingsbury's general presentation comports with this perspective, Matthew's "shaping principle," the implied author's cluster of reigning theological convictions, is muted in Kingsbury's methodological reflections on character. If characters reveal their author's commitments, and if Matthew's commitments are theological, how might we more firmly yoke Matthean theology and characterization?

Third: *the meaning and significance of Matthew's "roundness" or "flatness" of characterization need reassessment.* Literary-critical reflection has been so mesmerized by Forster's distinction between characters round and flat[31] that Kingsbury's adoption of it does not startle. Yet some caveats should be entered about this notion and its exegetical consequences.

(a) For Kingsbury, roundness of characterization is suggested by the abundance or variety of traits, and flatness is evoked by their paucity or homogeneity. This view does not betray Forster, who has identified flat characters as "types, and sometimes caricatures . . . constructed round a single idea or quality."[32] However, Kingsbury omits mention of Forster's test of characterization: "The test of a round character is whether it is capable of surprising in a convincing way. If it never

---

29. Springer, *Rhetoric of Literary Character*, 18. On the theological import of characters' interaction in the Gospels, see McCracken, "Character in the Boundary."

30. Price, *Forms of Life*, 1–23.

31. On the influence of Forster's theory, see Harvey, *Character and the Novel*, 192; Abrams, *Glossary of Literary Terms*, 21; Chatman, *Story and Discourse*, 131–34. For other theoretical ruminations, consult Ralph Cohen, ed., "Changing Views of Character," a special issue of *New Literary History* 5, no. 2 (1974); as well as the works cited above in n. 4.

32. Forster, *Aspects of the Novel*, 67.

surprises, it does not convince, it is [a] flat pretending to be round."[33] Contemplat-
ing Matthew, we need to consider the persuasiveness, on Forster's own terms, of
Kingsbury's identification of particular characters as round and flat.

(b) *Pace* Kingsbury, more recent theorists have expressed dissatisfaction with what
they regard as the superficiality of this theoretical distinction in its unmitigated form.
For example, Thomas Docherty complains that Forster's view is, well, flat: even in
"flat" characters, rejoins Docherty, a dynamism exists, without which such characters
would emerge as static, even lifeless.[34] Correlatively, we might ponder the degree to
which round characters exhibit a kind of regularity, or habitual pattern, without which
we could not properly recognize that figure's character or constellation of relatively
stable traits.[35] Moreover, Cornelis Bennema has demonstrated that characterization in ancient Greco-Roman literature is far more variegated and complex than has
been generally recognized, "capable of approaching modern notions of character at
times."[36] Obviously, some qualifications of Forster's theory are warranted.[37]

(c) Though never so expressed, Kingsbury's appraisal of Matthew's characters shares one of Forster's presuppositions: namely, round characters are more
perfectly realized as literary creations than their flat counterparts. In *Aspects of the
Novel* that bias is intimated by Forster's generous praise of Austen and his tepid
appreciation of Dickens;[38] in *Matthew as Story* a similar bias is revealed by Kingsbury's claim that Jesus and the disciples become, for the reader, "real persons"
and mouthpieces for the values espoused by the implied author.[39] Even if we
retain a modified version of Forster's theory, his implied valorization of round and
flat characters in the First Gospel invites reconsideration. The point is not that
Matthew favors Jesus over the religious authorities and, for that reason, renders
their respective characterizations as round and flat. At issue, rather, is a more
supple interaction of Matthew's characters and their narrative world. Given the
exigencies of a story's particular "governing principle," more or less flat characters
may achieve certain effects for their creators, conveying to their readers certain
insights that are different from those associated with their more rounded counterparts.[40] Wallace Martin has revised Forster's postulate in a perceptive exegesis
that merits citation in full:

---

33. Ibid., 78.
34. Docherty, *Reading (Absent) Character*, 47–48.
35. Springer, *Rhetoric of Literary Character*, 27–36.
36. Bennema, "Theory of Character," 395.
37. Refining Forster's influential typology, Hochman (*Character in Literature*, 86–140) posits a
taxonomy of characters comprising eight polar pairs: stylization/naturalism, coherence/incoherence,
wholeness/fragmentariness, literalness/symbolism, complexity/simplicity, transparency/opacity,
dynamism/staticism, closure/openness. Though I make no attempt to fit Matthew's characters into
these categories, the reader may recognize Hochman's figure in this chapter's carpet.
38. Forster, *Aspects of the Novel*, 71–73.
39. Kingsbury, *Matthew as Story*, 10–14.
40. Barnet (*Not the Righteous but Sinners*) analyzes the interplay of a narrative's readers with its
characters in the construction of meaning.

Because of his simplicity, Huck Finn might justly be called a flat character; his pangs of conscience, in two short passages in the novel, are prized by those who think round, "deep" characters are better, and often they cannot conceal their disappointment with his failure to grow. But the prejudice, violence, credulity, conformity, and even the humanity of the world he inhabits would not even be visible if we did not see them through the transparency of Huck's amoral eyes, which strip away the conventions of "sivilization" to reveal what we civilized readers would not otherwise see. If Huck were round, American literature would gain a slightly more interesting character but lose a world.[41]

My fourth caveat: while appreciation of the type and multiplicity of its characters' traits informs an analysis of Matthew, *the choices made by those characters is more clearly indicative of that Gospel's governing principle.* Some kinds of structural analysis focus on the functions performed by "actants" within a narrative;[42] alternatively, by compiling a comprehensive taxonomy of traits, Kingsbury invites us to explore the *ēthoi* evinced by Matthew's characters. Both of these approaches afford legitimate entrées into literary character; yet to many critics it is evident that action and *ēthos* stand in a reciprocal relationship. As Henry James mused, "What is character but the determination of incident? What is incident but the illustration of character?"[43] With this, Kingsbury would likely concur, inasmuch as the traits of the First Gospel's characters are to some degree manifested in his exposition of the Matthean plot.[44] Still, one wonders: how smoothly does Kingsbury's prolegomenon on persistent character traits meld with his account of those characters' actions, conjoined in a plot that is animated by theological considerations?[45]

For readers of Matthew, Springer's reflections again serve us well. In her judgment character is the kind of person suggested by a visible set of traits; those traits are the expression of regular or habitual *actions*, which are committed in accordance with certain antecedent *choices*. It is in the choices made by characters that the *values* shaping a narrative are revealed.[46] If "by their choices we shall know them," then Springer's hypothesis is crucially important

---

41. W. Martin, *Recent Theories*, 118. Note also Woods's acute observations (*How Fiction Works*, 167): "Flatness is more interesting than [Forster, *Aspects of the Novel*] makes it out to be" (as in Chekhov's short stories); "roundness is more complicated than he makes it out to be" (because a story's characters can never be the same as real people).

42. E.g., Greimas, *Semantique structurale*, 168–82.

43. James, "The Art of Fiction" (1884, repr. 1888); cited by W. Martin, *Recent Theories of Narrative*, 116. See also Chatman, *Story and Discourse*, 108–19.

44. Kingsbury, *Matthew as Story*, 9–28, 43–93, 115–45.

45. For instance, in his recital of the events of Matthew's story, Kingsbury (ibid., 3) observes that Jesus undergoes internal struggle at Gethsemane (26:36–46). However, in his ensuing treatment of characters (ibid., 11), Kingsbury judges the Matthean Jesus to be in complete alignment with God's values. The tension between these two assessments may owe, in part, to Kingsbury's less-than-felicitous distinction between "narrative events" and "trait-based characters."

46. Springer, *Rhetoric of Literary Character*, 27–35; Price, *Forms of Life*, xii et passim.

in construing Matthew's characters, for biblical narrative delights in subtlety, "the art of reticence."[47] Let us, then, weld a tighter bond among Matthean characterization, plot, and religious perspective: from their traits, we may be able to infer and to compare the choices made by Matthew's characters under conflicting circumstances. From those choices, in turn, it may be possible to deduce the theological principles that govern the First Gospel. The test of such a theory demands that we now return to Matthew and its characters.

Exegetical Assessments

The exegesis that interests me here concerns the degree to which Matthew's characters have been crafted in the service of his theological convictions.[48] My thesis is simple: *through the choices narrated or implied in the traits of its characters, Matthew's reader is confronted with various and conflicting degrees of fidelity to God and adherence to God's righteous sovereignty.*[49]

Lord of Heaven and Earth

We begin with a Matthean character that Kingsbury neither denotes as such nor considers separately: *God.* Throughout his treatment, Kingsbury consistently refers to God as an "actor," who intermittently but dramatically participates in Matthew's story: at Jesus' baptism (3:13–17), transfiguration (17:1–8), and resurrection (28:1–7). Through these events, God's normative perspective on Jesus is enunciated and reaffirmed.[50]

With Kingsbury I concur that, in Matthew, the implied author establishes as normative God's evaluative point of view. Yet Kingsbury is needlessly reticent to acknowledge God's status as a character in that Gospel. If God is an "actor" within the story, then in some sense God is a character, whose traits and actions

47. Though the phrase is Alter's (*Art of Biblical Narrative*, 114–30), the idea was most famously captured by Auerbach (*Mimesis*, 3–23), for whom "the whole [of biblical narrative, like Gen. 22:1–19] . . . remains mysterious and 'fraught with background'" (11–12).

48. Limitations of space forbid my examining Matthew's so-called minor characters. This omission is regrettable: many such characters exert an impact disproportional to their brevity of presentation. One thinks of John the Baptist, who anticipates and later fulfills Jesus' exhortation for righteousness, yet wavers while in prison in his estimation of Jesus (Matt. 3:1–15; 11:2–3); the Gentile centurion and Canaanite woman, who display extraordinary faith (8:5–13; 15:21–28); the Galilean women who endure to the bitter end with Jesus and proclaim the resurrection to the disciples (27:55–56, 61; 28:1–10). *Pace* Kingsbury, "ficelles," rather than "minor characters," is a better description of such figures: i.e., typical characters, well defined and individualized, that reveal the protagonist and, often, the values of the implied author (see Harvey, *Character and the Novel*, 62–68; Booth, *Rhetoric of Fiction*, 102–3; and chap. 6 below). Cotter (*Christ of the Miracle Stories*) offers a fine, form-critical study of such ficelles.

49. By "faith" in the First Gospel, I refer to trust that is manifested in obedience: fidelity to God's demands as revealed in the law and interpreted by Jesus (Matt. 8:5–13; 9:27–31; 17:20–21; 21:21–22). See Barth, "Matthew's Understanding of the Law," 112–16.

50. Kingsbury, *Matthew as Story*, 34, 51–52, 79, 90–91. *Pace* Hill ("Figure of Jesus"), who disputes God's normative point of view in the First Gospel, here I argue that Matthew supports such an interpretation.

betoken certain choices and normative commitments.[51] Admittedly, God's activity differs from that of other characters in both quality and degree; the Almighty in Matthew is not personified as are the Olympians in Homeric epic.[52] Nevertheless, God in Matthew's Gospel functions as a "framing character": a figure, notably active at the story's beginning and end, whose externality affects the reader's perception of that story (much as a frame, though extrinsic to the picture, influences our sense of what it encloses).[53]

Similarly, God is "relatively external" to Matthew's story in that God's characterization is known through the words and deeds of Jesus, God's supremely accredited agent (Matt. 1:22; 3:17; 17:5). Through Jesus, Matthew constantly reminds the reader of God's own character[54] as "the heavenly Father," whose righteous love is unmitigated and whose salvific fidelity to creation is wholeheartedly devoted, "mature" or "perfect" (τέλειος [teleios], 5:48; see also 5:21–47; 6:25–34; 7:7–12; 18:23–35; 20:1–16). By sending the beloved Son in a manner consistent with the Lord's past engagement with Israel (as suggested by the genealogy in 1:1–17, the echoes of Torah in 1:18–2:23, and the prophetic "formula quotations" throughout),[55] God's own integrity, or inherent faithfulness, is conveyed. Within this context, Gethsemane and Golgotha constitute a critical decision, not only for Jesus, but also for God: in both cases there is every indication that the Son of God is captured, deserted, and crucified, not through some error of the protagonist's judgment, but by God's own will (26:36–46, 56; 27:46; contrast Aristotle's famous "tragic flaw," *Poet.* 13.5–10.1453a).[56] Yet God's seeming abandonment of Jesus is overturned by the resurrection (Matt. 28:5–7): despite all appearances to the contrary, God ultimately keeps faith with the Son and, in a sense, with God's own self (cf. 16:21; 17:22–23; 20:17–19; 26:56).

Through the framing character of God, Matthew communicates the quintessential values that govern his story of Jesus: the salvific justice, loving faithfulness, and transcendent authority of God. Banal though it may sound—but of

51. Thus, too, Knowles ("Plotting Jesus," 121), for whom God is "the prime mover and agent behind the [Matthean] narrative and therefore, arguably, its main character." Knowles's study complements mine by its attention to Scripture as God's "voice" in Matthew.

52. Cf. Homer, *Iliad* 4.1–140; 5.1–518; 14.153–401; 21.385–513; 22.225–366.

53. Thus Springer, *Rhetoric of Literary Character*, 113–26, identifying Douglas of *The Turn of the Screw* (1898) and Alice Staverton of "The Jolly Corner" (1908) as "framing characters" in Henry James's fiction. I am suggesting, not that Matthew ignores God's activity during Jesus' ministry (thus, 4:11; 6:9–15, 30; 12:28; 17:5; 22:32; 23:22), but rather that God's decisive interventions for Jesus at the Gospel's beginning and end shape the reader's perception of the whole.

54. The same holds true in John, as noted by M. Thompson in "'God's Voice You Have Never Heard.'"

55. Matt. 1:22–23; 2:15b, 17–18, 23; 4:14–16; 8:17; 12:17–21; 13:35; 21:4–5; 27:9–10. Stanton, "Origin and Purpose," offers a valuable *Forschungsbericht* on Matthew's use of Jewish Scripture.

56. Such imbedded *hamartia* (ἁμαρτία) characterizes Oedipus, so ignorant of his own identity that he croons, "I want a girl just like the girl that married dear old Dad."

nonetheless primary importance—in Matthew, God never disappoints. God, after all, is indivisibly, predictably perfect (τέλειος [*teleios*]). In that respect *and by Matthew's design*, God is a flat character: the epitome of uniform, absolute righteousness.

The Devil

Diametrically opposed to God is *the devil*, or *Satan*, depicted in Matthew as the negation of all that characterizes the heavenly Father. God is perfectly righteous, the One whose name is to be consecrated (Matt. 5:48; 6:9); Satan is the transcendently "Evil One," the personification of hypocrisy and deceit (4:3, 6; 6:13; 13:19, 38). Whereas God and divine agents actuate health and wholeness, the devil and his minions promote disease and demonism (cf. 4:23–24; 8:1–17; 9:1–8, 18–35; 10:1–8; 12:22–32). Archenemy of the Son of Man (13:25, 37–39), the devil presides over a nefarious domain at war with God's dominion (13:36–43). Prior to the eschatological consummation and its attendant destruction of his kingdom (25:41), Satan's pernicious power suborns those of "this generation" who have been confronted with the call to God's righteous domain (12:39, 45c; 13:24–30, 38–39; 16:4, 23; cf. 5:37; 7:15–20; 15:19; 18:32; 24:12; 25:26).

Though he discusses "the arch-adversary of Jesus Messiah, the Son of God,"[57] Kingsbury no more identifies Satan as a "character" in the Matthean narrative than he describes God as such. The reasons for this are unclear. To be sure, we must exercise care in delineating this particular character: not unlike God, though to a lesser degree,[58] Satan assists in "framing" the story of Jesus in compliance with one of Matthew's governing, theological principles. In a narrative that chronicles the necessity and difficulty of subordination to God's righteous sovereignty, Satan personifies the attraction of humanity toward conduct that is self-serving, faithless, and arrogant—the same diabolical temptations that Jesus endures in the wilderness (Matt. 4:1–11). The characterizations of God[59] and of Satan in that pericope establish the antipodal extremes, anticipated in the nativity account (1:18–2:23), between which the action of the ensuing narrative will swing: the countervailing power exerted by good and evil, the "magnetic pull" of allegiance either to God or to Satan.[60] As Kingsbury observes, the Matthean narrative is driven by the clash between God and Satan, portrayed in the teaching of Jesus (5:33–37; 6:24; 7:15–23; 12:25–37, 43–45; 13:18–30, 36–43, 47–50; 25:31–46) and dramatized

---

57. Kingsbury, *Matthew* (PC), 77; cf. 75–78.

58. Matthew does not present Satan's wickedness as coextensive with God's righteousness; nor is Matthew's story triggered by a contest between God and Satan (cf. Job 1:1–2:13). At the risk of overworking Springer's metaphorical "framing character," the figure of Satan might be regarded as a "matte," which complements the character of God in framing the evangelist's picture of Jesus.

59. Note that, throughout his temptation by Satan, Jesus' rebuttals are centered, not on himself, but on his responsible fidelity to God (Matt. 4:4, 7, 10).

60. Though not theocentrically, Aristotle also notes that a distinction between "virtue" and "vice" is fundamental for both humanity and dramatic characterizations (*Poet.* 1.2.1–7.1448a).

through the surrogate altercation of Jesus with the religious leaders (9:10–13; 12:1–45; 15:1–20; 16:1–12, 21; 19:3–9; 20:18–19; 21:12–46; 22:15–46; 23:1–26; 26:1–5, 47–68; 27:1–2).[61]

Therefore, with respect to narrative function, the devil in Matthew's story is analogous to God in one sense: both are essentially flat, framing characters that typify the alternatives of fidelity and faithlessness, between which every other character must choose. As the unqualified, ever-flowing fountainhead of evil, Satan comprehensively defines the perfidious disobedience, intrinsically antagonistic to the will of a categorically righteous God, by which all other characters are tempted and to which some ultimately succumb.

God-with-Us

Perfect righteousness and fidelity to God are among the theological values that shape Matthew's story. The character of God, allusively portrayed, frames those normative principles. Among the major characters who advance the Matthean plot, *Jesus* is indubitably the one that most closely approximates those values. He exemplifies all the traits summarized by Kingsbury: compassion empowered by the authority to save, integrity of word and deed, complete steadfastness to God and to his disciples, fearless confrontation of evil forces, utterly self-giving service and love for humankind (cf. Matt. 1:21; 4:23; 8:23–34; 9:1–8, 35–36; 14:13–21; 16:13–21; 17:22–23; 20:17–19, 25–28; 28:20).[62] Russell Pregeant's assessment is on target: "as Son of God/Messiah, to whom 'all things' have been delivered and who can speak of the yoke of Torah as his own, [Jesus] occupies a vantage point that is as close as possible to God's own."[63]

Kingsbury's otherwise cogent assessment of Jesus' characterization in Matthew invites modifications. First, Kingsbury contends that, because of his multiple traits, Jesus emerges from the First Gospel as a round character. In my view—to the contrary—Matthew's characterization of Jesus is flat, since the many traits ascribed to him are manifestations of a single "root trait," diversely identified as "righteousness," "obedience," "faithfulness," or simply "goodness."[64] Second, this flatness of Jesus' character is neither accidental nor symptomatic of the evangelist's deficient literary creativity. Rather, it squares precisely with the implied author's governing theological principles: if kinship is expected between child and parent,

---

61. Similarly, Kingsbury, *Matthew as Story*, 56: "In Matthew's scheme of things, the world is the scene where two kingdoms, or spheres of power, are locked in cosmic battle (13:36–43)."

62. Ibid., 12–13, 45–48, 59–93.

63. Pregeant, "Wisdom Passages," 227. So also Kingsbury: "Matthew establishes Jesus as the thoroughly reliable exponent of God's evaluative point of view" ("Figure of Jesus," 6).

64. Here I apply to Matthew's characterization of Jesus a possibility suggested by Kingsbury with respect to the religious leaders: namely, a root quality may be manifested in a variety of traits (*Matthew as Story*, 18–19). Matthew's association of "goodness" with unwavering fidelity to God accounts for the abrasiveness and harsh vituperation occasionally attributed to a "good" character like Jesus (hence, Matt. 15:21–28; 23:13–36).

even as a disciple should resemble the teacher (Matt. 10:24), then Jesus, the Son of God (3:17; 17:5) and incarnation of God's wisdom (11:27), naturally embodies the perfection (τελείωσις [teleiōsis]) that characterizes his heavenly Father (5:48). The Matthean Jesus never surprises the reader acculturated to the norms of the First Gospel: from start to finish Jesus is predictably, statically, consistently obedient to the Father's purposes.[65] Overall the character of Jesus is flat, and deliberately so. As such, he personifies the whole-souled righteousness that looms large in the scheme of values undergirding Matthew's story.[66]

Though its full exploration is impossible here, another element of Matthean characterization deserves mention. As revealed by his choices, the righteous character of Jesus approximates—but is never completely interchangeable with—the evangelist's characterization of God as ultimately righteous. Matthew's Christology is high: Jesus is Emmanuel, "God with us" (1:23; cf. 11:27; 18:20; 28:20), and for that reason receives human veneration (2:8, 11; 8:2; 9:18; 14:33). Nevertheless, discriminations between the Son and the Father are subtly introduced and maintained throughout Matthew. (a) Matthew's story of Jesus is framed by miraculous events initiated, not by Jesus, but by God (the nativity: 1:18–2:23; the resurrection: 28:1–20; cf. 16:21; 17:22; 20:19). (b) Likewise, Jesus' teaching in Matthew focuses, not on himself, but on the kingdom of the heavenly Father (5:16, 45, 48; 6:1–18, 25–33; 7:7–12, 21–23; 10:20, 31–33; 12:50; 13:10–50; 15:3–6; 18:10–35; 19:10–15, 23–30; 20:1–16; 22:1–10, 15–22, 29–40; 25:1–13, 31–46). (c) Jesus explicitly differentiates the prerogatives, service, and knowledge proper to the Son and to the Father (19:17; 20:23, 28; 23:9–10; 24:36). In this connection, the crises at Gethsemane (26:36–46) and Golgotha (27:33–50) should be taken at their suspenseful face value: despite prior indications of his resolve (4:1–11; 16:21; 17:22; 20:17–19), Jesus' own will is sorely challenged by his Father's (N.B.: the anguish suggested by 26:37–38). Jesus *could* have aborted the mission to which he was called (N.B.: 26:39, 42, 53; cf. 20:28) and, on the cross, expressed abandonment by God when he chose not to do so (27:46).

As revealed by the choices of his ministry, therefore, Matthew's Jesus emerges as *largely* flat, or proximate to God's own faultless fidelity. Nevertheless, Jesus is not *completely* flat, nor is he flatly identified *as* God.[67] To the contrary: "'Call no one your father on earth, for you have one Father, who is in heaven'" (23:9 AT).

---

65. Cf. Culpepper's similar assessment of the Johannine Jesus (*Anatomy of the Fourth Gospel*, 103). At those points where Jesus surprises the Gospel's other characters, all can be attributed to his likeness to God (e.g., 9:2–4; 14:25–26; 15:25–26).

66. Thus Kingsbury, *Matthew as Story*, 111: "It is [Jesus] in Matthew's story in whom the greater righteousness comes to perfect expression: Single-hearted in his devotion to God, he loves the neighbor as self (5:48; 22:37–40)."

67. Again, John's Gospel offers an interesting parallel: for the fourth evangelist, as for the first, Jesus is the center of interest insofar as he directs the believer to an ultimate understanding of God (Barrett, "Christocentric or Theocentric?" 4).

Elders and Chief Priests and Scribes

As depicted in the First Gospel, *the religious authorities*[68] reflect a dark mirror image of Jesus. Whereas Jesus exemplifies authentic righteousness and insight into God's intention (Matt. 5:1–7:29), these officials display only the patina of righteousness and (for the most part) incomprehension of God's will (15:14; 16:1–4; 23:16–19, 24–28). "'Seeing, they do not see, and hearing, they do not hear, nor do they understand'" (13:13 AT): the Messiah, who by his heavenly Father's authority bestows new life on Israel, is regarded by the leaders as a blasphemous "deceiver," or messianic fraud, who at the behest of Beelzebul threatens Israel's destruction (9:3, 34; 12:24; 15:1–2; 26:59–65; 27:63–64). The irony is stunning: by treacherously imputing this character to Jesus, the religious leaders adopt for themselves those very attributes (12:30–37; 15:3–9, 19; 21:33–44; 22:29; 23:4–39; 27:41–43, 62–64; 28:11–15). Indeed, practically all of the leaders' traits, as itemized by Kingsbury, are exactly antithetic to those of the Matthean Jesus. He displays manifold goodness (genuine obedience, perspicacity, truthfulness, candor, fearlessness, innocence, and compassion); inversely, the religious leaders exhibit various forms of evil (legalistic error, blindness, calumny, manipulative deception, fearfulness, malicious conspiracy, injustice, and cunning heartlessness: see 9:10–13, 36; 12:1–14, 22–32; 15:1–20, 32; 21:33–46; 22:15–33; 23:4–7; 26:1–5, 55, 59–62; 27:11–12, 63–64; 28:11–15). Matthew's characterization of the religious leaders is, therefore, commensurate with that of Jesus: each flatly inverts the other.

With much of this analysis Kingsbury would agree;[69] we can advance the discussion farther. First, although their characterization is generally flat, the religious authorities in Matthew nicely exhibit the kinesis that Docherty discerns in such characters: the leaders' hostility toward Jesus does not remain fixed but steadily escalates as the story progresses (thus 9:3–4, 11; 12:1–14; 21:23–22:46; 26:3–5, 59–68; 27:1–2).[70] Second, this kinetic development is disclosed, not

---

68. I follow Kingsbury's lead in focusing on the Jewish religious elite, who are sharply etched in the First Gospel (*Matthew as Story*, 115–27). For Matthew, however, the primary point of contrast between them and Jesus is neither their Jewishness nor their religiosity (since both Pilate and Herod "the king [*sic*]" are similarly pitted against Jesus). Matthew evinces distrust of all *leaders*—Jewish, Gentile, or proto-Christian—who do not manifest righteous faith (2:1–18; 18:10–35; 19:28–30; 20:26–28; 27:11–24). In this context it is significant that the centurion's faith is measured by his self-subordination to Jesus' authority (8:5–13). For an astute assessment of this aspect of the Matthean perspective, see Amy-Jill Levine, *Social and Ethnic Dimensions*, 89–130; 241–71; note also Krentz, "Community and Character."

69. Kingsbury, *Matthew as Story*, 17–24.

70. In a correlative expression of "kinetic flatness," Jesus' response to the scribes and Pharisees becomes progressively vitriolic (Matt. 5:20; 15:1–20; 23:13–36; see Kingsbury, "Developing Conflict"; idem, *Matthew as Story*, 116–27; Simmonds, "'Woe to You!'"). At issue is not whether conflict between Jesus and his coreligionists intensifies in Matthew. Of course it does. That for which we should reach is a subtler concept of characterization that helps us better understand the discernible evolution of this Gospel's essentially static characters.

merely by sheer identification of the authorities' traits (*pace* Kingsbury), but more evidently by the *choices* those characters make throughout the narrative. The same deeds and words of Jesus are seen and heard by both the crowds and their leaders. The former respond with astonishment and the potential for faith; the latter opt to accuse Jesus of blasphemy and to align him with the prince of demons (9:2–8, 32–34; 12:22–24; 26:65–66).[71]

A third observation requires extended discussion that can be only adumbrated here. Kingsbury identifies an affinity that, for Matthew, exists between the religious leaders and Satan (12:34; 13:38–39).[72] What is interesting, however, is Matthew's refusal to equate the former with the latter.[73] If the evangelist had intended such an equivalence, it would be impossible to account either for Jesus' occasional concession of the scribes and Pharisees' righteousness, provisional authority, and scrupulosity (5:20; 23:2–3, 23), or for particular Jewish leaders in Matthew whose admirable traits betoken commendable choices (the scribe in 8:19; the ruler in 9:18; Joseph of Arimathea [perhaps] in 27:57–60).[74] In these passages the evangelist suggests that, while the religious elite demonstrate some faithfulness to God—certainly more than Satan, who is inherently demonic—that fidelity is truncated and requires amplification. Accordingly, the righteousness of scribes and Pharisees must be *exceeded*; zealous observance of legal minutiae must be consummated in concern for weightier, wholesome matters of justice, mercy, and faith.[75] Again, Matthew's characterization of the religious authorities parallels that of Jesus: though not interchangeable with God, by his choices Jesus tends toward righteousness that is utterly faithful; though not equivalent with Satan, by their choices Israel's leaders are inclined toward faithless, diabolical conduct. If upheld, this conclusion should bear on later allegations of Matthew's anti-Jewish ide-

---

71. In Matt. 23 the first woe (vv. 13–14) is addressed to the scribes and Pharisees' decided refusal to enter the kingdom or to permit that option for others. Likewise, the remaining woes are predicated on willful decisions made by Israel's leaders (23:16–39).

72. Kingsbury, *Matthew as Story*, 19, 116–18.

73. *Pace* Longenecker ("Evil at Odds"), who sees in Matthew a uniform "coalition of evil" among Satan and the Pharisees that threatens to pull the narrative apart.

74. In Matt. 8:19–20 the scribe's willingness to follow Jesus may intimate presumption or myopic arrogance; I am less certain than Kingsbury of a harsh repudiation embedded in Jesus' oblique response ("On Following Jesus"). Elsewhere (*Matthew as Story*, 67–68) Kingsbury acknowledges the difficulty that 23:2–3, 23 presents for construing Matthew's outlook on the scribes and Pharisees as totally disapproving.

75. Matthew's description of the leaders as "hypocrites" (15:7–8; 22:18; 23:13, 15, 23, 25, 27, 28–29; cf. 6:2, 5, 16; 7:5; 24:51) is significant even if hard to pin down. That term connotes more than a pious veneer covering an interior lack of righteousness (Wilckens, "ὑποκρίνομαι") or irresponsible interpretation of the law (Garland, *Intention of Matthew 23*, 111–17). For Matthew, ὑπόκρισις (*hypokrisis*) seems to describe a diminished fidelity (Kingsbury, *Matthew as Story*, 19–20), stemming from intentional self-deception (Via, *Self-Deception and Wholeness*, 92–98).

ology.[76] Doubtless owing to the internecine Jewish controversy from which the First Gospel sprang,[77] Matthew's Jesus and Jewish authorities are infuriated with each other, but the evangelist presents the leaders as neither completely flat nor homogenously evil.[78]

The Multitudes

Up to a point, Kingsbury's appraisal of *the crowds*[79] in Matthew is convincing. Receptive to Jesus yet imperceptive of his full significance (4:25; 7:28–29; 8:1, 18; 13:13, 53–58; 19:2; 20:29–31; 21:9), they typically present a contrast with both their leaders (who generally reject Jesus) and the disciples (who accept Jesus as their master). On the basis of their few character traits, Kingsbury deems the crowds to be a unified, flat character. If, however, we consider the choices they make and the degrees of faith implied by those choices, another assessment of the crowds emerges. Throughout most of the narrative, the crowds evince sympathy for Jesus, even when their leaders react antipathetically (Matt. 9:2–8, 32–34; 12:22–24; 22:23–34; cf. 15:10–12; 23:1–39). In the passion narrative the masses align themselves with their chief priests and elders in expediting Jesus' arrest, sentencing, and execution (26:47, 55; 27:1–2, 15–26, 39–44). Their bloodthirsty defection is startling, though in retrospect not without anticipation: as portrayed by Matthew, the depth of their dedication to Jesus has always been in question. Amazement is not the same as allegiance (thus 7:28; 9:33; 15:31; 22:33; cf. 13:53–58); mere physical "following" is not on par with costly discipleship (4:25; 8:1, 10; 12:15; 14:13; 19:2; 20:29 vs. 4:20–22; 8:22; 9:9; 10:38; 16:24; 19:27–29).[80] Nor is acclamation of Jesus as "a prophet" tantamount to confession of him as Christ, the

---

76. Among others, see Burnett: "It is debatable which writing in the New Testament . . . is the most anti-Jewish, but Matthew's Gospel certainly deserves a place at or near the top of the list" ("Exposing the Anti-Jewish Ideology,"155). Burnett's essay is an honorable stand against vicious Christians' terrorization of Jews that in my view misreads Matthew. If the First Gospel is inherently anti-Jewish, how does one explain its unreserved endorsement of Israel's Scripture and its refusal to dissociate emergent Christianity from Judaism (see Allison, *The New Moses*)? Nearer the crux is Luz: "[The church's] story of Jesus, in other words, should express gratitude toward Judaism rather than bitterness. We must consider the terrible consequences resulting for Jews from, for example, Matthew's Israel theology or from other books of the Bible and their Christian interpretation. These are the experiences that *we* must come to grips with—and they are quite different from Matthew's [intentions]" (*Theology of Matthew*, 156–57, italics original).

77. Scholarly investigation of this subject is practically bottomless. For a balanced overview and assessment, consult Stanton, *A Gospel for a New People*, 111–281.

78. *Pace* van Tilborg, *Jewish Leaders in Matthew*. Weaver ("You Will Know Them") elucidates Matthew's comparably complex portrait of Roman figures.

79. With Amy-Jill Levine (*Social and Ethnic Dimensions*, 265–68), I doubt that Matthew systematically differentiates οἱ ὄχλοι (*hoi ochloi*, "the crowds") from ὁ λαός (*ho laos*, "the [ethnic] people of God"; note the terms' apparent equivalence in 4:23–25; 26:47; 27:15–26). I am less confident than she that Matthew correlates certain crowds' reactions to Jesus with particular provenances (e.g., "Galilee" vs. "Jerusalem").

80. Kingsbury, "The Verb *Akolouthein*."

Son of God (cf. 16:13–14; 21:11, 46).[81] In each of these cases, the crowds' commitment to Jesus is real but inadequate and finally evanescent; like seed sown on rocky soil, they endure for a time[82] but instantly fall away with the onset of tribulation (13:20–21). Insofar as they may be analyzed collectively, the crowds are better regarded as fairly rounded characters: albeit their minimalist representation, they are lifelike in their unpredictable vacillation and divided loyalty to Jesus.[83] To be, in this manner, characteristically round is no compliment in the implied judgment of an author who decidedly favors flatly consummate (τέλειος) and unalloyed devotion to God's kingdom and God's Messiah.

These Twelve

In contrast with Jesus and the religious leaders, but like the crowds, *the disciples* in Matthew do not so much initiate action as react to others' decisions.[84] As Kingsbury suggests, their characterization is rounded: throughout the narrative their traits conflict, their loyalties shift, their choices unfold in unexpected ways. Simon Peter, Andrew, and the Zebedee brothers initially demonstrate unquestioning obedience to Jesus' summons (Matt. 4:18–22; 9:9; 10:2–4; 21:1–7; 26:17–19). Contrary to Israel at large (11:2–3, 16–19; 13:53–58; 21:9–11), the disciples perceive the secrets of the heavenly kingdom (13:11, 51; also 16:12; 17:13), spurn this world's quotidian security (19:27, 29), and recognize their leader as the Messiah and Son of God (14:33; 16:16–17; also 11:25–27). Consequently, they are esteemed as the foundation of a new people of God (16:18; 18:17; 19:28; 21:43), "brothers" of Jesus and of one another (12:49; 18:35; 23:8; 25:40; 28:10), and adoptive "sons of God" insofar as they do the Father's will (5:45; 13:38; cf. 6:9; 7:21). By virtue of their elect position, they are vested with missionary authority derived from Jesus' own (10:1, 5–15, 40–42; 16:19; 18:18; 28:18–20) and are subjected to attacks akin to those experienced by their master (9:14; 10:16–25; 12:1–2; 15:2; 24:3–25:46; 26:69–75; 27:64; 28:11–15). While obedient to God's kingdom, mediated through Jesus, the disciples also prove to be irresolute (8:21–22; 26:33–35, 69–75; cf. 10:34–39), fearful (14:26, 30), imperceptive (15:16; 16:9–11, 22–23; cf. 26:22), and lacking in trust (8:25–26; 14:16–17, 28–31; 15:33; 16:8;

---

81. Here Kingsbury's point is well taken (*Matthew as Story*, 24–25). Yet it is hard to see why one title ("Son of God"), however prominent in the First Gospel, must be regarded as the preeminent description, under which all other christological affirmations must be subsumed (ibid., 52–58, 102; idem, *Matthew* [PC], 33–65). See Meier, *Vision of Matthew*, 68, 217–19; Hill, "Son and Servant."

82. For that reason, *pace* Kingsbury (*Matthew as Story*, 24–25), I am not persuaded that the crowds entirely lack faith in Jesus. Contrast alternative exegeses of Matt. 21:8–11 by Meier (*Vision of Matthew*, 145–46) and Minear ("The Disciples and the Crowds").

83. A.-J. Levine (*Social and Ethnic Dimensions*, 266): "Matthew cannot state whether the crowds will eventually number among the disciples because the future era of the church is both new and open."

84. The disciples' typical responsiveness is evident in eleven "character-shaping incidents" (Matt. 4:18–22; 8:18–22; 13:51; 14:22–23; 16:5–23; 17:1–13; 19:23–20:28; 26:14–25; 26:30–35, 58, 69–75; 27:3–10; 28:16–20) studied by Edwards, "Characterization of the Disciples."

17:19–20; 21:18–22). As the plot advances toward crisis in Jerusalem, their will, already enervated, collapses altogether: resisting Jesus' example of discipleship as self-sacrificial service for others (16:21–28; 19:13–15; 20:20–28; 26:6–13), the disciples eventually betray their calling and desert Jesus in his time of greatest trial (26:14–16, 20–25, 30–56, 69–75).

No doubt the First Gospel's implied author encourages the reader to identify with the disciples and, in so doing, to adopt an evaluative perspective on disciple-ship—either in alignment or contradistinction with the disciples' evolving conduct and point of view.[85] In suggesting that Matthew's depiction of the disciples confronts the reader with a choice between undivided fealty to God and feckless capitulation to Satan's authority, Kingsbury is correct.[86]

To the preceding I would interpose three qualifications. First, the decision between obedience and infidelity constitutes a governing principle of the Matthean narrative; all of the characters in the First Gospel, not just the disciples, guide the reader in exploring the rewards and hazards of that choice. Second, as round characters, the disciples reveal, in Matthew's implied judgment, a theo-logical response that is undesirable or at least inadequate. On balance, they are ὀλιγόπιστοι (oligopistoi), "of little faith" (Matt. 6:30; 8:26; 14:31; 16:8; 17:20). Their allegiance to heavenly sovereignty (βασιλεία [basileia]) is greater than that of the crowds or their leaders; yet it does not attain the flatly rigorous perfec-tion demanded of a disciple who would be like his teacher, Jesus (5:48; 10:24–25; 18:15–17).[87] Third, I am less confident than Kingsbury that Matthew's Gospel ends on an unequivocally triumphant note of happy resolution, in which the reunited disciples "undertake the worldwide missionary task to which [the risen Christ] commissions them."[88] Where does the narrator say this? Although Jesus confers on the Eleven his ever-sustaining authority to make disciples, to baptize, and to teach among all nations (28:18–20), their decision to accept and to exercise this commission is left unreported. Even more, their anticipatory response to that charge is characteristically divided: to the mountain they go and worship Jesus, but some doubt (28:16–17; cf. 14:22–33). At the Gospel's conclusion, when confronted by Jesus' unwavering fidelity and his disciples' motley faith, doesn't Matthew's

---

85. Kingsbury puts the matter well: "It is through such granting or withholding of approval on cue, therefore, that the reader becomes schooled in the values that govern the life of discipleship in Matthew's story" (Matthew as Story, 14). See also Luz, "Die Jünger"; S. Brown, "The Mission to Israel"; Edwards, "Uncertain Faith."

86. Kingsbury, Matthew as Story, 131–42.

87. After the Twelve's desertion and Jesus' crucifixion, an ostensible religious leader (Joseph of Arimathea) and some members of the crowd (the women from Galilee) display a more perfect discipleship (Matt. 27:55–61).

88. Kingsbury, Matthew as Story, 17; note also 130, 144.

reader face for the last time the fundamental choice[89] that presides over the entire narrative: under whose sovereignty will you ultimately serve (cf. 6:24)?[90]

Summary

Characterization within the First Gospel does not stand as an independent, literary entity. Informing and governing the varying depth of Matthew's characters is a salient theological principle: the reader should render obedient faithfulness to God, whose own fidelity has been decisively manifested in Jesus Christ. Whereas a modern novel might track the psychological evolution or devolution of a central character,[91] Matthew takes another, most interesting tack: its narrative portrays the constancy and instability of trust, the waxing and waning of faith, through many different characters. By probing the dynamics of faith through figures both "historical" and "supernatural," the First Gospel's narrative world emerges as a complicated mixture of the representational and the illustrative: Matthew's story purports to be mimetically correlative with "the real world" of first-century Galilee and Judea, yet it is to a high degree theologically stylized.[92] God and Satan—and in lesser measure Jesus and the religious leaders—are flatly transparent to the poles of righteousness and disobedience between which the Gospel's story suspensefully swings. The disciples and the crowds display some of the rounded complexity of human life, torn between the summons to faithfulness and temptations to infidelity. To switch metaphors, Matthew evinces a talent for *chiaroscuro*: the light and shade of the First Gospel's characterizations are as subtly or starkly rendered as needed by the evangelist to convey the tenor of his religious confessions and, in so doing, to form his readers in steadfast righteousness.[93]

89. My phraseology intends to contextualize, not to resolve, the debate over the itinerant or domiciliary character of Matthean missiology (see also 10:5–11:1). With Kingsbury (*Matthew* [PC], 103–4; idem, *Matthew as Story*, 156–57) I concur that the evidence is ambiguous: prophets and teachers appear to have operated both within and beyond the Matthean church (7:15–20; 10:41; 23:8–12, 34).

90. Elsewhere some responses to charges by Jesus are explicitly negative (Matt. 19:21–22) or left unreported (8:21–22). Regarding their missionary ventures, Jesus' predictions of his disciples' conduct are not uniformly approving (10:21–22; 24:10; cf. 25:31–46). One may justly say of Matt. 28:16–20 what Tannehill has seen in Mark 16:1–8: "It is not clear how the story will develop from this point. . . . A positive development is indicated but negative possibilities are also suggested. The Gospel is open-ended, for the outcome of the story depends on decisions which the church, including the reader, must still make" ("The Disciples in Mark," 404).

91. While agreeing with practically all critics that "the developing character who changes inwardly is quite a late arrival in literature," Scholes and Kellogg conjecture that the Gospels may have been instrumental in nudging ancient narrative toward "inward development." "The inwardness of Christianity, as represented by Jesus' statement on adultery in the heart [Matt. 5:28], opens up one way for the consideration of the inner life" (*Nature of Narrative*, 165, 167).

92. On the relation between "real" and fictional worlds, see Scholes and Kellogg, *Nature of Narrative*, 82–88.

93. So also M. Thompson on John ("'God's Voice You Have Never Heard,'" 200–201): "The primary purpose of the Gospel is not 'informational' but 'formational.'"

RESIDUAL QUERIES AND REFLECTIONS

Where might we go from here? Three areas seem to me ripe for continued investigation.

1. How might the study of Matthean characterization inform our assessment of the First Evangelist's *Sitz im Leben*? To what degree, for instance, do the convoluted responses of the disciples and crowds symbolize the mixed reception that was accorded to the kerygma of the Matthean community, both within and beyond its own walls? Is the flat, uncompromising rigor of the Matthean proclamation the *cause* or the *result* of that *corpus mixtum* that Matthean Christians encountered among the Jews and Gentiles whom they missioned (Matt. 13:24–30, 47–50)? Do the First Gospel's characterizations afford us clues in answering, or more helpfully framing, that question? While in some quarters it is unfashionable to claim little if any correlation between a Gospel's historical origins and its narrative construction, I am inclined to think, with John Donahue,[94] that a work like Matthew can be responsibly adopted as both a window onto its provenance as well as a mirror held up to readers of every generation. To be sure, such doubled vision—as though gazing both into and through a "two-way mirror"—constantly courts distortion and must be constantly, carefully checked.

2. A cognate question: Could the study of characterization benefit historians in their attempt to reconstruct Jesus or other figures within the First Gospel? Although its answer is unclear, such a question is not preposterous. After all, as Wallace Martin has observed,[95] there is arguably more that unites than divides the genres of history and fiction (and one might add, religious biographies like the Gospels). In all cases, similar literary conventions are employed to naturalize stories and render them credible to us. Rather than separating us from reality, characters and plotted narratives actually *create* the reality that we experience, whether in historical reportage of the so-called real world or in its fictional and religious counterparts. Would it not be ironic if the tools of some literary criticism, which has customarily deflected historical issues pertaining to the Gospels, proved serviceable to historians in their reflection on, and construction of, the critical narratives in which they are interested?

3. Finally, the theological dimension of characterization, and of other literary conventions, is a field of Gospel research ripe for harvest. One may justifiably dissociate the techniques of literary analysis from the *methods* of ordinary redaction criticism; however, to neglect the redaction-critical *perspective*, with its salutary emphasis on the evangelists' theological concerns, is to risk distorting

---

94. John Donahue, "Windows and Mirrors."
95. W. Martin, *Recent Theories of Narrative*, 71–75.

the kind of narrative that the Gospels present.[96] Common to both literature and religious belief is their capacity to gather the threads of the past into a coherent weave for the future, to render perspicuous life's dark and joyful jumble.[97] To paraphrase Forster: theology, like fiction, is truer than history, because both move beyond the evidence.[98] Criticism of the Gospels that reckons with literary features like characterization apart from their theological implications is by no means illegitimate. It is, in my judgment, ultimately impoverished.

96. I have elaborated on this issue and my understanding of its significance in another context: *The Disciples according to Mark*, 254–87.

97. Walcutt (*Man's Changing Masks*) and MacIntyre (*After Virtue*) explore the interplay of narrative with a society's mores. On the convergence of narrative and theology in Christian communities, see Hauerwas, *A Community of Character*.

98. Forster, *Aspects of the Novel*, 63; see also Price, *Forms of Life*, 298–301.

Chapter Three

An Oration at Olivet

The loveliest thing we can experience is the mysterious. It is the basic feeling that stands at the cradle of true art and science.

Albert Einstein[1]

Mark's is a mysterious Gospel, and no portion of it bristles with more mysteries than the so-called Synoptic apocalypse in chapter 13.[2] Beyond discrete exegetical problems posed by its verses, interpreters have long pondered the material's derivation, either from the historical Jesus[3] or from some Jewish or Jewish-Christian prototype,[4] and the degree, if any, to which that material may properly be regarded as "apocalyptic." Curiously, few have studied one of Mark 13's most obvious features: its character and function as a rhetorical event.

Just at this point, George Kennedy's rhetorical approach[5] offers help. Following that lead, in this chapter I essay an assessment of the rhetoric of Mark 13. Here are my presuppositions. First, in line with the current scholarly consensus, I consider this chapter eschatologically oriented but not an "apocalypse" as such.[6] If we accept a helpful distinction drawn by John Collins,[7] we need not worry that Mark 13 fails to conform

---

1. Einstein, *Mein Weltbild*, 16 (AT).
2. For the chapter's modern history of exegesis, see Beasley-Murray, *Jesus and the Last Days*.
3. Beasley-Murray (ibid., 350–76) is highly optimistic in tracing the discourse back to Jesus himself.
4. Proposed by Colani (*Jésus Christ et les croyances messianiques* [1864]), the theory of a "little apocalypse" underlying Mark 13 has fallen on hard times in recent Synoptic study. The hypothesis was notably revived by Pesch, *Naherwartungen*, 207–23, and just as notably rejected by A. Y. Collins, *Beginning of the Gospel*, 73–91.
5. Kennedy, *New Testament Interpretation*, 3–38. See above, chap. 1.
6. Thus Schüssler Fiorenza, "Phenomenon"; Rowland, *The Open Heaven*, 9–72, 351–57. Dissenting while reasserting this pericope's formal "apocalypticism" is Brandenburger, *Markus 13*, 21–42.
7. J. Collins, "Towards a Morphology of Genre."

43

to the literary genre of an apocalypse (as the book of Daniel so obviously does); it is enough to recognize that Mark adopts an apocalyptic *perspective*, awaiting a cataclysmic end of the present age. A second assumption: analyzing Mark 13 in accordance with Greco-Roman rhetorical conventions is appropriate, owing to rhetoric's pervasiveness throughout Mediterranean antiquity.[8] Third, questions attached to the sources and authenticity of the Olivet Discourse are immaterial to the question of its rhetorical effectiveness.[9] It is the discourse in its canonical form, as presented by the Markan Jesus to the second evangelist's early Christian community,[10] that interests me.

A RHETORICAL ANALYSIS OF MARK 13

The Rhetorical Unit

For defining the limits of the speech in Mark 13, the markers of inclusio are obvious. At 13:5a we find a common Markan formula, "And Jesus began to say to them" (AT),[11] introducing Jesus' discourse, which commences at 13:5b. At 14:1 the narrator intervenes, shifting the time, characters, and circumstances. Accordingly, 13:37 may be regarded as the oration's end. Between these points lies an unbroken address of thirty-three verses (5b–37): the longest uninterrupted speech of Jesus in the Second Gospel.[12]

The Rhetorical Situation

According to Lloyd Bitzer, a rhetorical situation may be defined as that "natural context of persons, events, objects, relations, and an exigence which strongly invites utterance; this invited utterance participates naturally in the situation, is in many instances necessary to the completion of situational activity, and by means of its participation with [the] situation obtains its meaning and its rhetorical character."[13] Does this complicated state of affairs obtain in Mark 13?

Though its verification depends on closer inspection of the rhetoric in verses 5b–37, a provisional case can be made for its rhetorical situation.

---

8. Kinneavy, *Greek Rhetorical Origins*, 56–100, summarizes the evidence.

9. Broadly conceived, the question of sources is not entirely irrelevant. As we shall see, the *ēthos* of Jesus and the use of Septuagintal allusions enhance Mark's rhetorical force.

10. That community's geographical and social location remains uncertain. Marcus ("The Jewish War") mounts a vigorous case for Mark's Syrian provenance. Elsewhere I have suggested that traditional association of the Second Gospel with Rome in the 60s is not implausible ("Was Mark a Roman Gospel?" and *Mark: Images*, 224–50).

11. See also Mark 1:45; 4:1; 5:20; 6:2, 34; 8:31; 10:32; 12:1.

12. The only discourses of comparable length are Mark 4:3–32 and 7:6–23, both of which are repeatedly interrupted by the narrator (4:10–11a, 13a, 21a, 24a, 26a, 30a; 7:9a, 14a, 17a, 18a, 20a).

13. Bitzer, "Rhetorical Situation," 5.

1. As described by Mark, the audience is appropriate for the rather esoteric discourse that will follow. After a period of public instruction within the temple (11:27–12:44), the dramatis personae are reduced, first to Jesus and his disciples (13:1–2), then quite abruptly to Jesus and a quartet from among the Twelve (13:3). While reflecting a conjunction, evident in various rabbinic texts, of "public retort and private explanation,"[14] this movement is also typical of Mark's narrative: repeatedly therein, a small group of Jesus' intimates are permitted instruction or disclosures denied to the general populace (see 4:10–34; 7:17–23; 9:28; 10:10–12). On three occasions in Mark other than that recounted in 13:3, Peter, James, and John participate in events closed to others, even to the rest of the Twelve (5:37; 9:2; 14:33).[15] Thus Jesus' oration in 13:5b–37 is privately addressed (κατ' ἰδίαν [kat' idian], "by themselves," v. 3)[16] to a privileged inner circle, at least three of whom have been informed of their teacher's identity as Messiah (8:29; 9:41) and Son of God (9:7; note also 8:31, 38; 9:9, 31; 10:33, 45).

2. By the beginning of Mark 13, several events have converged in a manner that would render the ensuing speech natural, if not inevitable. In response to a disciple's comment on the temple's rock-solid stability (13:1),[17] Jesus' prophecy of its annihilation (13:2) announces Judaism's cultic destruction, foreshadowed by his prophetic activity (11:12–21) and subversive teaching within the temple precincts (11:27–12:44). Jesus' own destruction is also imminent: immediately after the Olivet Discourse, the plot for his arrest and crucifixion is hatched in earnest (14:1–11; cf. 3:6; 8:31; 9:31; 10:33–34; 12:12). In terms of both narrative and rhetorical logic, Jesus' address is appropriately situated at Mark 13:5b–37: its length and gravity, laden with images and phraseology that will be echoed in chapters 14–15,[18] correspond with the dark hues and deceleration of narrative speed in Mark's passion narrative.[19] Occurring on the eve of Jesus' execution, Mark 13:5b–37 is an *Abschiedsrede*: a "farewell address of a great man before his death," of which Semitic and Greek literature present numerous specimens.[20]

---

14. Daube, *New Testament and Rabbinic Judaism*, 141–50.

15. Simon Peter, Andrew, James, and John are the first disciples whom Jesus summons in Mark (1:16–20).

16. The audiences for this address seem incrementally enlarged in Matthew (24:3) and Luke (21:5–7).

17. Cf. Josephus, *Ant.* 15.11.1.380–7.425; idem, *J.W.* 5.5.1.184–8.247. Brandenburger (*Markus 13*, 91–115) may be right that Mark 13:1–2 originated as an independent "pronouncement story." Nevertheless, in their present literary position, these verses situate the address in vv. 5b–37.

18. See C. Black, *Mark* (ANTC), 276–338.

19. On "The Connexion of Chapter Thirteen with the Passion Narrative," see Lightfoot, *Gospel Message of St. Mark*, 48–59.

20. Cf. Gen. 49:1–33; Deut. 31:1–34:8; Josh. 23:1–24:30; 1 Sam. 12:1–25; 1 Kgs. 2:1–9; 1 Chr. 28:1–29:5; Tob. 14:3–11; 1 Macc. 2:49–70; John 14:1–17:26; Acts 20:18b–35; 2 Tim. 1:1–4:22; *1 En.* 91–105; *Jub.* 23:9–32; Plato, *Apology*; idem, *Crito*; idem, *Phaedo*; Xenophon, *Mem.* 4.7.1–10; and the pseudepigraphical *Testaments of the Twelve Patriarchs.* In *Prophecy in Early Christianity* (186, 399–400 n. 93), Aune notes the entwinement of various ancient genres in the introduction of Mark 13: peripatetic dialogue (13:1–2), the solicitation of an oracular response (13:3–4), and the *Tempeldialog* (13:1–4). All such *Abschiedsreden* display superior elegance but inferior pith when compared to the last words attributed to botanist Luther Burbank (1849–1926): "I don't feel good."

3. For Bitzer, an "exigence" refers to an actual or potential imperfection, marked by urgency, which is amenable to positive modification by discourse. The exigence that occasions the speech in Mark 13 is indicated by potential imperfection (v. 2: Jesus' prediction of the temple's toppling) and implied urgency (v. 4: the quartet's inquiry about the realization of these things). Implicit in both these elements is an intricate web of rhetorical associations. The prophecy in 13:2 tacitly locates Jesus among prophets who proclaimed the temple's desolation.[21] While seemingly detached from the proclamation of a singular catastrophe, the query in verse 4 (πότε ταῦτα ἔσται καὶ . . . ὅταν μέλλη ταῦτα συντελεῖσθαι πάντα; [pote tauta estai kai . . . hotan mellē tauta synteleisthai panta? "When will these things be and . . . when are all these things to be accomplished?" AT]) echoes the wording of Daniel 12:7 LXX (συντελεσθήσεται πάντα ταῦτα [syntelesthēsetai panta tauta, "all these things will be accomplished"]). The choice of Danielic expression suggests that the disciples' reaction to the prospect of the temple's collapse was colored by a degree of eschatologically generated excitement.[22] Delivered at a venue with eschatological associations (see Zech. 14:1–5), Jesus' response will attempt in part to bolster the confidence of an audience whose "soul" is agitated (Plato, *Phaedr.* 271a–d; Aristotle, *Rhet.* 2.5.1382a–83b).

As far as I can tell, rhetorical criticism of Mark 13 cannot in itself resolve the vexed question of whether the tragedy of 70 CE has already occurred. If Mark knew that the temple had already fallen, a *vaticinium ex eventu* ("prophecy" sprung from a known event) to that effect would have amplified the *ēthos* of Jesus (a rationale apparently at work in Luke 19:41–44; 21:20–24). On the other hand, a more precise statement of cultic collapse, reflecting the post-70 reality, could have heightened the eschatological tension that, as we shall see, Mark 13:5b–37 seems designed to relax. Rhetorical analysis cannot arbitrate this classic exegetical stalemate.[23]

Assessing this material's rhetorical situation does offer help in adjudicating another and no less contentious scholarly debate. On grounds both stylistic and substantive, the very existence of the Olivet Discourse, in its present location, has seemed intrusive to some scholars.[24] Quite the contrary: if the foregoing analy-

---

21. Mic. 3:10–12; Jer. 7:14; 26:6, 18; John 2:19; Acts 6:13–14; *1 En.* 90:28; *J.W.* 6.5.3.300–309; *b. Yoma* 4.1.39b.

22. Jewish reaction to the events of 70 CE was anything but uniform, though some associated the temple's destruction with divine judgment (*2 Apoc. Bar.* 7:1; 80:1–3; *Sib. Or.* 4:115–27) or eschatological hopes for Jerusalem's re-creation (*4 Ezra* [2 Esd.] 11:1–12:3).

23. Balabanski (*Eschatology in the Making*, 55–100) presents a guarded interpretation of Mark 13 as cognizant of Jerusalem's destruction. In "Apocalyptic Rhetoric" A. Y. Collins notes Bitzer's theories of "rhetorical situation" and "exigence" in arguing that the Olivet Discourse is best understood as a specific response to the first Jewish war against Rome, beginning in the spring and summer of 66 CE, after Menahem (Menachem), a son or grandson of Judas the Galilean (Acts 5:37), emerged as a messianic leader (*J.W.* 2.17.7.430–8.34). Like Balabanski, Collins acknowledges and responds to alternative proposals for the sociohistorical setting of Mark 13; to engage that debate is not my task here. Collins offers a sophisticated traditio-historical analysis, which is not dependent on rhetorical-critical premises. Her references to Bitzer are lagniappe for her argument, not integral to it.

24. E.g., Pesch, *Naherwartungen*, 48–73; Grayston, "Mark XIII."

sis be accepted, one may conclude that Mark 13 is propitiously situated, even powerfully so, however obtrusive it may seem to modern critical sensibilities.

The Rhetorical Problem

Scholars have long puzzled over the raison d'être of Mark 13. How might a rhetorical interpretation of this passage clarify the principal issues at stake?

1. Presupposing an association of the temple's ruin with the end of all things, the four disciples' questions in 13:4 invite neither a forensic evaluation of past facts nor a deliberative assessment of actions expedient for future performance. Essentially, their questions pivot on proper belief ("When will these things be?") and evidence to substantiate it ("What is the sign when these things are all to be accomplished?"). Jesus' address in 13:5b–37 responds to these issues of belief and its validation: certain virtues are extolled (wariness, endurance, preparedness, perspicacity), while specific, corresponding vices are censured (cf. Aristotle, *Rhet.* 1.9.1366a–b; Cornificius, *Rhet. ad Her.* 3.6.10–3.8.15; Augustine, *Doct. chr.* 4.4.6). Therefore, from among the various species of rhetoric,[25] epideictic most accurately captures the type of oration we find in Mark 13:5b–37.

Even if this judgment be accepted, it invites some qualifications. First, by typing the Olivet Discourse as epideictic, I am not suggesting that Jesus is engaged in oratorical display, calculated chiefly to please his audience (thus Aristotle, *Rhet.* 1.3.1358b; Cicero, *De or.* 2.84.340–85.349). By 300 CE Menander Rhetor (of Laodicea)[26] analyzed and systematized a rhetorical reality that had long existed: the complexity of epideictic as a rhetorical species. When viewed in the light of Menander's categories, Mark 13:5b–37 begins as a kind of *lalia*, or informal talk (Menander 2.4); as the speech unfolds, it embraces the concerns of *paramythetic*, or consolation (2.9), with *proemptic*, a speech for one departing on a journey (2.5). If our earlier conclusions be upheld, then the Olivet Discourse also functions as *syntactic*, a speech of leave-taking (2.15). I would not argue that Mark 13:5b–37 snugly occupies any of these ancient, oratorical pigeonholes, since the speech does not precisely accord with the topics germane to these types as Menander presents them. My point, rather, is that the presiding functions of this oration are generally epideictic, construed with respect to ancient norms.[27] Jesus intends neither to dazzle nor to delight his auditors, but to boost their confidence and to instruct them in modes of conduct that are essential in an eschatological age.

---

25. Classical discussions of this topic are found in Aristotle, *Rhet.* 1.3.1358b–1359a; Cicero, *Inv.* 1.5.7; Cornificius, *Rhet. ad Her.* 1.2.2; Quintilian, *Inst.* 3.4.1–16; 3.6.80–85.

26. For the text, consult Russell and N. Wilson, *Menander Rhetor.*

27. A. Y. Collins disagrees that the resemblance between Mark 13 and epideictic is as close as I suggest ("Apocalyptic Rhetoric," 10–13). Although she is obviously correct that Mark 13 "does not explicitly address [Jesus'] impending death or departure" (13), it is just as obvious that the speech does not refer either to Menahem's uprising, his royal pretensions, or specific Jewish-Roman hostilities in the summer of 66 CE, to which (she argues) the Olivet Discourse alludes (see above, n. 23).

A second qualification: as is often the case in epideictic discourse, portions of Mark 13:5b–37 shade into deliberative rhetoric: a concern for the disciples' actions in the future (vv. 10–11, 14–16). Both theoretically and practically, this is tolerable within epideictic. Classical theorists acknowledged fluidity among rhetorical species, granting that considerations of past and future often converge in epideictic (Aristotle, *Rhet.* 1.3.1358b; Quintilian, *Inst.* 3.4.15–16; 3.7.28). Within Mark 13:5b–37 Jesus responds in terms of circumstances to come, inasmuch as the exigence triggering the oration is oriented to the future (vv. 2, 4; see Quintilian, *Inst.* 3.8.25). Nevertheless, Jesus ultimately denies that the course of things to come, while providentially assured, can be locked into a timetable (vv. 32–37). Nor, on the basis of expedience or self-interest, can one prepare beforehand for impending distress (v. 11). Overall this speech—even the climactic exhortation of verses 14–16—relativizes activity without preempting it, emphasizing equanimity during that stressful period when "the gospel must first be preached to all nations" (v. 10 NIV).[28] Though tinctured with deliberative elements that carry persuasive weight, the center of gravity remains epideictic: an attempt by Jesus to instill and to enhance in his listeners particular attitudes and feelings in the present regarding things to come, as well as to denounce the converse of those values.

2. Another approach to the question of this unit's rhetorical problem is by means of stasis theory: identifying the point on which the speech pivots and to which the audience's attention is directed (Quintilian, *Inst.* 3.6.9, 12, 21). Though the discussion of stasis in antiquity was complex and at times chaotic,[29] our purposes are adequately served by Cicero and Quintilian's simpler parsing of the alternative rational questions that discourse attempts to answer: fact or conjecture (*an sit*, whether a thing is), definition (*quid sit*, what it is), and quality (*quale sit*, of what kind it is).[30] Which of these stases captures the primary question at issue in Mark 13?

For this audience, the facts concerning which Jesus prophesies are not at issue. That the temple will totter—and by extension, that other calamities foretold by Jesus will come to pass—appears intelligible to the disciples. Neither do their questions in Mark 13:4 deny the veracity of Jesus' pronouncements. Nor is the quality of these occurrences in dispute: whether God is justified in so designing or permitting this eschatological scenario is never broached. The principal question addressed by Jesus'

28. Similarly, Grayston, "Mark XIII," 378–79, who reaches this judgment independently of rhetorical premises. Such an interpretation casts doubt on W. Marxsen's well-known exegesis that Mark is a Galilean Gospel summoning Christians to flee to Pella for the Lord's Parousia (*Der Evangelist Markus*, 101–28). Yet, as Blount ("Preaching the Kingdom") notes, utter passivism is foreclosed by the mandate for evangelizing (κηρυχθῆναι τὸ εὐαγγέλιον [*kēryxthēnai to euangelion*]). Mark 13:10 is a form of nonviolent, revolutionary engagement.

29. Among numerous treatments, see Cicero, *Inv.* 1.8–14; 2.4.14–54.177; idem, *De or.* 2.24.104–26.113; Quintilian, *Inst.* 3.6.63–82; Cornificius, *Rhet. ad Her.* 1.11–16; Hermogenes, *On Stases* (in Nadeau, "Hermogenes, *On Stases*").

30. Cicero, *De or.* 2.25.104–9; Quintilian, *Inst.* 3.6.66–67. Classical theorists disagree on exact divisions among stases (Aristotle, *Rhet.* 3.17.1417b; Cicero, *Inv.* 1.8.10; Cornificius, *Rhet. ad Her.* 1.11.18–15.25; 2.12.17).

oration concerns the proper definition of facts whose realities are, or will be, conceded: When bogus prophets arise, when wars and rumors of wars circulate, how should they be interpreted? Will they constitute the final consummation, or will they be merely preliminary to it? Jesus maintains the latter interpretation. After the prophecy in 13:2, the disciples ask for more facts (v. 4). Jesus complies with their request, yet raises the discussion to another level: the proper definition of those facts (*quid sit*).

The Arrangement of the Olivet Address

The classical *taxis* or *dispositio* of an epideictic address includes three major components: the *prooemium* (proem or exordium), a narration (*narratio*) of topics, and the *peroratio* (or *epilogos*). Mark 13:5b–37 conforms with and creatively adapts this typical taxis.

1. A textbook exordium prepares the audience by informing it of the object(s) of the discourse and by disposing the listeners to receptiveness of what will be said (Aristotle, *Rhet.* 3.14.1415a; Cornificius, *Rhet. ad Her.* 1.4.6–7; Quintilian, *Inst.* 4.1.1–79). If Mark 13:5b is considered the introduction of the discourse (as appears to be the case, since the first of its topics is presented in 13:6), then the minimalism and abruptness of "Beware that no one leads you astray" seemingly flout the criteria for an appropriate *prooemium*. Despite its unconventionality, a case can be made for its suitability and effectiveness. Admittedly, 13:5b does not attempt to ingratiate the speaker to his audience. For that, however, there is no need. This oration is intended to be heard, not detached from, but within the context of the Gospel's previous twelve chapters, from which Jesus' mysterious authority has emerged. Nor need the orator at Olivet solicit his listeners' attention: he knows that he has it since they have already invited his response (vv. 3–4). Neither is any statement of the objects of the discourse necessary: they have been proposed in the disciples' questions, "When will these things be?" (a question of time) and "What will be the sign?" (a question of attendant circumstance). On the other hand, the sudden, authoritative command in 13:5b does satisfy the one indispensable requirement of an exordium: to capture the audience's attention for the ensuing discourse (Quintilian, *Inst.* 4.1.5). Conjoined with the questions of time and circumstance in verses 4a and 4b, Mark 13:5b accomplishes all that is needed to prepare this audience for this speech.[31]

2. The bulk of the address, Mark 13:6–36, is a *narratio*, comprising specific topics that have been carefully grouped for their fitness with the exordium, their internal coherence, and their maximum amplification. All of these characteristics invite comment.

---

31. With Mark 13 one may compare most of the speeches in Acts, whose exordia comprise a sentence or less: 1:16; 2:14b; 3:12; 4:8b; 5:35b; 7:2a; 10:34–35; 13:16b; 15:7a, 13b; 17:22b; 19:35; 22:1; 24:10a; 25:24a; 27:21; 28:17b. Four speeches in Acts contain an extended *prooemium* (4:24b–26; 20:18–27; 24:2–4; 26:2–3); three have no *prooemium* at all (5:29–32; 11:4–18; 25:14–21).

As a beginning, notice a chiastic relationship between the implied objects of the *prooemium* (the questions in v. 4) and the kinds of topics treated in the *narratio* (vv. 6–36). The disciples' second query ("What is the sign?") is addressed by roughly the first three-quarters of the *narratio* (vv. 6–27). The remainder, 13:28–36, takes up their first question ("When will these things be?"). Thus the observation of the fifth-century commentator, Victor of Antioch, is not quite correct: "They asked one question; he answers another."[32] In fact, they asked *two* questions. Jesus responds to both, but in such a way—disproportionately and in inverse order—that realigns the disciples' assumptions about their inquiries' force and significance.

We notice a second thing in the arrangement of Mark 13:6–36: the topics therein are formally repetitive but materially progressive. Aside from the pathetical lament and petition in 13:17–18, Jesus' statements in this *narratio* assume one of four basic forms, which recur in varying juxtapositions throughout this address:

1. Exhortation, usually to vigilance (vv. 9a, 10, 23a, 28a, 33a, 35a)
2. Prediction of future occurrences (vv. 6, 8a, 9b, 12–13a, 19, 22, 24–27)
3. Commission or prohibition, preceded by a temporal or relative conditional clause (vv. 7a, 11, 14–16, 21, 28b–29)
4. Authoritative pronouncement (vv. 7b, 8b, 10, 13b, 20, 23b, 30–32, 33b–34, 35b–36)

Concentrations of one form or another occur at certain points: thus verses 24–27 are uninterruptedly predictive; verses 30–36, nearing the end of the address, are for the most part pronouncements, peppered with exhortations. Most striking, however, is the high degree of recurrence and entwinement of these four forms throughout the speech. For rhetorical effect, the repetition of these forms tacitly offers the listeners some consistent and regular points of orientation in grappling with equivocal occurrences and uncertain responsibilities in an eschatological age.

Yet for all of their formal repetitiveness, the topics in Mark 13:6–36 are substantively distinguishable and logically progressive. Responding to his disciples' question of "the sign" attending the eschatological consummation (13:4b), Jesus arranges four topics:

1. General earthly calamities to be experienced by all (vv. 6–8)
2. Particular earthly calamities to be experienced by believers (vv. 9–13)
3. Particular human responses to the calamitous "great tribulation" (vv. 14–23)
4. Particular supernatural responses to the "great tribulation" (vv. 24–27)

In reply to the question of the time of "these things" (13:4a), two topics are considered:

---

32. Cited by Nineham, *Gospel of St. Mark*, 343–44.

1. Predictable imminence and assurance of the time (vv. 28–31)
2. Unpredictable suddenness and ignorance of the time (vv. 32–36)

The formal regularity of these six topics assists in reassuring the disciples, who receive a more intricate response than their simplistic questions envisioned or invited.

A third aspect of this *narratio* warrants mention: its arrangement of eschatological topics escalates to a climax. Jesus does not mention "troubles" at random; rather, they advance from more familiar, abstract disturbances—the beginning of the world's labor contractions (vv. 6–8)—through more intense, personal suffering (vv. 9–13), ultimately culminating in breathtaking, cosmic turbulence (vv. 24–27). This rhetorical technique is known as ἀπ' ἀρχῆς ἄχρι τέλους (*ap' archēs achri telous*), a progression "from beginning to end."[33] With the completion of circumstantial topics at 13:27, the speech has reached its emotional climax. From there until the end, the address proceeds with somewhat quieter, thoughtful caution. This is more characteristic of Greek than of Roman oratory, which tended to reserve its full passion until the conclusion. Doubtless this arrangement also reflects one of Mark's theological convictions: the need for Christians' grace under eschatological pressure. The *narratio* of this address exemplifies Quintilian's standards of lucidity, brevity, and plausibility (*Inst.* 8.2.1–2). The latter criterion is better satisfied by the oration's invention and style, to which we shall turn momentarily.

3. Although a one-sentence conclusion is unusual in classical rhetoric, that's what we find in Mark 13:37.[34] By Aristotelian standards (*Rhet.* 3.19.1419b–20b), verse 37—"And what I say to you, I say to all: Watch!" (NKJV)—does just what needs to be done. Repetition of "I say" encourages the audience's favorable estimation of the orator—and by implication discourages its trust in "false messiahs and false prophets" (v. 22) who might attempt to vitiate his pronouncements. The extension of Jesus' address, from "you" to "all," amplifies the force of his points, broadening their significance beyond a small coterie of disciples to the larger Markan community. The audience's emotions are suitably stirred by the final command, "Watch!" Although Mark 13:37 does not summarize the various arguments of the discourse, it forcefully recapitulates the oration's principal refrain: "Beware" (βλέπετε [*blepete*], vv. 5, 9, 23, 33). At 13:37 Mark accomplishes several rhetorical objectives in one pointed stroke. He directs the reader's attention to the passion narrative, immediately following, which will detail the consequences for disciples who fail to "watch" (14:32–42). The abrupt command on which Jesus' speech concludes in 13:37 (γρηγορεῖτε

---

33. Rabe, ed., *Hermogenes: Opera*, 47.
34. Alternatively, one might classify Mark 13:32–37 as the *peroratio*. Such an assessment is problematic: it all but relegates the critical issue of time (v. 4a) to the *epilogos* without the topic's having been previously developed in the *narratio*. Moreover, vv. 32–37 restate nothing that has preceded them, other than what v. 37 adequately recapitulates: the admonition to "watch."

[*grēgoreite*], "watch") formally and substantively balances the equally pointed impera-
tive in 13:5b (βλέπετε [*blepete*], "Beware"), which opened the address. The form and
content of this *peroratio* are utterly apposite: the speech ends as suddenly and without
warning as "the master of the house" will come (vv. 35–36). While disturbing some
classical sensibilities, this curt conclusion upholds others: with "emphatic concision"
(βραχυλογία [*brachylogia*]: Cornificius, *Rhet. ad Her.* 4.54.68), Mark 13:37 preserves
the "internal economy" of the address (Quintilian, *Inst.* 7.10.16–17) and dramatically leaves its audience at the threshold of decision (Aristotle, *Rhet.* 3.18.1420b;
Cornificius, *Rhet. ad Her.* 3.10.18).

What does the foregoing analysis contribute to the larger scholarly conversation, conducted from different critical premises, about the arrangement of Mark
13:5b–37? In general, rhetorical criticism provides some standards, contemporaneous with the biblical material, by which competing scholarly assessments of
a passage's literary structure may be adjudicated. Mine is by no means the only
possible rhetorical analysis of the arrangement of Mark 13. I suggest only that
such principles, and the sort of interpretive outcome to which they lead, may be
used to corroborate and to refine results reached by other interpreters, primarily
on the basis of form and composition criticism.[35] By attempting to construe the
Olivet Discourse as a literary whole, not as a patchwork arising from its composite
origins, rhetorical analysis may throw light, in specific cases, on the persuasive
function of problematic or seemingly ill-fitted verses.[36]

Rhetorical Invention in Mark 13

"Of the . . . tasks of the speaker, invention is the most important and the most
difficult" (Cornificius, *Rhet. ad Her.* 2.1.1). Equally challenging is the analysis of
inventio, the devising of arguments, or proofs, that lend conviction to a case. The
inventional strategies inherent in Mark 13:5b–37 are intricate; only some of their
more conspicuous features may be noted here.

1. Inartificial (ἄτεχνοι [*atechnoi*]) proofs, not created by the orator (e.g., laws,
contracts, witnesses, and oaths), were more characteristic of judicial rhetoric (Aristotle, *Rhet.* 1.15.1375a). Their general absence from the Olivet Discourse is under-
standable. If, however, "law" be broadly understood as any testament to which

---

35. Cf. the reconstructions by Lambrecht, *Redaktion der Markus-Apokalypse*, 285–97; Standaert,
L'Évangile selon Marc, 231–53; Brandenburger, *Markus 13*, 13–20.

36. If the prediction concerning usurpers of Christ (Mark 13:6) falls within the purview of "general
earthly calamities," then it probably does not allude to an intramural, Christian aberration. Moreover,
the putatively intrusive pronouncement regarding universal evangelism (v. 10) is to be coordinated
with particular persecutions that believers will undergo (cf. vv. 9–13). Thus Hooker ("Trial and
Tribulation," 85–88) correctly intuits the evangelist's intentions in both cases, for which my analysis
offers theoretical support.

one appeals for substantiating or refuting a claim, then Mark 13's numerous Septuagintal allusions function as inartificial proofs of Jesus' position.[37]

Scholars have long recognized the scriptural echoes reverberating within Mark 13. Noteworthy in this regard is Lars Hartman's thesis that the chapter is a midrash on Daniel.[38] Whatever we make of that proposal, insufficient attention has been paid to *the rhetorical effect* of such biblical appropriation. To hint at such a range of Scripture without explicit citation pays tacit tribute to the biblical literacy of one's audience, if the listeners' recognition of those allusions was presupposed. Second, and more important, enlisting scriptural testimony for construing disruptive prospects could generate considerable consolation among Mark's anxious auditors.

2. Artificial (ἔντεχνοι [*entechnoi*]) proofs, constructed by the rhetor from circumstances of the case (Aristotle, *Rhet.* 1.2.1355b–1356a; Quintilian, *Inst.* 3.8.15), bear the persuasive brunt of Mark 13. As is typical of epideictic, neither inductive nor deductive logic looms large in this oration. The various events, recounted by Jesus in the first four topics (Mark 13:6–8, 9–13, 14–23, 24–27), are comparable to Aristotle's historical arguments by "examples" (παραδείγματα [*paradeigmata*]);[39] however, because Jesus' topics are couched as predictions of the future, not yet actual history, the analogy is imprecise. Closer to the Aristotelian model are examples in the last two topics (vv. 28–31, 32–36): the image of the fig tree (vv. 28–29) is an "illustrative parallel" (*Rhet.* 2.20.1393b = *similitudo* in Quintilian, *Inst.* 5.10.1);[40] the story of the traveler (vv. 34–36), a "fable" (*Rhet.* 2.20.1393b–1394a).[41] Although these παραδείγματα are intended to persuade (v. 28a, "from the fig tree learn the parable" [AT]), in fact they do not prove anything. And while this speech evinces careful arrangement, as we have seen, it does not proceed in accordance with the dictates of deductive or enthymematic logic.[42] On the other hand, the address has been

37. The following catalog is illustrative: for v. 7 ("this must take place"), cf. Dan. 2:28–29; for v. 8a ("nation against nation"), cf. 2 Chr. 15:6; v. 8b ("birth pangs"), cf. Isa. 26:17; 66:8; Jer. 22:23; Hos. 13:13; Mic. 4:9–10; for v. 9c, cf. Ps. 119:46; for v. 12, cf. Isa. 3:5; 19:2; Ezek. 38:21; Mic. 7:6; for v. 14a ("the abomination of desolation" [KJV]), cf. Dan. 9:27; 11:31; 12:11; 1 Macc. 1:54; 6:7; 2 Macc. 6:2; for v. 14c ("Let them head for the hills" [AT]), cf. Gen. 14:10; for v. 19, cf. Dan. 12:1; for v. 22, cf. Deut. 13:1–3; for vv. 24–25, cf. Isa. 13:10, 13; 34:4; Ezek. 32:7–8; Joel 2:10, 31; 3:15; Hag. 2:6; for v. 26, cf. Dan. 7:13–14; for v. 27 ("from the end of the earth to the end of heaven" [AT]), cf. Deut. 13:7; 30:3–4; Zech. 2:6; 4:10; 6:5.

38. Hartman, *Prophecy Interpreted*, 145–77; more recently, Pilgaard, "Apokalyptik."

39. Aristotle, *Rhet.* 2.20.1393a; see also Quintilian, *Inst.* 5.10.125–11.44; Anaximenes, *Rhet. ad Alex.* 7.17.1428a–8.13.1430a.

40. Mark 13:28–29 should be correlated with 11:12–21; consult Telford, *Barren Temple*, 213–18.

41. Alternatively, the ὡς ([*hōs*], "as") clause in 13:34 can be taken as a simile (Quintilian, *Inst.* 8.3.72–76). On the tradition-history of 13:34–36, consult Beasley-Murray, *Jesus and the Last Days*, 470–74.

42. Mark 13:20b contains the speech's only enthymeme (see Aristotle, *Rhet.* 2.22.1395b–23.1400b; 2.25.1402a; Quintilian, *Inst.* 5.10.1–6; 5.14.1–35; 8.5.9–11). Although it can be syllogistically reconstructed, its major and minor premises would not be considered probable, much less universally true, by those not already disposed to accept the validity of Jesus' definitions: (a) Those human beings who will be saved are the elect. (b) God shortened the days for the sake of those who will be saved. (c) Therefore, God shortened the days for the sake of the elect.

partially motivated by a logical fallacy: that of confusing fallible signs (persecutions and spurious prophecies) with infallible signs (that will demonstrably
attend the Parousia of the Son of Man; cf. Aristotle, *Rhet.* 1.2.1357b). Thus
the force of Jesus' argument, while not rigorously logical, does aim to expose a
logical fallacy.

To that end, it is worth observing that Mark 13:5b–37 employs, in effect if not
by design, several of Aristotle's general lines of argument, or "commonplaces"
(κοινοὶ τόποι [*koinoi topoi*]: *Rhet.* 2.18.1391b–19.1393a; *loci*, in Quintilian, *Inst.*
5.10.20–125). Against misapprehensions concerning the timing and circumstances of the end, Jesus constructs the following conventional arguments:

1. *The division of genus into species:* Against a mistakenly realized eschatology,
Jesus introduces a "periodized tribulation." He deflects attention away from "the
end," generically conceived, onto various species of eschatological events (general
calamities, believers' trials, the great tribulation, the coming Son of Man).[43]

2. *The relationship of antecedent and consequence:* The species of events into which
the eschatological genus is divided occur, not haphazardly, but in a particular
chronological sequence, with certain consequences following specific antecedents
(thus v. 8c: "This is [only] the beginning of the birth pangs").

3. *The relationship of contradiction:* Against antagonists who would short-circuit
God's appointed chronological progression with illegitimate claims that the end
is either imminent or calculable, Jesus invokes contradictory propositions ("The
end is not yet" [v. 7b AT]; "You do not know when the time will come" [v. 33;
see also v. 35]).

4. Jesus contends, not that the end is indefinitely delayed (cf. v. 30), but
that all the penultimates must become manifest before the final reclamation of
God's elect. This is one form of *the circumstance of future fact:* if the antecedents of
something are present, then the natural consequences will occur (Aristotle, *Rhet.*
2.20.1393a).

Not once in this discourse appears a common form of rhetorical argument: the
interrogation of one's opponents. Although constructions from silence are always haz-
ardous, the accepted use of question-and-answer in classical rhetoric (Aristotle, *Rhet.*
3.17.1419a; Cornificius, *Rhet. ad Her.* 4.15.22–16.24), as well as the prevalence of this
technique by Jesus elsewhere in Mark (some fifty-seven occurrences), may confirm our
earlier assessment of the rhetorical situation of Mark 13. This speech resonates, not as
an apologetic rejoinder within an already schismatic situation in the Markan community, but as pedagogical, even pastoral consolation for uneasy Christians.[44]

---

43. A similar strategy is adopted in 2 Thess. 2:1–12, analyzed by Holland, *Tradition That You
Received*, 134–39.

44. Similarly, Grayston, "Mark XIII," 375–76; contra Weeden, *Mark—Traditions in Conflict*,
52–100.

Logos is only one of the modes of internal persuasion evident in this address. Of far greater persuasive power are *pathos*, the emotions stirred among the audience, and *ēthos*, the rhetor's character.[45] Incorporated within Jesus' eschatological scenario are fearsome occurrences (wars, persecutions, familial infighting, cosmic ruptures), for which an effective counterfoil is the arousal of pity for those especially vulnerable (expectant and nursing mothers [v. 17], endangered travelers [v. 18];[46] see Aristotle, *Rhet.* 2.8.1385b–86b; Cicero, *De or.* 2.52.211). So vividly rendered are these images that they might be considered examples of ἐνάργεια (*enargeia*: Quintilian, *Inst.* 4.2.63–64; 8.3.61–67; cf. Cornificius, *Rhet. ad Her.* 4.55.68–69) or *visiones* (Quintilian, *Inst.* 6.2.29–36; Longinus, *Subl.* 15.1–12): graphic exposition that excites the imagination and stirs the emotions. If the exigence and situation of this address have been properly construed, we may wonder what purpose is served by depicting such horrifying prospects. The answer seems to lie in the recurrent assurances and exhortations to endurance in Mark 13:7, 11, 13b, 20, 23, 27, and 30–31: the bolstering of confidence presupposes, and to some degree is dependent on, a clear-eyed acknowledgment of fearful potentialities (thus Aristotle, *Rhet.* 2.5.1382a–83b). By rhetorically creating in his listeners' minds the experience of terrors to come, Jesus can now reassure "the elect" of the ultimate triumph of God's providence, while equipping them for future trials and tribulations (see *Rhet.* 2.5.1383a).

Implied in this address, indeed throughout the Second Gospel (1:27–28; 4:41; 9:14–15; 12:32), is an estimation of Jesus "as [one] possessing genuine wisdom and excellence of character" (Quintilian, *Inst.* 4.12.1; see also 1.pr.9–12; 1.2.3; 2.15.33; 12.1.1–45). Jesus' *ēthos* lends persuasive weight to this oration's various pronouncements (KJV: 13:9, "for my sake"; v. 13a, "for my name's sake"; see vv. 23b, 26, 31, 37). Even the self-professed qualification of his knowledge (v. 32) redounds to "the Son's" credit, insofar as it magnifies the surpassing knowledge of God. So powerful is Christ's *ēthos* that it can backfire on gullible believers: when suborned by pseudo-christs and fake prophets, that *ēthos* may be wielded as an instrument of deceit (vv. 5–6, 21–22), whose potential damage can be thwarted only by authoritative forewarnings of the authentic Christ (vv. 5b, 23). On balance, the *logos* and *pathos* of the Olivet Discourse depend ultimately upon its orator's *ēthos*.[47]

---

45. For both Cicero (*De or.* 2.43.182–46.194) and Quintilian (*Inst.* 6.2.7–27), *ēthos* and *pathos* can constitute varying degrees of similar proof.

46. With Pesch (*Markusevangelium*, 2:293), I take χειμῶνος (*cheimōnos*, "in winter") to refer to the season of heavy rains, when passage across the wadis would have been impeded.

47. Aristotle (*Rhet.* 1.2.1356a) considered *ēthos* to be internal to a speech. However, as Kennedy notes (*New Testament Interpretation*, 15), since the speaker's authority was brought to the rhetorical occasion, *ēthos* in the Bible functions largely as an external means of persuasion.

Rhetorical Style in the Oration at Olivet

Kindred to the invention and arrangement of this address is its *elocutio*: "fitting the proper language to the invented matter," as Cicero puts it (*Inv.* 1.7.9). The following observations are based on Theophrastus's four virtues of style: correctness, clarity, ornamentation, and propriety.[48]

1. For classical theorists, correctness (ἑλληνισμός [*hellēnismos*], *purus*) seems to have referred mainly to appropriate grammar (Cicero, *De or.* 3.40). If "Atticism" were taken as a grammatical touchstone, as was the case in Roman oratory of the mid-first century BCE,[49] then Mark 13:5b–37 would be regarded as deficient at several points. The Olivet Discourse harbors constructions that by classical standards would be considered inelegant: ὅτι (*hoti*, "that") recitative following λέγειν (*legein*, "to say"; vv. 6, 30); the use of εἰς (*eis*, "into") in constructions where ἐν (*en*, "in") would be favored (vv. 9, 10); the impersonal use of a plural verb, with no subject expressed (vv. 9, 11); the conjunction of an attributive participle in the masculine case with a neuter noun (v. 14); the use of ἄν (*an*, a particle indicating contingency in subjunctive constructions) with a verb in the indicative mood (v. 20); various "Semitisms" (redundant pronouns [vv. 11c, 19]; the use of ἐγώ εἰμι [*egō eimi*], "I am"] followed by a participle [vv. 13a]; and probably at least one Latinism (ἀλεκτοροφωνίος [*alektorophōnios*]: "the third night-watch" [lit. 'cock-crowing'; v. 35c]). There are also instances of asyndeta, the absence of connecting particles (vv. 5b–6, 7bc, 8abcd, 23ab, 33a).[50] Matthew and Luke may have considered some of these constructions infelicitous; that would account for their alteration of Mark's grammar in the Synoptic parallels.[51]

In defense of the overall "correctness" of the style in Mark 13, one may offer the following rejoinders. First, with respect to Koine Greek, an "ideal" standard

---

48. These criteria were anticipated by Aristotle (*Rhet.* 3.2.1404b–1405b) and later taken up by Cicero (*Or.* 75–121; *De or.* 3.9.37–39; 3.52.199), Quintilian (*Inst.* 1.5.1; 8.1–11.1; 12.10.58), and Hermogenes (*Peri ideōn*). For discussion, see Kennedy, *Art of Persuasion*, 273–90.

49. Kennedy, *Art of Persuasion*, 330–40.

50. M. Black (*Aramaic Approach*, 42) reckons some of these items as Mark's imputation of an Aramaic pattern.

51. Among other adjustments: both Matt. 24:5 and Luke 21:8 delete ὅτι (*hoti*), "that," from Mark 13:6; Matt. 10:17 (ἐν ταῖς συναγωγαῖς [*en tais synagōgais*], "in the synagogues") lightly refines Mark 13:9 (εἰς συναγωγάς [*eis synagōgas*], "in synagogues"); cf. Luke 21:12; likewise, Matt. 24:14 (ἐν ὅλῃ [*en holē*], "throughout [the] whole") is smoother than Mark 13:10 (εἰς πάντα [*eis panta*], "in all"); Matt. 24:15 sets in agreement a neuter participle (ἑστός [*hestos*], "standing") with a neuter noun, whereas Mark 13:14 places a masculine participle (ἑστηκότα [*hestēkota*], "standing") after a neuter noun; πεσοῦνται (*pesountai*, "will fall") in Matt. 24:29 sharpens ἔσονται πίπτοντες (*piptontes*, "will be falling") in Mark 13:25a; both Matt. 24:42 and Luke 12:38, 40 delete the allusion to Roman "watches" in Mark 13:35. However, Matthew and Luke agree with Mark in preserving some impersonal plurals ("they," as in Mark 13:9, 11 = Matt. 10:17 = Luke 21:12; Mark 13:26 = Matt. 24.30 = Luke 21:27) and the phrase, λέγω ὑμῖν ὅτι [*legō hymin hoti*], "I say to you that" (Mark 13:30 = Matt. 24:34 = Luke 21:32). Note also Matthew's preservation of the conditional ἄν plus the indicative mood (24:22a = Mark 13:20a).

of Attic purity is as unrealistic as it is unsuited. Second, the line of demarcation between "classical" and "semitizing" Greek was not hard and fast: for example, the construction of a *casus pendens* with a resumptive pronoun (cf. Mark 13:11c) is not unknown in classical Greek,[52] and (as we shall presently see) asyndeta need not be automatically identified as "Semitisms."[53] Third, assuredly in the case of Mark 13:19 (cf. Dan. 12:1) but possibly elsewhere, the Semitic flavor of this address owes much to Mark's inventional mimicry of the Septuagint. Fourth, Mark 13:5b–37 lacks many of the syntactical excesses often attributed to that evangelist (the heaping of participles, prepositions, and adverbs; excessive use of the historical present and double negatives).[54]

On balance, the syntax of Mark 13:5b–37 betokens, if not "classical purity," then the direct simplicity of Koine Greek. If it does not evince the elegance of the Epistle to the Hebrews, then neither does it manifest Revelation's "barbarism."

2. For Quintilian (*Inst.* 8.2.22) the primary stylistic virtue is clarity (*perspecuitas*, τὸ σαφές [*to saphes*]). Here the oration at Olivet merits high marks. In Mark 13:6–36 most of the referents are clear enough, if not in every case their precise significations. The "examples" in verses 28, 34–36a are less obscure than the parables in Mark 4:3–32 (cf. *Inst.* 8.6.52). Verse 14 presents a glaring exception to this assessment. As we shall see, however, its obscurity may be calculated.

3. It is with respect to ornamentation (τὸ μεγαλοπρεπές [*to megaloprepes*], *ornatus*) that the style of Mark 13 holds the greatest surprise. Classical theorists divided style into two parts. First, there is *lexis* (diction), the choice of words for forceful expression, including metaphors and tropes ("turnings," in which one word is substituted for another). Second, synthesis: verbal compositions that manipulate clusters of sounds or words ("figures of speech") or ideas ("figures of thought") in striking or unexpected ways.[55] The following table offers a conspectus of the diction and composition employed in Mark 13:5b–37 (AT).[56]

52. See Moulton, *Prolegomena*, 69–70, and the Attic evidence cited therein.
53. On the slippery subject of "Semitisms" (infiltrations of Semitic constructions into classical and Koine Greek), consult the temperate appraisal by Moule, *Idiom Book*, 171–91.
54. For a good précis of Markan vocabulary, syntax, and style, see V. Taylor, *St. Mark*, 44–66.
55. Classical treatments of ornamentation include Aristotle, *Rhet.* 3.1.1403b–12.1414a; Anaximenes, *Rhet. ad Alex.* 22.1434a.35–28.1436a.13; Longinus, *On Sublimity*; Demetrius, *De elocutione*; Cicero, *De or.* 3.37.149–42.168; Quintilian, *Inst.* 8.6.1–76; 9.1.1–3.102. For modern study of classical canons of style, consult Lausberg, *Handbook of Literary Rhetoric*, 242–411.
56. I have translated excerpts from Mark 13 as literally or as freely as necessary to convey stylistic features of the Greek. Where a play on words or sounds exists in the original that can be rendered in English only clumsily, I have reproduced the corresponding Greek words or phrases.

Tropes

A. Metaphor (*translatio*), the transference of a word, applying to one thing, to another that is similar (Cornificius, *Rhet. ad Her.* 4.34.45):

"If the Lord had not cut short the days . . ." (v. 20a)

"From the fig tree learn the parable." (v. 28a)

"He is near, at the very gates." (v. 29)

"For you do not know when the lord of the house is coming. . . ." (vv. 35b–36)

B. Synecdoche (*intellectio*), the suggestion of the whole or genus of something by its part or species (Quintilian, *Inst.* 8.16.19):

"for my name's sake" (v. 13a)

C. Metonymy (*denominatio*), the substitution of some attribute or suggestive word for what is actually meant (Cornificius, *Rhet. ad Her.* 4.32.43):

"all flesh" (v. 20a)

"my words" (v. 31)

Figures of Speech

A. Parallelism, the collocation of related words, phrases, or clauses of similar structure:

"and . . . you will be flogged [δαρήσεσθε (*darēsesthe*)], and . . . you will be made to stand [σταθήσεσθε (*stathēsesthe*)]" (v. 9bc)

"The Lord cut short the days . . . / . . . He cut short the days." (v. 20ad)

"Let those in Judea flee . . . , let the one on the roof not descend . . . , let the one in the field not turn back." (vv. 14–16)

"the sun . . . the moon . . . the stars . . . the powers" (vv. 24bc–25ab)

B. Homoeoptoton (*exornatio*), the appearance, in the same sentence, of two or more words with like terminations (Cornificius, *Rhet. ad Her.* 4.20.28; cf. Quintilian, *Inst.* 9.3.78):

"He will send out the angels [ἀποστελεῖ τοὺς ἀγγέλους (*apostelei tous angelous*)], and he will gather together the elect [ἐπισυνάξει τοὺς ἐκλεκτούς (*episynaxei tous eklektous*)]." (v. 27).

C. Reduplication (ἀναδίπλωσις, *anadiplōsis*), immediate repetition of one or more words of identical syntax, in order to amplify (Cornificius, *Rhet. ad Her.* 4.28.38; Quintilian, *Inst.* 9.3.28):

"as soon as . . . you know that [it] is near . . . / as soon as . . . you know that [he] is near" (vv. 28bc, 29bc)

D. Transplacement (*traductio*), the reintroduction of a word used in various functions (Cornificius, *Rhet. ad Her.* 4.14.20–21; Quintilian, *Inst.* 9.3.41–42):

"that he watch" / "watch" (vv. 34d, 35a)

E. Polyptoton, establishing a contrast by varying a word's declension or inflection (Quintilian, *Inst.* 9.3.37):

"You may hear [ἀκούσητε (*akousēte*)] of wars and rumors [ἀκοὰς (*akoas*)] of wars." (v. 7a)

"of creation that he created" (v. 19)

"the elect whom he elected" (v. 20b)

F. Epanaphora, repetition of the same word at the beginning of successive clauses (Cornificius, *Rhet. ad Her.* 4.13.19):

"There will be . . . , there will be . . ." (v. 8bc)

"Look . . . , look . . ." (v. 21bc)

G. Antistrophe (ἐπιφορά [*epiphora*]), repetition of the same word at the end of successive clauses (*Rhet. ad Her.* 4.13.19):

" . . . will pass away, . . . will not pass away" (v. 31ab)

"to you I say, to all I say" (v. 37ab)

H. Homoeopropheron, syllabic correspondence in the beginning of two or more words in close succession (cf. *Rhet ad Her.* 4.12.18):

"pseudomessiahs and pseudoprophets" (v. 22a)

I. Homoeoteleuton, syllabic correspondence in the ending of two or more sentences (Quintilian, *Inst.* 9.3.77):

"Be wary [βλέπετε (*blepete*)]. Be chary [ἀγρυπνεῖτε (*agrypneite*)]." (v. 33a)

J. Epanalepsis, repetition of a word at the beginning and end of a clause (*Inst.* 8.3.51):

"nation . . . against nation, and kingdom against kingdom" (v. 8a)

"Brother will betray brother." (v. 12a)

K. Asyndeton (*dissolutio*), absence of connecting particles (*Inst.* 9.3.50):

"Beware . . . ; many . . ." (vv. 5b–6)

"Do not be alarmed: this must happen." (v. 7bc)

"There will rise up . . . ; there will be . . . ; there will be . . . ; [the] beginning" (v. 8abcd)

"But you beware; I have told you everything beforehand." (v. 23ab)

"Pay attention—stay alert." (v. 33a)

L. Polysyndeton, superfluity of connecting particles (*Inst.* 9.3.50–52):

καί- (*kai*)-parataxis (redundant "and" in successive clauses; in vv. 9c–13a and 24c–27ab)

"no one . . . , neither . . . nor . . ." (v. 32ab)

"whether" [ἤ (*ē*)] . . . "or whether" [ἤ] . . . "or whether" [ἤ] . . . "or whether [ἤ]" (v. 35bc)

M. Alliteration, repetition, in adjacent words, of initial or medial consonants (cf. Cornificius, *Rhet ad Her.* 4.12.18):

Δοὺς τοῖς δούλοις [*Dous tois doulois*], "vesting the vassals" (v. 34b).

N. Assonance, repetition, in adjacent words, of similar vowel sounds conjoined with different consonants (*Rhet. ad Her.* 4.12.18):

μὴ θροεῖσθε· δεῖ γενέσθαι [*mē throeisthe; dei genesthai*], "be not dismayed; plans have been made" (v. 7bc)

ἐξουσίαν, ἑκάστῳ τὸ ἔργον [*exousian, hēkastō to ergon*], "power, to each person a performance" (v. 34bc)

O. Hyperbaton, transposition of word order for emphasis (Cornificius, *Rhet. ad Her.* 4.32.44; Quintilian, *Inst.* 8.6.62–67):

"[the] beginning of the birth pangs, these" (v. 8d)

"very near is summer" (v. 28c)

P. Chiasmus (cf. *commutatio*: Cornificius, *Rhet ad Her.* 4.28.39), the reversal of grammatical structures in adjacent phrases or clauses:

"They will betray you to sanhedrins, and in synagogues you will be flogged." (v. 9b)

"and a father, [his] child, and . . . children against parents" (v. 12ab)

"now if he had not cut short . . . , all flesh would not have been saved; but for the sake of the elect, . . . he cut short" (v. 20abcd)

Q. Antithesis, juxtaposition of contrary ideas (*Rhet. ad Her.* 4.15.21; *Rhet. ad Alex.* 26.1435b.25):

"This must happen, but the end is not yet." (v. 7cd)

"Don't be anxious beforehand what you will say, but . . . say that." (v. 11bc)

"For it is not you who are speaking, but rather the Holy Spirit." (v. 11d)

"And you will be hated . . . , but the one who endures . . . will be saved." (v. 13ab)

"Heaven and earth will pass away, but my words will by no means pass away." (v. 31)

"No one knows, . . . except for the Father." (v. 32ac)

"Therefore, watch—for you do not know." (v. 35ab)

R. Parenthesis (*interpositio*), the interruption of the flow of discourse by the insertion of a remark (Quintilian, *Inst.* 9.3.23):

"And in all the nations the good news must first be preached." (v. 10)

"Let the reader understand." (v. 14b)

S. Ellipsis, deliberate omission of a word, which is implied by the context (*Inst.* 9.3.58):

"and kingdom [will rise up] against kingdom" (v. 8a)

"and father [will betray unto death his] child" (v. 12a)

T. Apposition, juxtaposition of coordinate elements, the second of which modifies the first:

"the powers, those in the heavens" (v. 25b)

"no one . . . , neither the angels in heaven nor the Son" (v. 32ab)

"to the slaves [he gave] authority, to each his assignment" (v. 34bc)

Figures of Thought

A. Aposiopesis, the incompletion of a thought (Cornificius, *Rhet. ad Her.* 4.30.41; 4.54.67; Quintilian, *Inst.* 9.2.54–57; 9.3.60–61):

"As a fellow on a journey, . . . he charged the porter to keep watch." (v. 34)

B. *Controversia*, ambiguous phraseology designed to excite suspicion or entice discovery (Quintilian, *Inst.* 9.2.65–95):

"When you see the sacrilege that desecrates, standing where he ought not be . . ." (v. 14a)

C. *Echphrasis*, vivid description (Cornificius, *Rhet. ad Her.* 4.38.51):

"and then you will see . . . from the four winds, from earth's end to heaven's end" (vv. 26–27)

"when the lord . . . comes, . . . perhaps early" (v. 35bc)

D. Arousal (ἀνάστασις [*anastasis*]), the stirring of emotion (*Rhet. ad Her.* 4.43.55–56):

"Pray that it not happen in winter!" (v. 18)

E. Pleonasm, emphatic superfluity (Quintilian, *Inst.* 9.3.46–47):

"But you—watch yourselves." (v. 9a)

"But you—pay attention." (v. 23a)

F. Simile, comparison of implicitly similar figures (Cornificius, *Rhet. ad Her.* 4.49.62):

"as a fellow on a journey, . . . [so also, you]" (vv. 34–35)

I assume that the preceding lists are incomplete—which only makes so sweeping a range of ornament in a speech of moderate length the more striking. Equally impressive is the skill with which the tropes and figures have been blended: they do not attract to themselves undue attention; most would probably be missed by those who silently read the speech but did not hear it recited aloud. At the time of the oration's performance, even its auditors would not have been entirely conscious of this panoply of ornament; at a subliminal level, however, the various techniques would register with persuasive effect (Cicero, *De or.* 3.50.195). The diction and composition of Mark 13 are not merely decorative; they are also functional devices, integral to the purpose of securing an audience's agreement in matters of faith that are beyond deductive, logical proof.[57]

4. The fourth of Theophrastus's virtues, propriety (τὸ πρέπον [*to prepon*], *decorum*), refers to stylistic appropriateness to the speech's circumstances, the orator's

---

57. On the interplay of figures and argument, see Quintilian, *Inst.* 9.1.19, 21; note also the discussion in Perelman and Olbrechts-Tyteca, *The New Rhetoric*, 167–79.

ēthos, the audience's mood, and the character of the address. In these respects the Olivet Discourse would likely have been judged successful by a rhetorician of Mark's age. From among the Ciceronian levels of style,[58] "the middle way" (*medius et quasi temperatus*: *Or.* 6.21; *De or.* 3.45.177) tends to control Mark 13: befitting a "cautious" or "restrained" eschatology, the argument and diction are neither grandiloquent (cf. *De or.* 5.20) nor plain (cf. *Or.* 6.20). Although its precise rhythm, based on metrical quantities in pronunciation, is probably irretrievable,[59] overall this oration evinces a style more "free-running" than disjointedly "periodic" (cf. Aristotle, *Rhet.* 3.9.1409ab; Quintilian, *Inst.* 9.4.19–147). While that would be expected in a didactic presentation, a "running" style seems especially appropriate for an address that counsels cautious discernment of a lengthy train of eschatological events: the longer the phrases and clauses, such as we find here, the less hurried and more deliberate the rhetorical effect (Cornificius, *Rhet. ad Her.* 4.19.26–20.28).[60] The masterly character of the rhetor would be enhanced by his command of ornament, whose varying clarity and obscurity are congenial with an eschatological scenario that can be broadly forecast (Mark 13:23) yet not pinpointed (v. 32).

When compared to studies of its arrangement and "logical" argument, the style of Mark 13:5b–37 has been relatively neglected in recent scholarship. Here is another area in which Greco-Roman rhetoric may throw fresh light on familiar texts. The classical theory and practice of style afford us a useful set of conceptual tools with which to frame some new inquiries, as well as to reexamine some perennial problems of interpretation.

A case in point is the notorious *crux interpretum* at Mark 13:14: τὸ βδέλυγμα τῆς ἐρημώσεως (*to bdelygma tēs erēmōseōs*), "the desolating sacrilege." Beyond a general consensus on its allusiveness to a similar phrase in Daniel and 1 Maccabees, commentators have despaired of precisely identifying to what or to whom Mark intends for this epithet to refer.[61] Rhetorical criticism is equally unable to answer the question of reference. That, however, is neither the sole nor arguably the most productive question to be raised of this phrase. Within

58. Cicero, *Or.* 5.20–6.21; 21.69–29.101; idem, *De or.* 3.52.199–200; 3.45.177; see also Cornificius, *Rhet. ad Her.* 4.8–11; Quintilian, *Inst.* 12.10.58–72; Augustine, *Doctr. chr.* 4.19.38; 4.24.54–26.56.

59. As Kennedy notes (*New Testament Interpretation*, 30), analysis of NT prose rhythms is precluded by the lack of systematic differentiation between long and short syllables in pronouncing Koine Greek. Still, the Olivet address exhibits some almost poetic features: μὴ θροεῖσθε· δεῖ γενέσθαι (*mē throeisthe*; *dei genesthai*: "Fear not; this must be," v. 7ab); καὶ τότε ἀποστελεῖ τοὺς ἀγγέλους / ἐπισυνάξει τοὺς ἐκλεκτούς (*kai tote apostelei tous angelous / episynaxei tous eklektous*: "and then he will send the angels / he will gather together the chosen," v. 27a).

60. In *Inst.* 9.4.83, 91, Quintilian speaks of the different effects created by short and long syllables, rather than by phrases and clauses of varying lengths. Such clauses and phrases, however, are implied in Demetrius's discussion of the degrees of elevated diction (*Eloc.* 2.36–52).

61. See, e.g., Beasley-Murray, *Jesus and the Last Days*, 408–16; Pesch, *Naherwartungen*, 139–44.

a rhetorical framework, the significance of τὸ βδέλυγμα τῆς ἐρημώσεως resides largely in its provocative mystery and its concomitant resistance to clear interpretation. The technique is known as *controversiae*, much admired by clever declaimers in the first century CE, "whereby we excite some suspicion to indicate that our meaning is other than our words would seem to imply; yet in this case our meaning is not contrary to that which we express, as is the case in irony, but rather a hidden meaning that is left to the hearer to discover" (Quintilian, *Inst.* 9.2.65).

However unsafe or unseemly it might have been for Mark to speak more plainly at 13:14, for him to have done so would have assuredly been less provocative for his audience. This approach may also help to explain the presence in the same verse of the admonition, "Let the reader understand." As rhetorically inept as it may at first appear, that mysterious injunction may have been intended to seize the imaginations of those in Mark's community who were "overhearing" Jesus' oration, teasing them to unravel the secret of "the desolating sacrilege who [*sic*] stands" (cf. *Inst.* 9.2.78).[62] That the evangelist's rhetorical strategy was indeed successful is confirmed by the captivated creativity that it has exercised on generations of the Gospel's exegetes.

Evaluating Mark 13 by Ancient Literary Norms

Judged by first-century standards, does the Olivet Discourse constitute "good rhetoric"? As in any form of criticism, the answer depends on weighing various criteria. The bobtailed *prooemium* and *peroratio* of Jesus' address in Mark 13, as well as its grammatical roughness, would have jarred most classical rhetoricians. Moreover, those, like Aristotle, who esteemed the persuasive value of closely reasoned proof would probably have found this speech disappointing. Judged in strict accordance with such canons as these, Mark 13:5b–37 is a flawed declamation.

On the other hand, this discourse is by no means bereft of rhetorical effectiveness and sophistication. It seems appropriate to its situation and exigence: while directly responsive to their queries, the speech encourages its listeners to ponder related questions of a higher order. It is less concerned with dispensing and verifying abstruse information than with allaying anxiety, strengthening confidence, and instilling vigilance among timorous disciples. To those ends both the form and substance of the address are tailored: the audience is afforded, not only an anticipatory, vicarious experience of the vicissitudes and rescue to come, but also the reassurance and stability tacitly conveyed through familiar, rhetorical

---

62. Daube, *New Testament and Rabbinic Judaism*, 426, anticipated my proposal.

conventions. Audience contact is immediately established and then is maintained by a chiastic, coherent, and climactic narration. Upon an implicitly logical substructure, a speech of powerful pathos and *ēthos* has been crafted, whose wide-ranging stylistic devices are not merely decorative but deftly functional. Characteristic, perhaps, of one disposed to open or equivocal conclusions (see 15:39; 16:8), the evangelist does not say how Jesus' original audience reacted to the oration at Olivet. While Mark is no Cicero, one wonders if in every respect Quintilian would have disapproved.

FINAL REFLECTIONS

En route to my own *epilogos*, I have ventured judgments on the contributions and limitations of a rhetorical analysis, assessed within the context of other scholarship on Mark 13. Whether those judgments will hold, only time and continued investigation into Mark's Gospel will tell. In any case the following seem to me appropriate points on which to end this chapter.

1. Much scholarship on the Olivet Discourse has gravitated toward either reconstructing its tradition-history or analyzing its literary composition. Regarding the latter, the usefulness of Greco-Roman rhetorical theory, particularly on the subject of *taxis* (arrangement), should be evident. From the vantage point of tradition-history, rhetorical study may seem largely irrelevant; throughout most of the history of exegesis, however, precisely the reverse of this assessment would have been more common! It is highly unlikely that the second evangelist and his original audience would have envisioned, much less favored, an interpretation of the address on Olivet based on discriminating antecedent traditions from their subsequent redaction. Later generations of listeners and readers have made sense of Mark 13 and similar passages by appropriating the material in the rhetorical manner in which it is patently presented.[63] Furthermore, framing our interpretive questions of Mark 13 redaction-critically may as often play us false as true: discrepancies that modern exegetes have construed as evidence of Mark's use of composite sources may have stemmed instead from the evangelist's need to provide significant aural clues to a Gospel that was originally heard, not read.[64] Rhetorical theory provides excellent guidelines from antiquity for understanding and articulating the power of ancient address *as* address.

---

63. Ever since 1863, Lincoln's Gettysburg Address has profoundly moved North Americans, most of whom know nothing of its traditional antecedents, which stretch from the oratory of Edward Everett (1794–1865) to the Greek funeral orations of Pericles and Gorgias. See G. Wills, *Lincoln at Gettysburg*, 211–59.

64. Achtemeier, "*Omne verbum sonat*," esp. 26–27; Shiner, *Proclaiming the Gospel*; Wire, *The Case for Mark*.

2. On the other hand, modern reclamation of classical rhetoric requires correction by, and coordination with, other interpretive perspectives. This is necessitated by the complexity of biblical texts, molded by a broad array of historical, literary, and religious pressures. Thus, as we have witnessed, rhetorical criticism of Mark 13 entails recognition of the degree to which the Olivet Discourse creatively adapts or even flouts rhetorical norms, owing to its location within the larger narrative of Mark's Gospel and its subjection to not one but many generic constraints.

3. If the essence of this essay's argument be accepted, then a reconsideration of Mark's rhetorical versatility seems in order. In content and format Mark 13 is like nothing else in that Gospel, which at points deprecates the power of verbal persuasion (see 4:10–12; 8:14–21).[65] Nevertheless, in chapter 13 Mark modifies his customary approach and attacks the problems and prospects raised by an apocalyptic eschatology with extraordinary directness, depth, and rhetorical sophistication. As far back as Papias (130 CE; Eusebius, *Hist. eccl.* 3.39.15) and as recently as George Kennedy,[66] the construction of Mark's Gospel has paled alongside those of the other evangelists. May we justly conclude that the Second Gospel's narrative rhetoric is uniformly "fairly crude," as Mary Ann Tolbert has suggested?[67] Alternatively, does Mark remain for us, rhetorically as well as theologically, "a master of surprise," an evangelist who relentlessly brings his interpreters up short just when they think they have his little Gospel pinned down?[68]

4. If this chapter's analysis has treated Mark 13 accurately and with fairness, it may also be worth pondering the possibility that, in the address at Olivet, the second evangelist has created a miniature rhetorical masterpiece. Apocalypticism strikes most moderns along today's religious mainline as essentially brazen, irrational, and primitive. Mark, as always, bewilders us with a very different point of view. The unexpected care with which the Olivet Discourse has been crafted is, in a sense, congruent with the equally off-putting significance of apocalypticism in Markan theology.[69] In chapter 13 Mark administers his audience

---

65. Recall Mark 13:11, where the value of practiced rhetorical endeavor seems undercut by Jesus' admonition that his disciples should not rehearse their apologia but leave all persuasion to the Holy Spirit in the moment of crisis (cf. Exod. 4:1–17; Num. 22:35; Jer. 1:6–10). For different reasons, Plato exhibits a similar paradox: the rhetorician who distrusts rhetoric (*Phaedr.* 257b–58e; 275d–76a).

66. For Kennedy, Mark's Gospel tends toward "radical Christian rhetoric," a form of "sacred language" that presupposes the believer's immediate and intuitive apprehension of truth without assistance from the art of persuasion (*New Testament Interpretation*, 97–113, esp. 104–7).

67. Tolbert, *Sowing the Gospel*, 59, 78. The outcomes of her perceptive study seem to me ambivalent: for all of the evangelist's touted lack of literary sophistication, Mark remains, in her view, a work of extraordinary subtlety and power (311–15 et passim; see my review in *CBQ* 54 [1992]: 382–84).

68. Thus Juel, *A Master of Surprise*.

69. See, among others, Marcus, *Mystery of the Kingdom*; A. Y. Collins, *Beginning of the Gospel*, 1–38.

a straight shot of apocalyptic pastoral care: the comfort of a distraught Christian community by revitalizing a vision that sweeps all affairs of heaven and earth under God's mysterious, faithful, restorative dominion.[70] That pastoral objective, pervading Mark's Gospel, is achieved nowhere with greater clarity, finesse, and power than that which we and the disciples experience in an oration at Olivet.

---

70. For further reflections in this vein, see C. Black, "Ministry in Mystery"; idem, *Mark* (ANTC), passim.

Chapter Four

Theophilus, Meet Theophrastus

Despite his influence in my life, Oscar Hammerstein II is not my idol. . . . The truth is that in Hammerstein's shows, for all their revolutionary impact, the characters are not much more than collections of characteristics—verbal tics and quirks, like Southern accents or bad grammar, which individualize a character only the way a black hat signifies a villain—and his lyrics reflect that naïveté.

Stephen Sondheim[1]

Lazarus and "Dives" (Luke 16:19–31) and the Pharisee and the tax collector (18:9–14) are only four of the unforgettable characters in the parables of Luke's Jesus. Having loosed the bonds of their stories, two other figures from Luke's distinctive parable tradition have entered everyday discourse as character types: the Good Samaritan (10:29–37) and the Prodigal Son (15:11–32). No other Gospel contains parables more vivid than Luke's, and much of that liveliness percolates from their colorful characters. One wonders: How would such characters in Luke's parables have registered for "Theophilus" (1:3; cf. Acts 1:1) and that Gospel's larger audience of "God-lovers"? Is there a definable literary context in which that question may be situated and answered?

THEOPHRASTUS AND HIS CHARACTERS

The Study of Character in Antiquity

The peculiar stamp on an ancient Greek coin was its *charaktēr*: the marks that differentiated its value from other currency (LSJ 1977a). By extension Herodotus

---

1. Sondheim, *Finishing the Hat*, xix.

used the term in referring to a person's distinguishing facial, bodily, or dialectical features: "While the boy was still speaking, Astyages . . . thought he saw something in the character of his face like his own, and there was a nobility about the answer he had made" (*Wars* 1.116.1). Without using the term *charaktēr*, Aristotle illustrates shamelessness with cowards who throw down their arms and flee from battle, the licentious who are unable to curb their carnal lust, and those so greedy that "[they] would pick a corpse's pocket" (*Rhet.* 1383b.12–1385a.15). Aristotle tended toward general descriptions of virtue and vice (*Eth. Nic.* 1106b.16–1108b.6). By contrast, his trusted successor as head of the Peripatetic School, Theophrastus (ca. 370–ca. 285 BCE), "gives us a real occasion, and instead of an anonymous agent, a real individual" occupying a specific time and place: daily life in early fourth-century Athens.[2] Thus, with *Characters*, Theophrastus has innovated a genre— a satirical taxonomy of behavioral types—that was updated centuries later by such literati as George Eliot (*Impressions of Theophrastus Such*, 1879) and William Makepeace Thackeray (*The Book of Snobs and Other Contributions to Punch*, 1895). Just what purpose Theophrastus intended his *Characters* to serve remains an open question. Though most of his works have not survived, from Diogenes Laertius (*Eminent Philosophers* 5.42–50 [second century CE]) we learn that Theophrastus was an esteemed educator and prolific philosopher who delved into hundreds of aspects of human inquiry including botany, chemistry, physics, politics, ethics, logic, metaphysics, and rhetoric.[3] His *Characters* occupies an unusual place in that author's output. Two theories for its purpose seem credible. One is that it was a jeu d'esprit, written for his amusement and that of his friends. The anecdotes could also have been injected into his lectures on ethics as comic relief.[4] (Perhaps the format of *Characters*, a taxonomical catalog, is Theophrastus's takeoff on his own more influential *Inquiry into Plants* and *On the Causes of Plants*.) Another suggestion is that, while the book offers no overt ethical analysis, *Characters* implies a moral and ideological stance, "a common sense of separateness and superiority,"[5] that the author's community of scholars would have shared. This interpretation of the book chimes with a comment by Plutarch: "For according to Theophrastus, jest [*skōmma*] is a concealed rebuke for error. Consequently the listener supplies mentally on his own what is missing, just as if he knows and believes it" (*Quaestiones convivales* 631d–e).

---

2. Diggel, *Theophrastus: Characters*, 7.

3. As Kennedy notes ("Theophrastus and Stylistic Distinctions"), Theophrastus essayed a treatise on three aspects of style. In chap. 3, on Mark, we have acknowledged this contribution; with reference to John, we shall return to it in chap. 5.

4. Diggel, *Theophrastus: Characters*, 15–16; and (more cautiously) Jebb, *Characters of Theophrastus*, 37–40.

5. Millett, *Theophrastus and His World*, 31. "Theophrastus has created for his audience an implied code of conduct: a perspective on honor and shame, co-operation and conflict as they might impinge on upper-class citizens with reference to the civic society peculiar to democratic Athens" (ibid., 105).

The *Characters*: A Closer Look

The book comprises thirty cameos of everyday Athenians, sketched by Theophrastus with an eye for telling details. The author categorizes human foibles by assigning each character type a one-word classification, which I translate loosely here without intending to mislead.

Table 1: Theophrastus's Characters

The Dissembler (*eirōn*)	Mr. Superstitious (*deisidaimōn*)
The Toady (*kolax*)	The Griper (*mempsimoiros*)
The Chatterbox (*adoleschēs*)	Mr. Distrustful (*apistos*)
The Country Bumpkin (*agroikos*)	Mr. Gross (*dyscherēs*)
Mr. Obsequious (*areskos*)	Mr. Tasteless (*aēdēs*)
The Shameless Opportunist (*aponenoēmenos*)	The Petty Ambitious (*mikrophilotimos*)
The Talker (*lalos*)	The Cheapskate (*aneleutheros*)
The Gossip (*logopoios*)	The Braggart (*alazōn*)
The Shameless Sponger (*anaischyntos*)	Mr. Arrogant (*hyperēphanos*)
The Penny-Pincher (*mikrologos*)	The Coward (*deilos*)
The Boor (*bdelyros*)	The Oligarch (*oligarchos*)
Mr. Tactless (*akairos*)	The Old Fool (*opsimathēs*)
The Overdoer (*periergos*)	The Slanderer (*kakologos*)
The Blockhead (*anaisthētos*)	The Scoundrels' Friend (*philoponēros*)
The Grouch (*authadēs*)	The Chiseler (*aischrokerdēs*)

For a taste of this feast of folly, try the twelfth on this menu: "Mr. Tactless." Theophrastus's description, *akairos*, literally means one who is "unseasonable": a person with no sense of timing or sensitivity to what suits the circumstances:

[Tactlessness hits its mark {at a time} aggravating to those one meets.]

Mr. Tactless is the sort who comes for extended conversation when you are busy. And serenades his sweetheart when she's feverish. And comes to you when you have just forfeited your security deposit and asks you to stand bail for him. And arrives to offer evidence after the case is closed. And while he's a guest at a wedding, he launches a tirade against the female sex. And when you have just come back from a long trip, he invites you for a walk. And, as your broker, he has a knack for bringing along a higher bidder after the sale is over. And after the audience has gotten the point, he gets up to explain it all over again. And he overzealously tries to secure what you don't want but haven't the heart to refuse. And when people are offering public sacrifice at great expense, he comes to collect a payment with interest. And standing and watching while a slave is being whipped, he announces that a boy of his own once hanged himself after such a thrashing. And when assisting at arbitration he puts the parties at loggerheads, even though both want a reconciliation. And when he wants to dance he grabs a partner who is not yet drunk. (trans. Diggel, *Theophrastus: Characters*, alt.)

This character is illustrative of the rest. Theophrastus's technique is not hard to analyze.

1. We begin by noting that this and the book's other character sketches do not open with Theophrastus's own words. Interpolated at the beginning of the book, then at the top of each of these cameos, are superfluous, moralistic prologues whose vocabulary and style reveal the hand of a later editor.[6] Nine of the thirty cameos conclude with equally flat-footed epilogues. As originally worded,[7] each of Theophrastus's definitions wastes no words on tiresome exposition. He is a master of showing, not telling: sketching a figure that invites observers to draw the obvious conclusion about his conduct.

2. None of these definitions is lengthy; most are rendered in a few hundred words. Most expansive are The Toady, "the sort who says to someone walking with him, 'Are you aware of the admiring looks you are getting?'" (2.2); Mr. Superstitious, who, "if a weasel runs across his path, . . . will not proceed further until someone else has covered the ground or he has thrown three stones across it" (16.3); and The Chiseler, who "borrows money from a visitor staying with him" (30.3)—not out of avarice, but because he relishes taking advantage of others.

3. Although the subject occupies a sliver of his publications, Theophrastus was arguably the most consequential Hellenistic philosopher in the field of rhetoric.[8] To judge from his influence on Cicero (*De or.* 3.37–38; *Or.* 79) and Quintilian (*Inst.* 8.1–11.1), whose works were written just before or during the era of the NT's composition, Theophrastus left his deepest mark on ancient rhetoric in the areas of style and delivery. His theory emerged from practical experience: he is said to have lectured to as many as two thousand students at once, and to have paid attention to the technique of speaking, grooming and attire, and careful gestures.[9] His criteria for good style were good grammar (*hellēnismos*), clarity (*to saphes*), suitability for the circumstances (*to prepon*), and restrained ornamentation (*kataskeuē*).

---

6. Diggel (*Theophrastus: Characters*, 16–19) provides a well-balanced assessment of the work's authenticity and integrity.
7. "Original wording" should be understood generously: the text of this work is corrupted. For consideration of the manuscript's convoluted transmission in antiquity, consult Diggel, *Theophrastus: Characters*, 37–51.
8. Kennedy, *A New History*, 84–85.
9. For primary attestation of these reports, see Kennedy, *Art of Persuasion in Greece*, 273.

Though the occasion for these *Characters* is obscure, the book's style scores high alongside its author's other values.

4. While each of the cameos concentrates on a dominant human foible, the differences between Theophrastus's types are not rigid. For instance, the element most definitive of Mr. Tactless is his irrepressible talent for doing the wrong thing at the wrong time. Nevertheless, the *akairos* shares traits with other personality types: his verbal clumsiness intersects with that of The Chatterbox (#3), The Talker (#7), The Gossip (#8), and The Slanderer (#28);[10] his preoccupation with money, with that of The Shameless Sponger (#9), The Penny-Pincher (#10), The Cheapskate (#22), and The Chiseler (#30).[11] His repulsiveness to his girlfriend and women in general is similar to that of The Boor, "who raises his clothes and exposes himself in front of ladies" (11.2), and of Mr. Tasteless, "who at dinner narrates how he was cleaned out from top to bottom after drinking hellebore [laxative], the bile from his feces blacker than the broth on the table" (20.6; trans. Diggel). His inordinate zeal resembles that of The Overdoer, "who promises more than he can deliver" (13.2). In one so incompetent that he infuriates litigants who really want a settlement, there's more than a touch of The Blockhead, who wanders the countryside while being tried in court as the defendant (14.3).

5. All of Theophrastus's character types are identifiable in everyday society: they reveal their essential natures by their interactions with others at home, with their acquaintances, and in civic settings like lawcourts, weddings, auctions, public lectures, religious observances, and dances. Etiquette is foreign to them. They are notably proficient in springing their own traps when talking and handling money (anticipating two primary concerns in the Epistle of James, as in 2:1–17; 3:1–12; 4:11–5:6). The Talker's children plead, "Papa, talk to us so that we may fall asleep" (7.10). If he throws a party, The Penny-Pincher counts the number of cups from which each guest drinks, to prevent the caterer from dunning him (10.3–4).

6. There is nothing criminal or genuinely evil in the conduct of Theophrastus's characters. These are fools, not knaves; irritants, not menaces. An exception may be The Scoundrels' Friend (*philoponēros*), "apt to champion riffraff" while conspiring on juries to warp justice (29.6). Even so, in ancient Athens *ponēros* was a convenient label, applied to any legal or political cause of which one happened to disapprove.[12] Most of Theophrastus's targets are not of the sort that can or should be jailed. Rather, they are the kind of people that, if you saw them approaching, you might look for a convenient alley by which to avoid them.

---

10. Some distinctions: The Chatterbox is the logorrheic master of disconnected trivialities; The Talker, the know-it-all for everyone. The Gossip broadcasts tall tales he has fabricated about others; The Slanderer lives to defame.

11. More distinctions: The Sponger shamelessly takes advantage of others; so also The Chiseler, who disgracefully profits by it. The Penny-Pincher is an inveterate skinflint. The Cheapskate's miserliness is out of all proportion to his wealth.

12. Diggel, *Theophrastus: Characters*, 499.

7. The obvious should be stated. All of these characters are unsavory, misfits, and annoying. There's not a pleasant customer in the bunch; refined persons would never wish to emulate them and would be abashed to discover that others thought them just so.

8. Theophrastus's *Characters* is a humorous book. Like the New Comic playwright Menander of Athens (late fourth century BCE)—whose plays bear such titles as *Agroikos* (*The Country Bumpkin*), *Apistos* (*Mr. Distrustful*), *Deisidaimōn* (*Mr. Superstitious*), and *Kolax* (*The Toady*)—Theophrastus finds a way to send up those everyday personalities he deplores. "[He] seems to have had a very keen sense of the ridiculous, . . . [and his] descriptions are written as if their principal aim was to amuse."[13] Theophrastus achieves this effect by piling on acerbic details in short space. There is something of the stand-up comic's shtick in Theophrastus's august lexicon: one hears it in the patter of clauses that begin with a repetitive "and" (*kai*-parataxis) and end as punch lines, with pauses at the end of colons to be filled in by laughter (one may imagine). "Mr. Tactless" builds to a neat climax: the first trait (the fellow who opens his heart to you when you are busy) instantly captures the essential personality being skewered; the last (grabbing a dance partner who is still sober) would be a confusing attribute on which to open but makes perfect sense by the time one has reached the end. In that final line there's a wink to the audience, invited to tease out why an inebriated partner is to be preferred when dancing. In the same spirit lies the fine detail of serenading one's mistress when she complains of fever (cf. Alexis Comicus 150.10–11; Ovid, *Ars amatoria* 1.8.73–74), the classical equivalent of the immemorial excuse, "Not tonight; I have a headache."

LUKE'S PARABLES

Surveying the Terrain

Ever since Adolf Jülicher applied his magnifying glass to the Gospels' text near the turn of the twentieth century,[14] it has proved notoriously hard to define a "parable" (*hē parabolē*). As remembered in the Synoptics, Jesus' teaching was vibrantly imagistic and assumed different forms: comparisons (Luke 10:3; 12:6–7, 22–31, 54–59), aphorisms (7:35; 9:57–58, 60, 62; 11:33; 12:32, 34), metaphors (6:43–44a; 11:34–36; 13:32), figures of speech (6:44b; 11:21–22), example stories (10:29–37; 12:16–21), and allegory (20:9–19).[15] Although we confine ourselves to narratives for the purpose of this chapter's investigation, one may count as many as

13. Jebb, *Characters of Theophrastus*, 29.
14. Jülicher, *Gleichnisreden Jesu* (1899; repr. 1963).
15. See Theissen and Merz, *Historical Jesus*, 324–45.

twenty-seven parables in Luke.[16] In the following catalog of Lukan parables, those found in all the Synoptics are set in normal type; those Luke shares with Matthew (and not with Mark) are <u>underlined</u>; those appearing only in Luke are set in **bold-face**. Asterisked items(*) have parallels in the *Gospel of Thomas*.

Table 2: Luke's Parables

1. <u>Wise and Foolish Builders</u> (6:47–49)
2. <u>Children in the Marketplace</u> (7:31–34)
3. **Two Debtors** (7:41–43)
4. A Sower* (8:5–8; interpreted, 8:11–15)
5. **A Neighborly Samaritan** (10:25–37)
6. **A Friend at Midnight** (11:5–8)
7. <u>A Father's Good Gifts</u> (11:11–13)
8. **A Rich Fool*** (12:16–21)
9. <u>Waiting and Ready Slaves</u> (12:35–38)
10. <u>Wise and Foolish Slaves</u> (12:42–46)
11. **A Farmer's Barren Fig Tree** (13:6–9)
12. The Mustard Seed* (13:18–19)
13. <u>A Woman's Use of Leaven*</u> (13:20–21)
14. <u>Futile Appeals to the Householder</u> (13:23–29)
15. <u>A Lavish Banquet*</u> (14:16–24)
16. **Building a Tower** (14:28–30)
17. **A King Who Goes to War** (14:31–33)
18. <u>A Lost Sheep*</u> (15:4–7)
19. **A Lost Coin** (15:8–10)
20. **Lost Children and Their Father** (15:11–32)
21. **A Shrewd Manager** (16:1–8)
22. **The Rich Man and Lazarus** (16:19–31)
23. **A Dutiful Slave** (17:7–10)
24. **Ruthless Judge; Persistent Widow** (18:2–8)
25. **A Pharisee and a Tax Collector** (18:10–14)
26. <u>Trading on the Boss's Investments</u> (19:12–27)
27. Wicked Tenant Farmers* (20:9–19)

1. Given Mark's paucity of parables, one is not surprised to find in Luke only three in the triple tradition: The Sower (#4: Mark 4:3–8 = Luke 8:5–8 = Matt. 13:3–8), The Mustard Seed (#12: Mark 4:30–32 = Luke 13:18–19 = Matt. 13:31–32), and The Wicked Tenants (#27: Mark 12:1–12 = Luke 20:9–19 = Matt. 21:33–46).

2. Ten parables apparently stem from Q: Wise and Foolish Builders (#1: Luke 6:47–49 = Matt. 7:24–27), Children in the Marketplace (#2: Luke 7:31–34 = Matt. 11:16–19), A Father's Gifts (#7: Luke 11:11–13 = Matt. 7:9–11), Waiting Slaves (#9: Luke 12:35–38 = Matt. 13:34–37), Wise and Foolish Slaves (#10: Luke 12:42–46 = Matt. 24:45–51), Leaven (#13: Luke 13:20–21 = Matt. 13:33), Stringent Salvation (#14: Luke 13:23–29 = Matt. 7:13–14 and 25:10–12), The

---

16. This figure errs toward maximalism. There is little narrative built into Luke 7:31–35 (#2) or 11:11–13 (#7). Likewise, 13:18–19 (#12) and 13:20–21 (#13) are vignettes that, when collocated, create a sequential impression rather than a narrative as such. I include these to lend greater depth of field to this analysis; moreover, standard scholarly treatments also include them (e.g., Jeremias, *Parables of Jesus*, 146–49, 160–62; Scott, *Hear Then the Parable*, 87–88, 321–29, 373–87; Hultgren, *Parables of Jesus*, 202–12, 234–40, 392–409).

Banquet (#15: Luke 14:16–24 = Matt. 22:1–14), The Lost Sheep (#18: Luke 15:4–7 = Matt. 18:12–14), and The Pounds (#26: Luke 19:12–27) or Talents (Matt. 25:14–30).

3. The remainder and plurality of the Third Gospel's parables—fourteen—are distinctively Lukan (##3, 5, 6, 8, 11, 16, 17, 19, 20, 21, 22, 23, 24, 25). Of these, only the parable of the Rich Fool (#8) intersects with the *Thomas* tradition (logion 63); the remaining Thomasine intersections are with Q (##13, 15, 18)[17] or the triple tradition (##4, 12, 27).[18]

General Patterns and First Impressions

1. The fourteen distinctively Lukan parables demonstrate some interesting formal qualities. First, each has a firm narrative spine, whether it be a brief anecdote embedded within a large form-critical unit (7:41–43 in 7:36–50) or a complex story with multiple scenes (15:11–32), which simultaneously serves as the climax of a series of three parables of lost creatures (cf. 15:3–7, 8–10). Second, longer parables typically unfold in obedience to folklore's rule of three (##5, 9 [N.B.: 12:37, 38], 18–20, 21, 26[19])—sometimes breaking the pattern for unexpected effect (##4, 11 [N.B. 13:7–9], 15, 20 [15:25–32 as completing 15:11–24], 27). Third, Luke's parables often contrast the conduct or circumstances of paired characters: two builders (#1); two debtors (#3); fathers human and divine (#7); slaves who do and do not know how to proceed during their master's delay (##9, 10); the preparations of a builder (#16) and a potentate (#17); two prodigal sons (#20); rich man, poor man (#22); a resistant judge versus a relentless widow (#24), the latter's conduct chiming with that of another parable's importunate friend (#6); two worshipers in the temple (#25). (Note also, in #2, the paired contrast between the receptions of John the Baptist and the Son of Man [7:33–34].) Fourth, twenty-two of the twenty-seven parables in Luke (##5–26; around 81%), including all but one of the uniquely Lukan parables (#3), are situated in that Gospel's central travelogue (9:51–19:27): the heart of Jesus' teaching in this Gospel. Moreover, the preponderance of this travelogue's second half (roughly, 14:25–19:27) is dedicated to a large number of uniquely Lukan parables (##16–17, 19–25). Fifth, in most cases Bultmann's dictum holds true: "Some passages . . . *do not have a conclusion*, if, that is, it is

---

17. The parable of the Leaven appears in *Gos. Thom.* 96; the Banquet, in 64; the Lost Sheep, in 107 (also in *Gospel of Truth* 31–32).

18. The parable of the Sower appears in *Gos. Thom.* 9; the Mustard Seed, in 20; the Wicked Tenants, in 65–66.

19. Even though items 9, 18, and 26 stem from Q, not L, they illustrate the phenomenon at issue. When necessary to clarify other points, elsewhere in this paragraph I blur tradition-critical lines.

self-evident and not relevant."[20] Jesus is clear that the requests of both widow (#24) and tax collector (#25) were upheld (18:5, 7–8a, 14a), and we know all of the Samaritan's conduct (#5) necessary to answer the important question (10:36). On the other hand, in Luke we never learn whether the rich fool died that very night (#8), or if the barren fig tree bore fruit the next year (#11), or if the elder son accepted his father's invitation to attend his brother's homecoming celebration (#20).

2. Given the incontestable truism that "the kingdom [or dominion] of God" is typical of Jesus' teaching, it is interesting to note that expression's mention in only two of the twenty-seven items listed above: #13, the mustard seed of the triple tradition, and #14, the woman's leaven in Q. Both of these are introduced with the question "To what shall I compare the kingdom of God?" (13:20) or similar rhetoric (13:18). That royal metaphor is attached to #14 (the aphorism of "reclin[ing] at table in the kingdom of God" [13:29 AT], appended to the preceding parable in 13:23–28), to #15 ("Blessed is the one who shall eat bread in the kingdom of God" [14:15 AT] as preface to the parable of the Banquet [14:16–24]), and to #26 (the Pounds, 19:12–27), which refers to a nobleman's departure to secure a kingdom (19:15) and whose set-up is a supposition "that the kingdom of God was to appear immediately" (19:11). The five parables in Luke in which "God's reign" receives explicit mention stem in one case from the triple tradition (#12; cf. *Gos. Thom.* 20), while the remaining four evidently issue from Q (##13 [*Gos. Thom.* 96], 14, 15 [*Gos. Thom.* 64], 26). It is by no means true that Jesus' parables or overall teaching in Luke downplay the kingdom of God: the topic is stated (e.g., 4:43; 6:20; 7:28; 10:9; 11:20) or implied (e.g., 1:33; 11:2; 12:31, 32; 23:42) forty-six times in the Third Gospel. Instead, the point to recognize is that the Q (9:60; 10:9, 11; 16:16; 23:29–30, among others) and triple traditions (for instance, 8:10; 9:27; 18:16–17, 24–25, 29; 22:18; 23:51) of which the third evangelist avails himself are imbued with language about God's kingdom.[21] It is these traditions that create the eschatological ambience in which Luke's readers hear Jesus' parables, whether those pericopes expressly refer to the kingdom or not.

3. Let us turn the preceding inquiry around. Do some themes in the distinctively Lukan parable strata stand out when compared with those of the other Synoptics? If the kingdom of God is not the explicit focus of this evangelist's parables, save in a general way established by their narrative context, on what issues *do* the Lukan parables concentrate? The following are readily identifiable:

---

20. Bultmann, *History of the Synoptic Tradition*, 190 (emphasis as in Marsh's translation). Many of Bultmann's other observations on the parables' formal characteristics—for instance, their concision and the law of "end-stress" (188–92)—remain perceptive and invite reacquaintance.

21. In several cases Luke adds "the kingdom of God" to inherited traditions to point up its importance: 8:1; 9:2, 11; 9:62; 17:20–21; 21:31; 22:16. The expression occurs six times in Acts (1:3; 8:12; 14:22; 19:8; 28:23, 31; cf. 1:6; 20:25).

a. Debts and their forgiveness (##3, 21, 25)
b. Readily discharged responsibility to one's peers or superiors (##5, 21, 23)
c. Persistence in prayerful petition (##6, 24)
d. Misplaced confidence in worldly possessions (##8, 22)
e. God's forbearance before judgment (#11)
f. Discipleship's exacting demands (##16, 17)
g. Recovery of lost valuables (##19, 20, 21)
h. Profound reversals in status (#22, 25)

While distinctively Lukan, these themes are not *uniquely* so. One may see itera-tions of them in Q and the triple tradition: thus the topics of readiness (##1, 9) and unpreparedness (##1, 10), responsibility to a superior (#26), and recovery of the lost (#18). Eschatological reversals are especially prevalent in all traditions (##4, 12, 14, 15, 26, 27, and more obliquely, #2).[22] Also noteworthy is the fact that several of the themes identifiable in Luke's special parable tradition entwine and effectively comment on one another. The transvaluation of what should be sought (g) and relinquished (d) exemplifies social reversals both now and in the age to come (h). Discipleship's exacting requirements (f) and persistent petition (c) are particular instances of the disciple's general responsibility to the Lord (b), whose gracious judgment (e) may be expressed in the forgiveness of debts (a). Thus Luke's parables suggest a coherent theology and anthropology, even if they do not articulate that coherence in an obvious or systematic manner.

A SHADY DEALER CONVERSES WITH MR. TACTLESS

If the parable of the Prodigal Son (15:11–32) is Luke's most famous and most beloved, then that which immediately follows it, traditionally known as "The Unjust Steward" (16:1–8), is the third evangelist's most infamous, exegetically confounding, and theologically disturbing parable.

> And [Jesus] said to the disciples, "There was a rich fellow who had a business manager. Now charges were brought to him that this [manager] was squandering his assets. So [the rich man] called him and said to him, 'What's this I hear about you? Surrender your books;[23] you can't manage

---

22. "Great reversals" are also conspicuous in distinctively Matthean traditions: 18:23–35; 20:1–16; 21:28–32; 25:1–13, 31–46. Regarding delay before judgment, Matthew's parables of Wheat and Tares (13:24–30 [cf. 13:36–43]) and the Dragnet (13:47–50) intersect with Luke 13:6–9. Luke leans toward prudence in one's eschatological preparation (7:41–43; 14:28–30, 31–33; 17:7–10; though cf. 16:1–8; 19:12–27); Matthew's special tradition adopts a go-for-broke attitude (13:44, 45–46).

23. Literally, *ton logon*, "the word," which in this context is as figurative an expression of "account statement" as the translation suggested here.

anymore.'[24] Now the manager said to himself, 'What am I going to do now that my boss[25] is taking my position away from me? I'm not strong enough to dig. I'm ashamed to beg. I know what I'll do—so that, when I'm canned from management, they'll take me into their houses.' So, calling his boss's debtors one by one, he said to the first,

'How much do you owe my boss?'

'Eight hundred gallons of oil.'

'Take your bill, sit down fast, and write "four hundred."'

Then he said to another,

'Okay, you: how much do you owe?'

'A thousand bushels of wheat.'

'Take your bill and write "eight hundred."'

"Now the boss praised the dishonest manager because he had acted shrewdly, because this world's boys are shrewder than the fair-haired children[26] of their own generation." (AT)

The parable proper ends there at 16:8, if not already with its first clause ("because he had acted shrewdly"). Internal commentary on the parable continues for another five verses:

"Now I'm telling you: make friends for yourselves by means of unlaundered money, so that when it runs out they will take you into durable homes.[27] The one who's trustworthy in the least little thing is also trustworthy in many things. Now if you haven't been trustworthy with dirty money, who's going to entrust you with the real thing? And if you haven't been faithful in what belongs to another, who's going to give you your own? No one can slave for two bosses: Either he will hate the one and love the other, or he will be devoted to the one and despise the other. You cannot slave for God *and* for money." (AT)

There's little gain in rehearsing here the wailing and gnashing of teeth among interpreters of Luke 16:1–13.[28] In general, most of the consternation centers in three areas: (1) What of pertinent first-century economic practice can be imported into the parable to make sense of its narrative? (2) Just how does the internal commentary in verses 9–13 (or vv. 8–13) illuminate the parable in 16:1–8 (or 16:1–7)?[29] (3) How does one reconcile the moral and religious implications of this material with Luke's point of view, expressed throughout this Gospel?

24. "You're fired" would deliver the sense in modern English, while muffling an important irony as the story develops.

25. Literally, "my lord," *ho kyrios mou*.

26. Literally, "the sons of this age are shrewder than the sons of light."

27. Literally, "Make friends for yourselves by means of unrighteous mammon, so that when it fails they may receive you into the eternal tabernacles."

28. Representative are Marshall, *Gospel of Luke*, 614–24; Fitzmyer, *Luke (X–XXIV)*, 1094–1104; Johnson, *Luke*, 243–49. We shall return to this parable in chap. 8.

29. Precisely where the parable yields to internal commentary remains a debated point. See Fitzmyer, *Luke (X–XXIV)*, 1096–99.

Economics 101

Considerable exegetical energy is expended on the cultural aspects of the debt-reduction scheme (vv. 5–7). Somebody wins (the debtors come out ahead); somebody loses (the boss, who isn't repaid the full loan and may also lose interest on it; and his manager, who may be sacrificing his percentage commission).[30] Some have argued that the tacit effect of the manager's backroom negotiations with his boss's clients is to enhance the financier's prestige: what the entrepreneur would forfeit in cash he would more than realize in social status for his generosity.[31] While many of these explanations are based on practices in modern peasant societies, there is exegetical nobility in attempting to understand Luke's parable on its first-century terms. At least two problems immediately surface with such proposals. First, they tend toward reasonable conjecture lacking firm corroboration from the literature of the world being interpreted. Second, unless the exegete is careful, one may undermine some of the very points made by one such first-century witness: Luke.

However profound our ignorance of most first-century social cues, finally the parable tells us everything we need to understand its basic point: *at every turn we are dealing with scoundrels*. While there is no evidence that the accusations of embezzlement are based in fact—for all we know, the accusers may also be rogues[32]—their target's response is not that of an upright man. He does not contemplate defending his innocence; rather, his first thought is how to save his skin without losing face. One of this parable's many ironies is that the manager's self-salvage ends up justifying the charges lodged against him: by lowering everyone's debt, he swindles his boss. Implied in the CFO's insistence that the first of a series of debtors proceed quickly (*tacheōs*, v. 6) is the idea that the books will be cooked before their surrender to the CEO (v. 2b). There's no suggestion that the manager expects this expedient to preserve his former job; by reducing their obligations, he is blatantly ingratiating himself to those in position to return him a huge favor (thus v. 4 and its allegorical interpretation in v. 9). By colluding in fraud—it is *they* who fudge the numbers without resisting the manager's directives—the debtors hardly emerge as moral paragons; by unlawfully amending their contracts to reduced debts, they may remain in position to rationalize their theft. ("The bastard overcharged us anyway; he's so rich, he'll never miss it; it all washes out.") Because Luke repeatedly warns the reader to regard wealth askance (1:53; 6:24; 8:14; 12:13–21, 22–34;

---

30. Consult, e.g., Derrett, *Law in the New Testament*, 48–77; Kloppenborg, "The Dishonoured Master."

31. Moxnes, *Economy of the Kingdom*, 76–79. Bailey (*Poet and Peasant*, 101–2) and Hultgren (*Parables of Jesus*, 151–52) compound this conjecture's interest: the manager has maneuvered his boss into an inability to undo renegotiated contracts without losing face.

32. The verb *diaballein* ("to bring charges") is cognate with *ho diabolos* ("the devil") and the adjective *diabolos* ("libelous"). Cf. the LXX translation (*ho diabolos*) of the Hebrew *ha-śāṭān* in Job 1:6.

14:33; 16:19–31; 22:5), there is no reason to suppose that the rich man in 16:1–8 is an upright citizen. Nor does he prove to be: assuming his manager's guilt without proof, he summarily cashiers him (16:2); nothing within the parable's frame suggests that the manager is later reinstated. Whatever the motivation for the boss's response in 16:8a,[33] by his fruits we know him (6:43–45): what elicits praise for the manager is *not* the latter's integrity—he is plainly *adikia*, unscrupulous (16:8)—but rather his crafty (*phronimōs*) ploy in turning a self-interested profit. To laud what is shrewd yet unrighteous effectively stains the laudator of such con artistry. In 16:8b–13 is Jesus himself doing the same?

Does the Lord's Explanation Make Things Better or Worse?

An important key for understanding the quasi-allegorical interpretation of 16:1–8 (cf. 8:4–15; 20:9–18) lies in its conclusion: "No one is able to serve ['or be in thrall to,' *douleuein*] God and mammon"[34] (16:13b AT). Previously announced in Luke (6:20, 24; 12:13–21), the harsh dichotomy between entrusting oneself to worldly riches instead of God's kingdom is reiterated in 16:9 ("unrighteous mammon . . . that peters out" versus "eternal habitations"[AT]), in 16:10–11 ("unrighteous mammon [that amounts to] very little" versus "true riches" [AT]), in 16:12 ("the extraneous versus the internal" [paraphrased]), and in 16:13a (the despicable master to be hated versus the beloved master worthy of devotion). The interpretation in 16:8b–13 makes clear that capitalism as such is not being extolled. What disciples learn from the manager's cunning is the desperate need for humanity—creditors, managers, debtors all—to risk its future on God's grace (see also 11:5–13).[35] To be led home to God by way of a dingy parable is ample reason to befriend the cupidity with which it brims (16:9). As Adlai Stevenson II (1900–1965) mused, "A lie is an abomination unto the Lord and a very present help in time of trouble."[36]

---

33. Among many suggestions: mercy (Bailey, *Poet and Peasant*, 98), face-saving (ibid., 101–2; Hultgren, *Parables of Jesus*, 151–52); tempered admiration for having been outfoxed (Talbert, *Reading Luke*, 154); appreciation for promotion of his honor at the expense of his wealth (Tannehill, *Luke*, 247). Again we are crippled by ignorance of how a first-century Middle-Eastern audience would have viewed the middleman's cheating his boss. Can we be sure that the outcome allows the rich man to save face? Since all interested parties know exactly what happened and how, it seems as likely that the patron's business associates would consider him the sort of schmuck that President Lyndon Johnson (1908–1973) recognized: "While you're saving your face, you're losing your ass" (Jonathan Green, *Political Quotes*, 174).

34. A Semitic term for wordly property: *māmôn* (Hebrew/Aramaic) or *māmônā'* (Aramaic, emphatic state); see Fitzmyer, *Luke (X–XXIV)*, 1109.

35. Similarly, see Beck, *Christian Character*, 28–54.

36. Jonathan Green, *Political Quotes*, 212.

A Manager for All Seasons

Far from being the oddball among the parables, Luke 16:1–8 is its own tour de force. With astonishing twists it consolidates key themes running through all of this Gospel's parables. The story of the shrewd manager is premised on social reversal (vv. 3–4), now and in the age to come (v. 9; cf. ##15, 22, 25). Calculation (cf. ##16, 17) and debt forgiveness (cf. ##3, 25) drive the plot (vv. 5b–6, 7). As accountable to their Lord (5:8, 12; 11:1; 12:41) as the household steward is to his master (v. 1b; cf. ##5, 9, 10, 23, 26), Jesus' disciples (v. 1a) are positioned beside a character confronted by crisis (v. 2b; cf. #1), the terror of being lost (vv. 2a, 4; cf. ##8, 14, 18, 19, 20), and a need to keep petitioning for help (vv. 5a, 7a; cf. ##6, 24). The parable ends with gracious judgment (v. 8a; cf. ##7, 11; 13), upending all expectations (v. 9; cf. ##2, 4, 5, 12, 19, 20, 25, 26, 27). Properly relocating wealth within God's economy restores theological equilibrium (vv. 10–13; cf. ##8, 22).

The canny manager thus epitomizes Luke's other parabolic figures, much as Mr. Tactless has served our consideration of Theophrastus's *Characters*. In their magnificent loathsomeness these characters also resemble each other. With fine precision both illustrate coherent, well-developed patterns constructed by their authors. There, however, their similarities end. Mr. Tactless is definitely not what the cunning manager clearly is—on top of the situation. The former has no sense for an action's proper timing: he is literally *akairos*, "out of season." The latter, by contrast, says to himself, "I know what to do" (Luke 16:4a). Indeed he knows, and does it. In hindsight we recognize his patron's ironic misjudgment: "You can't manage anymore" (16:2b). To the contrary: the steward proves himself to be a masterly tactician. Well intentioned, Mr. Tactless is incredibly clumsy. Devious to a fault, the business manager is nimble under pressure.

The similarities and differences between Theophrastus's character sketches and Luke's parables run far deeper than that, however. There's no evidence that Luke knew the *Characters*, but for our purpose that makes no difference. Over a century separates Henry Fielding (1707–1754) from James Joyce (1882–1941). Both, however, stand in a recognizable tradition (the novel), whose presentation of character these authors crystallized, then exploded, at different moments in literary history (*Tom Jones*, 1749; *Ulysses*, 1922). The same may be said of Theophrastus and the third evangelist. Both creatively adapt existing genres (taxonomy; *bios*) by incorporating picaresque vignettes suggesting, without laboring, an ethics of character. These episodes throw refracted light on the manners and mores of ancient society: farming, commerce, dinner parties, religious ceremonies, judicial proceedings. Masters of style, both authors create a sensibility of which readers are invited to make sense by drawing their own conclusions.

Luke's sensibility, however, is not that of Theophrastus, and that variance makes all the difference. Some consider "the magnanimous soul" (*megalopsychos*) of Aristotle's *Nicomachean Ethics* (1123a.34–1125a.16) the moral touchstone from which Theophrastus's *Characters* express thirty varieties of deviation.[37]

> The magnanimous person, then, would appear to be one who thinks himself worthy of great things and is in fact worthy of them. . . . Since the magnanimous person is worthy of the greatest things, he is the best person. . . . He is especially concerned with honors and dishonors, and, when receiving great honors from excellent people, he will be moderately pleased. . . . Yet he will be neither immoderately pleased by good fortune nor immoderately distressed by ill fortune, since he does not regard even honor as the greatest good. . . . Because concealment is proper to a frightened person, the magnanimous person is open in his hatreds and his friendships. . . . He will allow no one, save a friend, to determine his life. . . . He is not prone to marvel, . . . nor is he a gossip. . . . In particular he avoids laments or entreaties about meager matters. . . . Taking few things seriously, he is in no hurry; counting nothing great, he is not strident.[38]

This is hardly the profile of Luke's business manager, who runs scared from loss of social standing, cheats a patron whom he has allowed to define his life, and connives with other clients in weaving a golden parachute. The difference lies in the evaluation. For Luke, the unjust steward's conduct is commendable: Wall Street's flimflammers do what it takes to save their skins (16:8b). From them Jesus' disciples can learn that their real (not merely economic) salvation demands comparable wiles, faithfulness, and devotion to the Lord of lords (Luke 16:8–13). When "a person should never own anything he can't get into a coffin" (Fred Allen,[39] tuned into Luke 12:16–21), why should worshipers of God Almighty be outpaced by devotees of the Almighty Dollar (16:10–11)?

Here we arrive at the matter's crux. As a humorous catalog of human pettiness, Theophrastus's *Characters* benefits by ingestion in small dosage. When read from start to finish, its snarky tone grows tedious, its stuffiness admitting no likelihood that its cultured audience would ever exhibit the boorishness, flattery, cowardice, stupidity, shamelessness ad nauseam of the figures it lampoons. Not only can Theophrastus himself come across as Mr. Fault-Finder; his cameos also are so hyperbolic that modern readers can be lulled into a dangerous self-satisfaction, reassured that they never would act "that way." "Informed members of Theophrastus's audience might combine a sense of pleasure in philosophical recognition, denied to outsiders, with a feeling of moral superiority over the Characters themselves: 'At least I don't behave like that, but then I've read and understood my Aristotle.'"[40] To bolster that belief, Theophrastus renders characters that are caricatures: Oscar Hammerstein's

---

37. Jebb, *Characters of Theophrastus*, 30–37; Millett, *Theophrastus and His World*, 105.
38. Translated (alt.) by Irwin in *Aristotle: Nicomachean Ethics*, 97, 99, 100, 102, 103.
39. Allen, *"all the sincerity in hollywood,"* 107.
40. Millett, *Theophrastus and His World*, 31.

"collections of characteristics [with] verbal tics and quirks." A scholar of Athens's Peripatetic school could easily join hands with a Pharisee at Jerusalem's temple and say, "God, I thank thee that I am not like other men, extortioners, unjust, adulterers, or even like this tax collector" (Luke 18:11 RSV).

The third evangelist begins from a different vantage point, where human evil is tinctured with occasional goodness (Luke 11:11–13), confessed sinners are vindicated instead of the self-satisfied (18:9–14), and God's kingdom underwrites a radically new realm of responsibility (6:17–49). Accordingly, the rogues in the Third Gospel's gallery are more angular and less predictable than Theophrastus's *Characters*. In Luke a wealthy host demonstrates none of a sinful streetwalker's hospitality (7:36–50), religious schismatics demonstrate kindness lacking in the religious elite (10:29–37; cf. 9:51–53), society's scrawny denizens wear down its fat cats (18:2–8), and an entire family proves itself prodigal—in waste, indignation, and mercy (15:11–32). Luke's parables stand out, not only from Theophrastus's *Characters*, but also from parables in the other Gospels. Though all of the Synoptics are symphonies of God's kingdom, the evangelists do not sing in unison; they harmonize, often discordantly.[41] Most of the figures in Mark's parables are as mysteriously elusive as his view of the kingdom (3:23–27; 4:3–8, 21–32; cf. 4:10–12). Matthew's parabolic protagonists and antagonists enact a drama of judgment: the hammer is ever ready to fall, sometimes wrapped in graceful velvet (18:23–35; 20:1–16; 21:28–32; 22:1–14; 25:1–46).[42] Even when we can see the conclusion coming (e.g., Luke 11:5–8; 16:19–31)—and very often when we cannot (13:6–9; 19:12–27)—the characters in Luke's parables never lose their capacity to *surprise*. "If he'll not get up and give whatever is needed because a friend is asking, he'll do it because of the guy's shameless persistence" (11:8 AT). "Boss, let it go for another year while I fertilize it; if it's fruitful, okay—if not, just cut it down" (13:8–9 AT). "If they aren't listening to Moses and the prophets, somebody raised from the dead will never persuade them" (16:31 AT). "The boss congratulated his dishonest manager for being a smooth operator" (16:8a AT). Intensity and depth, that "certain shock to the imagination" that Amos Wilder discerned in Jesus' parables,[43] are conspicuously absent from Theophrastus's *Characters*. Luke's parables have them in spades.

---

41. Donahue, *The Gospel in Parable*, highlights this quality. For another, recent use of ancient types of characterization in a Gospel's interpretation, consult Wright, "Greco-Roman Character Typing."

42. Even so, God holds the hammer, and God's carpentry does not adhere to human architecture (see Zimmermann, "Die Ethico-Ästhetik der Gleichnisse Jesu").

43. Wilder, *Early Christian Rhetoric*, 71–88, esp. 72.

Chapter Five

"The Words That You Gave to Me I Have Given to Them"

Style is the regard that *what* pays to *how*.
Edmund L. Epstein[1]

Among many notable differences between John and the Synoptics is the distinctive discourse of the Johannine Jesus. Lacking the other Gospels' pithy sayings (e.g., Luke 9:58-60, 62), parables (Mark 4:3-8, 26-32), and pronouncement stories (Matt. 22:15-22), in John "Jesus speaks in a more elevated, hieratic, even pretentious, style" with "nearer echoes in 1 John than in the other Gospels."[2] Both of these observations by Moody Smith are germane to this chapter's twofold task. First, we shall consider some salient features of John's literary style from the standpoint of particular theories of discourse in antiquity. Second, we shall extend this study to the form and function of the rhetoric in the First Letter of John, which stands alongside the Fourth Gospel as a significant witness to first-century Johannine Christianity. Such analysis prompts reflections on the shape of Johannine theology and some challenges presented by its interpretation. In effect, this chapter invites the reader to ponder the report about Jesus, apologetically filed by the temple police in John 7:46: "Never has anyone spoken like this!" To what degree is this assessment true? In what sense is it inaccurate? And what difference do such questions make to an interpreter of the First Epistle of John and the Fourth Gospel?

---

1. Epstein, *Language and Style*, 1.
2. D. M. Smith, *John* (PC), 4. See also Aune, "Oral Tradition"; Gerhardsson, "Illuminating the Kingdom."

83

THE RHETORIC OF THE JOHANNINE JESUS

Investigation of Johannine style is hardly novel.[3] The heyday of its exploration dawned in the late nineteenth and early twentieth centuries, when the critical paradigm was governed by questions about sources: specifically, the origin of the Fourth Gospel in either Semitic or Synoptic tradition, and the unity or disparity of authorship of John and 1 John.[4] Such questions still provoke debate, and John's peculiar style remains important for understanding that Gospel. While the Fourth Gospel has been extensively probed with a variety of literary-critical instruments,[5] the theory and practice of classical rhetoric seem to me especially appropriate to the task of appraising Johannine discourse. Like George Kennedy, I am primarily interested in trying to hear John's words "as a Greek-speaking audience would have heard them," which involves an appreciation of rhetoric in antiquity.[6] Much as Charles Rosen conceives historical and analytical criticism of music, one may say of rhetorical criticism of biblical texts: "not as the attempt to find new and ingenious things to say about the music of the past, but to account for the way music has been experienced, understood, and misunderstood."[7] We are no more required to assume that the fourth evangelist received formal education in rhetoric than we must presuppose his enrollment in the Qumran community to account for similarities in thought between John and the Dead Sea Scrolls.[8] Our only a priori point is undeniable: the NT's authors and readers lived in a culture whose speech and literature were suffused by techniques of persuasive discourse.[9]

Classical Conceptions of Rhetorical Grandeur

At least[10] by the time of Aristotle (384–322 BCE; see *Rhet.* 3.1403b–12.1414a), style (φράσις [*phrasis*] or *elocutio*) is considered one of the principal components

---

3. Festugière's *Observations stylistiques* is the most comprehensive study; Louw's "On Johannine Style" is a brief orientation.

4. Thus, among others, Burney, *Aramaic Origin*; Dodd, "First Epistle of John"; Howard, *The Fourth Gospel*, 213–27, 276–96.

5. Culpepper (*Anatomy of the Fourth Gospel*) and Segovia (*Farewell of the Word*) provide a sampler of strategies. Ashton (*Studying John*, 141–65, 184–208) offers incisive critique of some narrative-critical trends in Johannine interpretation.

6. Kennedy, *New Testament Interpretation*, 10. Stube (*Greco-Roman Rhetorical Reading*) presents the most detailed analysis of John 13–17 as a specimen of classical rhetoric with a missionary impetus.

7. Rosen, in a letter to *The New York Review of Books* 39 (April 9, 1992): 54; cited in Ashton, *Studying John*, 161.

8. Thus the variously inflected conclusions represented in Charlesworth, *John and Qumran*. With those essays one may contrast Ashton's bold, if unproven, proposal that the fourth evangelist had been an Essene (*Understanding the Fourth Gospel*, 232–37).

9. For a reliable overview of vast terrain, see Kennedy, *A New History*. G. Anderson, *The Second Sophistic*, considers rhetoric's social dimensions during the era of the NT and afterward.

10. In what follows, most of the Greek and Latin texts are available in the LCL series. Unless otherwise indicated, this chapter's translations (with minor modifications) are those of D. C. Innes (Demetrius), D. A. Russell (Longinus and Hermogenes), and M. Winterbottom (Cicero and Quintilian) in Russell and Winterbottom, *Ancient Literary Criticism*.

of rhetorical artistry. Quintilian (ca. 40–95 CE) highlights the stylistic properties of discourse in his own definition of rhetoric: *bene dicendi scientiam*, "the knowledge of how to speak well" (*Inst.* 2.15.38). As theorized by such critics as the celebrated Dionysius of Halicarnassus (*De compositione verborum*, ca. 20 BCE), style was subdivided into two categories: diction, or word selection; and composition, the arrangement of words in various configurations and rhythmic patterns. These categories were further broken down into tropes (verbal "turnings") and figures of speech or of thought (see, e.g., Cornificius, *Rhet. ad Her.* 4.19–69 [ca. 85 BCE]).[11] Although John is rich in these devices, some of which we shall note, our study will be concentrated on the general style of Jesus' discourse in that Gospel.

To get our bearings, we begin with *On Style*, produced perhaps in the first century BCE. Conventionally attributed to Demetrius, this work offers the most systematically developed treatment of four primary styles: the plain, the grand, the elegant, and the forceful. Force is the hallmark of Demosthenes (*Eloc.* 5.240–304); in elegance lie charm and wit (3.128–89); trivial subjects invite plain style (4.190–239). The rhetorical style of the Johannine Jesus most closely resembles what Demetrius calls magnificence or grandeur (τὸ μεγαλοπρεπές [*to megaloprepes*]; 2.38–127). Though it can spring from ornate diction or word arrangement, "grandeur also derives from the subject-matter, for example an important and famous battle on land or sea or the theme of the heavens or of earth" (*Eloc.* 2.75; cf. 2.38–74, 77–113). For Demetrius, diction is plastic and should be suitable to one's subject, like wax that can be molded into various animal shapes (2.106; 5.296).

More common among classical theoreticians was a simpler system of three rhetorical styles, which we find in Cicero's *Orator* (ca. 50 BCE): the plain, the middle, and the grand. "The third type of orator is the full, copious, weighty, and ornate. Here, surely, lies the most power": the *gravis* to storm or to creep into the feelings, to sow new ideas and to uproot the old (*Or.* 28.97). Like Demetrius, Cicero regards style as more than mere ornament; it must be intelligently conformed to its subject matter. "Surely [the orator] will be capable of feeling and speaking everything more sublimely and more magnificently when he returns to humanity from the heavens" (*Or.* 34.119). In his compendious *Institutio oratoria* (12.10.58–80), Quintilian elaborates Cicero's treatment of three "characters" (χαρακτῆρες [*charactēres*]) of style. The plain (*subtile*; ἰσχόν [*ischon*]) is best suited for imparting information; the flowery (*floridum*; ἀνθηρόν [*anthēron*]), for charming or conciliation. Emotions are moved by a style that is grand or robust (*grande*, or ἁδρόν [*hadron*]):

> The grand style is the sort of river that whirls rocks along, "resents bridges," carves out its own banks; great and torrential, it will carry along

---

11. Lausberg's magisterial *Handbook of Literary Rhetoric* (271–41) compiles an exhaustive, potentially exhausting inventory of rhetorical figures; briefer and more sparkling is Vickers, *In Defence of Rhetoric*, 294–339. Caird (*Language and Imagery*, 131–97) tilts the discussion toward biblical literature.

even the judge who tries to stand up to it, forcing him to go where he is taken. Such an orator will call the dead to life . . . and cause the state to cry aloud or sometimes . . . to address the orator himself. He will lift the speech high by his amplifications and launch into exaggeration. . . . He will come near to bringing the gods themselves down to meet and talk to him. . . . He will inspire anger and pity; and as he speaks the judge will grow pale, weep, follow tamely as he is snatched in one direction after another by the whole gamut of emotion. (*Inst.* 12.10.61–62)

The Homeric prototype for this highest eloquence is Ulysses (cf. *Iliad* 3.223; *Odyssey* 8.173), with "strength of voice and force of oratory that in its flow and onrush of words resembled the snows. No mortal, then, can compete with such an orator: people will look to him as a god. This is the force and swiftness that Eupolis admires in Pericles, which Aristophanes compares to thunderbolts. This is the capacity for real oratory" (Quintilian, *Inst.* 12.10.64–65).

On Sublimity, an anonymous first-century CE treatise customarily ascribed to Longinus, takes up the character and creation of τὰ ὕψη (*ta hypsē*), "the heights": "a kind of eminence or excellence of discourse [that] is the source of distinction of the very greatest poets and prose-writers. For grandeur produces ecstasy rather than persuasion in the hearer; and the combination of wonder and astonishment always proves superior to the merely persuasive and pleasant" (*Subl.* 1.3–4). Sublimity elevates the orator's audience: it offers intellectual food that requires prolonged rumination and must be digested over time (7.2–3). Much of *On Sublimity* consists of practical aids in crafting noble diction, figures, and composition (10.1–43.6); for Longinus, however, grandeur's primary sources are the grasp of great thoughts and strong, inspired emotion (8.1). Greatness of thought inclines toward representation of the gods, though not all discourse about heavenly things excites awe: the *Iliad* blazes with the poet's power at high noon; the *Odyssey* reveals Homer at artistic sunset (9.5–15). Remarkably, for a pagan author, real sublimity is attained in Genesis 1 by "the lawgiver of the Jews—no mean genius, for he both understood and gave expression to the power of divinity as it deserved" (*Subl.* 9.9).[12]

Lastly, Hermogenes of Tarsus (b. ca. 160 CE) devotes a large portion of his rambling treatise, *On Types of Style*, to the analysis of grandeur (μέγεθος [*megethos*]), one of seven elemental qualities of style. According to Hermogenes, grandeur itself comprises various components: solemnity, "things said of the gods *qua* gods" (*Per. id.* 242–54); asperity, vehemence, and florescence, all of which are differently nuanced expressions of criticism (255–63, 269–77); brilliance, "inherent in those acts that are remarkable and in which one can gain luster" (264–69); and amplification (or abundance, περιβολή [*peribolē*]), the expansion of thought by extraneous ideas (277–96). "Fullness [μεστότης (*mestotēs*)] is nothing other than

---

12. Translation by Russell, *"Longinus": On the Sublime*, 93–94.

abundance taken to an extreme, or what one might call 'abundant abundance'" (*Per. id.* 291).[13] By the injection of these properties, discourse that captures great thought is rescued from the trite or the commonplace (222, 241).

Before turning to John, let us summarize our findings thus far. (1) Reconstruction of positions espoused by rhetorical theorists of the imperial period amply reinforces a modern reader's intuition of the Johannine Jesus' lofty style. Though variously defined, grandeur or sublimity receives extensive consideration from classical rhetoricians. (2) Grand style excites within an audience strong if varied responses: powerful feelings, intellectual stimulation, religious wonderment. (3) Like other types of style, grandeur is more than merely decorative. It inheres in thought that was itself considered to be sublime. (4) Chief among these majestic conceptions, and eminently appropriate for grand stylization, are matters pertaining to divinity. Oddly, the effects Quintilian attributes to the ideal orator who speaks in grand style—inciting the state to outcry, raising the dead, calling down the gods for conversation, tossing his judge on a tide of emotion—are enacted by Jesus on the stage of the Fourth Gospel (5:18; 7:14–44; 11:43–44; 12:28–29; 18:28–40).

A Sublime Leave-Taking: John 14–17

To consider, in this chapter's limited space, the whole of John's rhetorical style is out of the question. Representative of its elevated rhetoric are the farewell address and intercessory prayer in John 14–17. When viewed through a classical prism, this longest speech of Jesus in the Fourth Gospel most closely resembles the oratorical species known as epideictic, whose primary concern is the induction or bolstering of beliefs and values held among one's audience in the present (Aristotle, *Rhet.* 1.3.1358b; Cicero, *Inv.* 2.59.177–78). Characteristic of epideictic address (Cornificius, *Rhet ad Her.* 3.6.10–3.8.15), John 14–17 is not a tightly argued exercise in formal logic; instead, it is a quasi-ceremonial elaboration (13:1) of four main topics:[14]

A. Jesus' departure and return (14:1–3, 15–17, 18, 27–28; 16:4b–7)
B. Relationships that obtain between Jesus and believers (14:15–17, 18–21, 23–24; 15:1–10, 15; 17:6–26), between Jesus and the Father (14:24, 28; 15:9–10, 15, 23–24; 16:5, 15, 32b; 17:1–2, 4–5), between the Father and believers (14:23; 15:27; 17:3, 11, 17), between believers and the world (14:30; 15:18–25; 16:8–10, 28, 33; 17:9, 14–16), between believers and one another (15:12–14, 17; 17:21–23)

---

13. Translations in this paragraph are by Wooten, *Hermogenes' On Types of Style*, 33, 51.
14. Kennedy in *New Testament Interpretation*, 73–85, develops a comparable assessment. Alternatively, in *Farewell of the Word* (291–308), Segovia suggests that John 13:31–16:33 consists of four discrete units, each with a detectable arrangement of argument tailored to fluctuating rhetorical objectives.

C. Peace (14:27; 16:33), joy (14:28; 15:11; 16:20–22, 24; 17:13), loyalty (16:1–4a, 32; 17:6), and glorification (14:13; 15:8; 16:14; 17:1, 4–5, 10, 22–24)

D. Knowing (14:4–7; 16:25, 29–30; 17:3, 7–8, 23–25), seeing (14:8–10, 17–19; 15:24; 16:10, 16–22; 17:24), asking (14:13–14; 15:7, 16b; 16:23–24, 26), and loving obedience (14:21–24; 15:1–10, 16a; 17:6)

Jesus' discourse in John 14–17 generally conforms to a subspecies of epideictic later classified as leave-taking (συντακτικός [syntaktikos]), which expresses the love, gratitude, praise, and prayers of the one departing for those left behind.[15]

1. A striking aspect of Jesus' rhetorical style in the Fourth Gospel is its circular redundancy of clauses and topics, of which John 17:22–23 is but one concentrated instance that embraces most of the topics just tabulated: "The glory that you have given me I have given them, so that they may be one, as we are one, I in them and you in me, [so] that they may become completely one, so that the world may know that you have sent me and have loved them even as you have loved me." How can language so repetitious and monotonous be the vehicle of a discourse long regarded as a religious masterpiece?[16]

Ancient literary critics suggest an answer. The technical term for John's vertiginous style is *amplification* (αὔξησις [auxēsis], *amplificatio*), a primary ingredient of grandeur (Cicero, *De or.* 3.26.104–27.108; Cornificius, *Rhet. ad Her.* 4.8.11; Quintilian, *Inst.* 8.4.26–27). Although classical theorists differed among themselves on how amplification should be defined—whether "vertically," as a heightening of effect (Aristotle, *Rhet.* 1.9.1368a), or "horizontally," as an extension of thought (Longinus, *Subl.* 12.1)—its fundamental quality and consonance with sublimity is undisputed: "Amplification is an aggregation of all the details and topics that constitute a situation, strengthening the argument by dwelling on it; . . . you wheel up one impressive unit after another to give a series of increasing importance" (*Subl.* 11.1; 12.2). As John 17:22–23 illustrates, the objective of *amplificatio* is not to construct an impeccably logical proof but to wield influence upon one's audience (Cicero, *Part. or.* 8.27).

The essence of amplification lies in figures, conventional patterns of repetition in thoughts and in words (Demetrius, *Eloc.* 2.59–67). Structurally, the rhetoric of John 14–17 is balanced to a fare-thee-well (so to speak), with its thoughts and words presented in parallel formulations:

---

15. Russell and N. Wilson, *Menander Rhetor* (2.15.430–34). The "farewell address of a departing leader" (*Abschiedsrede*) is a well-attested literary genre in antiquity: see, e.g., Gen. 49:1–33 (Jacob); Deut. 31:1–34:8 (Moses); Plato's *Apology* (Socrates); *1 En.* 91–107 (Enoch); the second-century BCE corpus *The Testaments of the Twelve Patriarchs*; and Mark 13:5–37, which is explored in chap. 3 above. For useful surveys of the genre, see Stauffer, "Abschiedsreden"; Munck, "Discours d'adieu"; and Segovia, *Farewell of the Word*, 5–20. Kurz, *Farewell Addresses*, offers perceptive exegesis of NT specimens.

16. R. Brown, *John (xiii–xxi)*, 582, notes but does not resolve the tension. For Schnackenburg the "long-pondered theology of John" underlies its "colourless" diction (*St. John*, 1:111–12). Challenging such interpretations is Popp (*Grammatik des Geists*), for whom Johannine repetition, variation, and amplification constitute a "grammar of the Spirit." On the exegetical significance of Johannine repetition, see also van der Watt, "Johannine Style."

A   On that day you will ask nothing of me. (16:23a)

   B   Very truly, I tell you, if you ask anything of the Father in my name, he will give it to you. (16:23b)

A´ Until now you have not asked for anything in my name. (16:24a)

   B´ Ask and you will receive, so that your joy may be complete. (16:24b)

A   I will do

   B   whatever you ask in my name. . . . (14:13a)

   B´ If in my name you ask me for anything,

A´ I will do it. (14:14)

A   If I had not come and spoken to them,

   B   they would not have sin; (15:22a)

      C   but now they have no excuse for their sin. (15:22b)

         D   Whoever hates me hates my Father also. (15:23)

A´ If I had not done among them the works that no one else did,

   B´ they would not have sin. (15:24a)

      C´ But now they have seen

         D´ and hated both me and my Father. (15:24b)

Sometimes the parallelism is honed even to the same number of words and syllables in a clause (technically known as isocolon [Cornificius, *Rhet. ad Her.* 4.20.27–28]):

> ἵνα ὦσιν ἓν καθὼς ἡμεῖς ἕν (*hina ōsin hen kathōs hēmeis hen*).
> so that they be one, [just] as we are one. (17:22b)

Also prevalent in John 14–17 is antithesis, the juxtaposition of contrary ideas in parallel structure (Anaximenes, *Rhet. ad Alex.* 26.25–38; Cornificius, *Rhet. ad Her.* 4.15.21; Quintilian, *Inst.* 9.3.81–86):

> You did not choose me
>   but I chose you. (15:16a)

> You will weep and mourn,
>   but the world will rejoice;
> you will have pain,
>   but your pain will turn into joy. (16:20)

> I am asking on their behalf;
>   I am not asking on behalf of the world,
> but on behalf of those whom you gave me,
>   because they are yours. (17:9)

Repetition, the other main component of *amplificatio*, assumes many different configurations, most of which are present in John 14–17.

A. Refining (*expolitio*) "consists in dwelling on the same topic and yet seeming to say something ever new" (Cornificius, *Rhet. ad Her.* 4.42.54). This technique may simply repeat an idea ("A little while, and you will no longer see me, and again a little while, and you will see me" [John 16:16, 17, 19]; see also 14:1a, 27b; 14:10–11a), or it may descant on the thought ("This is my command-ment, that you love one another *as I have loved you*" [15:12; cf. 15:17; see also 14:2b–3; 14:15, 23]).

B. Antanaclasis (*reflexio*), the punning repetition of a word in two different senses (Cornificius, *Rhet. ad Her.* 4.14.21; Quintilian, *Inst.* 9.3.68), is nicely illustrated by Jesus' (and Thomas's) references to "the way" in John 14:4, 5, and 6.

C. Polysyndeton (the purposeful multiplication of conjunctions) and asyndeton (their deliberate omission) "make our utterances more vigorous and emphatic and produce an impression of vehemence" (Quintilian, *Inst.* 9.3.54; see also Demetrius, *Eloc.* 2.63–64; Cicero, *Part. or.* 15.53–54; Cornificius, *Rhet. ad Her.* 4.30.41; Longinus, *Subl.* 19.1–21.2). Both figures amplify Jesus' farewell address: "Those who love me will keep my word, and my Father will love them, and we will come to them and make our home with them" (John 14:23; see also 14:3–4, 6–7, 12b–13a; 16:22–23a; 17:10–11a); "I am the vine, you are the branches" (15:5a; see also 14:1b).

D. Distribution (*distributio*), enumerating the parts of a whole (Cornificius, *Rhet. ad Her.* 4.35.47), describes the analysis of and warrants for the Paraclete's convic-tion of the world in John 16:8–11.

E. Synonymy (*interpretatio*: Cornificius, *Rhet. ad Her.* 4.28.38), the interchange of different words with similar meaning, is evident in John's alternations of πορεύομαι (*poreuomai*, "go") and ὑπάγω (*hypagō*, "go away"; 14:2–5, 12, 28; 15:16; 16:5, 7, 10, 17, 28), of λόγος (*logos*, "word") and ἐντολή (*entolē*, "com-mandment"; 14:15, 21–24; 15:10, 20; 17:6), of ἀγαπάω (*agapaō*) and φιλέω (*phileō*), "love" (e.g., 14:15, 21, 23–24; 15:12, 17, 19; 16:27; 17:23, 26), and of λέγω (*legō*) and λαλέω (*laleō*), "say" or "speak" (e.g., 14:29–30; 15:11, 15, 20, 22; 16:4, 6–7, 12–13, 17–18, 25–26; 17:1).

F. Jesus' rhetoric in John also rings the changes on a hypnotic range of repetitive figures: "Peace I leave with you; my peace I give to you" (14:27 [an example of epanaphora: Cornificius, *Rhet. ad Her.* 4.13.19]); "As you have sent me into the world, so I have sent them into the world" (17:18 [antistrophe: *Rhet. ad Her.* 4.13.19]); "Believe in God, also in me believe" (14:1 AT [epanalepsis: Quintilian, *Inst.* 9.3.29]); ". . . that I go to prepare a place for you? And if I go to prepare a place for you . . ." (14:2b–3 [reduplication: Cornificius, *Rhet. ad Her.* 4.28.38; Quintilian, *Inst.* 9.3.28]); "If you know me [perfect tense], you will know [future] my father also; from now on you [at present] do know him" (14:7 [polyptoton: Longinus, *Subl.* 23.1–2]); "I am in the Father and the Father is in me" (14:11 [antimetabole: Cornificius, *Rhet. ad Her.* 4.28.39]).

2. Beyond amplification, a panoply of other rhetorical devices, regarded by classical theorists as evocative of sublime thought, are displayed by the farewell discourse in John.

A. Some words inherently carry heft, fullness, and sonority (Cicero, *Part. or.* 15.53). Strength, like beauty, is in the beholder's eye. Nevertheless, it is hard to read or to hear John 14–17 without being impressed by the gravity of such words as "orphaned" (14:18), "abide" (μένω [*menō*]; 14:10, 17, 25; 15:4–10, 16), "glory/glorify" (14:13; 15:8; 16:14; 17:1, 4–5, 10, 22, 24), the portentous "day" (14:20; 16:23, 26) and "hour" (16:2, 4, 21, 25, 32; 17:1), "joy" (15:11; 16:20–24; 17:13), "sorrow" (16:6, 20–22), and "[make] holy" (14:26; 17:11, 17, 19). Of equal force is "I am" (ἐγώ εἰμι [*egō eimi*]), which here, as elsewhere in John (6:20; 8:24, 28, 58; 13:19; 18:6), implies Jesus' oneness with God (14:6; 15:1, 5; cf. Exod. 3:14; Isa. 43:10–11, 25; 51:12).[17]

B. Sometimes in John 14–17 Jesus draws comparisons (14:28; 15:13); more often he augments the force of his comments (14:12, 18, 21; 15:15, 18; 16:15; 17:4–5). Through expressions of reassurance under particular conditions (see 14:3, 12–15, 21, 23; 15:7; 16:7b–8, 13, 33; 17:7–8), Jesus offers consolation dressed in enthymeme (a proposition with a supporting reason: Aristotle, *Rhet.* 1.2.1356b). By such formulations discourse on grand topics acquires luster (Quintilian, *Inst.* 8.4.3–14; 5.9–11).

C. Rhythmic flow, created by the length of a sentence's constituent phrases, is another stylistic trait considered by classical rhetoricians. Among them, a rough consensus holds that sentences with long clauses (e.g., John 14:3; 15:19), and the yoking of shorter clauses into longer periods (e.g., John 16:12–15; 17:20–23), sustain sublimity (Demetrius, *Eloc.* 1.5; 2.44; Longinus, *Subl.* 40.1–43.5; Hermogenes, *Per. id.* 251–54).

D. Notwithstanding the ancients' universal esteem for clear expression (Aristotle, *Rhet.* 3.1404b; Cicero, *Or.* 23.79; Quintilian, *Inst.* 8.1.1–2.24; Hermogenes, *Per. id.* 226–41), most of them acknowledged a place within grand style for purposeful obscurity (ἔμφασις [*emphasis*]). Hermogenes, for instance, held that discourse about divine subjects depends on "the use of suggestive hints to indicate darkly, in the manner of the mysteries and initiations, something within the sphere of solemn thoughts. By appearing to know, but to be unable to reveal, we give an impression of grandeur and solemnity" (*Per. id.* 246; cf. Cornificius, *Rhet. ad Her.* 4.53.67; Quintilian, *Inst.* 8.3.83–86). Such comments throw light on the more obscure "figures" (παροιμίαι [*paroimiai*], 16:25, 29) in John 14–17: its similes (16:21–22) and metaphors (14:6; 15:1, 5, 15; 17:12 [see Demetrius, *Eloc.* 2.77–90; Quintilian, *Inst.* 8.6.4–18; Longinus, *Subl.* 32.1–7]), its allegorical tendencies (14:2–3, 23, 30; 15:2–4, 6, 8, 16 [see Quintilian, *Inst.* 8.6.44–53]), and its jarring non sequiturs (14:5 and 16:5; 14:31b and 15:1; 15:15 and 20). Like others from among his interlocutors in John (3:4, 9; 4:11–12, 15; 7:32–36; 8:21–23), Jesus' disciples can scarcely fathom his meaning (14:5, 8, 22; 16:17–18); they are attuned to the lower level of discourse whose divine nuances are pitched at a frequency inaudible without a boost from God (cf. 16:29–31). The sublimity exhibited by Jesus in John "contains much food for reflection" (Longinus, *Subl.* 7.3), mysterious depths to be plumbed (Quintilian, *Inst.* 9.2.65), reverberations of a "dialogue between heaven and earth."[18] Whatever may have been the

---

17. Consult Schweizer, *Egō Eimi*; and Harner, *The "I Am."*
18. Wilder, *Early Christian Rhetoric*, 50. On religious obscurity in classical and early Christian discourse, consult Kustas, *Byzantine Rhetoric*, 63–100, 159–99; and Thielman, "Style of the Fourth Gospel."

tradition-history of John 14–17,[19] the disjunctures, scattered topics, and frequent repetition within its canonical form can be appreciably explained on rhetorical-critical grounds.[20]

Thus far, two claims of our study appear mutually confirmatory. (1) Orators and critics roughly contemporary with the fourth evangelist meticulously developed a notion of rhetorical grandeur, expressly associating that style with stirring consideration of divine topics. (2) Jesus' leave-taking in John 14–17, devoted to transcendent concerns for his disciples, evinces such rhetorical sublimity to an equally explicit and impressively precise degree. To argue that Johannine style corresponds with modes of Greco-Roman discourse should not lead us to underestimate Semitic influences on John, much less flatly reassert C. H. Dodd's thesis that the Fourth Gospel was directed to adherents of "the higher religion of Hellenism."[21] If John's milieu now appears to many scholars more Jewish, then its exhibition of Hellenistic rhetoric is no more anomalous than that to be found in the contemporaneous writings of Josephus and Philo.[22] Nor should we become preoccupied with style at the expense of substance, which would distort both John and the rhetoricians. "Magniloquence," Longinus reminds us, "is not always serviceable: to dress up trivial material in grand and solemn language is like putting a huge tragic mask on a little child" (*Subl.* 30.2; cf. Aristotle, *Rhet.* 3.1408a; Demetrius, *Eloc.* 2.114–27). Before proceeding further, we should ponder the stylistic suitability of Jesus' valedictory to the theology of John 14–17.

The grandeur of this address is, on the one hand, synchronized with the peculiar dialectic exhibited by the Fourth Gospel's presentation of Jesus. To that Christology every reader's port of entry is John 1:1–18, whose conceptual and stylistic similarities with the farewell discourse cannot be accidental.[23] The heart of that Christology beats with the belief that Jesus of Nazareth is "the only-begotten God in the bosom of the Father" (1:18 AT), the incarnate Word whose acceptance confers eternal life (1:1, 14, 16–18; 14:9; 20:28). If one asks why the speech of the Johannine Jesus differs so vastly from that of Jesus in the Synoptics, a *rhetorical* explanation—as distinguished from a tradition-critical estimate—would be that a

---

19. The twentieth century's most influential attempt at such reconstruction of the Johannine Farewell Discourse is that of Bultmann, *Evangelium des Johannes*. On ancient dramatic and rhetorical grounds, Parsenios's study (*Departure and Consolation*) properly challenges some tradition-critical conclusions.

20. O'Brien ("Written That You May Believe," 301) believes that John is by design "a gappy text," placing readers in the position of characters in the narrative that experience faith as an uneven process. Kellum (*Unity of the Farewell Discourse*), however, argues that the Johannine Farewell Discourse manifests internal coherence at a degree underestimated in contemporary scholarship.

21. Dodd, *Interpretation of the Fourth Gospel*, 3–130.

22. See Balch, "Two Apologetic Encomia"; Conley, *Philo's Rhetoric*. Likewise, Daube ("Rabbinic Methods") argues for the influence of Hellenistic rhetoric on norms of rabbinic exegesis ascribed to Hillel (ca. 50 BCE–10 CE).

23. See Lausberg, *Der Johannes-Prolog*.

metahistorical Christology[24] requires for its expression a metahistorical rhetoric. Befitting one who does not merely orate about heaven and earth (Demetrius, *Eloc.* 2.75; Cicero, *Or.* 34.119) but actually bestrides them, the grandeur of Jesus' discourse in the Fourth Gospel is the rhetorical analogue of John's theological paradox: "even when on earth [the Son of Man] is in heaven."[25] Jesus *speaks* as Jesus *is*: in flesh, while *sub species aeternitatis* (John 3:13, 34; 6:63, 68b–69; 14:10, 24; 17:6–8, 14). This paradox is vividly articulated in John 3:13–14: of the Son of Man's descent and ascent, Jesus speaks (to Nicodemus) at once retrospectively and apodictically. In the Johannine Jesus time and space intersect, precisely because the Son of Man is the ladder, the avenue of intercourse between earth and heaven (1:51).[26]

Even more: the sublimity of John 14–17 comports with, even transports, Jesus' concern for his followers' consolation, the fortifying of their resolve under fire, and the maintenance of their integrity in love after his departure. The discourse develops all these ideas (14:1–3, 18–21; 15:9–17; 15:18–16:4; 16:19–24, 31–33; 17:13–26), as any reader or listener can verify. Less obvious and more subliminal—for that reason more powerful (see Longinus, *Subl.* 17.1)—is the communication of these values by the style of Johannine rhetoric. Jesus identifies this world as the theater, not the origin, of his disciples' witness (John 15:19; 17:14–18; cf. 16:28; 17:11). Yet he *establishes* that distinction by means of sublime discourse that evokes a "wondrous strange," though not perspicacious, response (16:29–30; cf. *Subl.* 1.3–4).[27] Jesus does not simply say, "Let not your hearts be troubled" (14:1, 27c AT); *the pervasive balance of the rhetoric itself* conveys the steady tranquility to which the content refers. Not merely does Jesus command that his followers love one another (15:12–17); *the grand reciprocity of John's rhetorical style*, with its spiraling repetition and verbal inversions, activates for the Gospel's audience the mutuality that inheres between Jesus and God, among Jesus and his "friends" (15:15; cf. 14:20–21; 15:9; 17:10–11, 21–23, 26). "I have given them your word," prays Jesus to the Father (17:14)—and John's sublime stylization of the word, imparted by the

24. Thus D. M. Smith, *Johannine Christianity*, 184–88. Syreeni ("*Incarnatus est?* Christ and Community," 263): "If we feel uncomfortable with John, it may be because we moderns prefer to have myth and history separated, not mixed as in John."

25. See Barrett, "Christocentric or Theocentric?" and "Paradox and Dualism," in his *Essays on John*, 1–18 and 98–115 (esp. 110). Brodie's exegesis (*Gospel according to John*, 507)—"What is being portrayed, therefore, [in John 17] is a Jesus who is not exclusively either on earth or in heaven, but who in some sense is moving from one to the other, who is ascending and is coming closer to the Father"— harmonizes with his exposition of John as a map of stages in human life and belief (31–39).

26. My interpretation approximates that of Stibbe, "The Elusive Christ," in idem, *John as Literature*, 231–47. Following Käsemann, Stibbe stresses with fewer qualifications than I the Johannine Jesus' unmitigated divinity. Contrast the better nuanced exegesis of D. M. Smith, *Theology of John*, 101–3, which details the merging in John of three distinguishable perspectives on Jesus: the cosmic, post-resurrection, and historical.

27. For both its profundity and its sublime presentation, John was regarded as a "spiritual Gospel" (*Hist. eccl.* 6.14.7) by the church's early doctors, many of whom were well versed in rhetoric. Compare the analyses of Wiles, *The Spiritual Gospel*; Sider, *Ancient Rhetoric*; and Kennedy, *Greek Rhetoric*, 180–264.

Word (1:1) and radiant with glory (17:22), amplifies the divine reality (or truthfulness, ἀλήθεια [alētheia]) in which both Jesus and his disciples are consecrated for mission (17:17–19). That word is truly a gift: the rhetoric of chapters 14–17, as of Jesus' discourse throughout John, does not arrive at, much less aim for, logical proof of Jesus' claims. Rather, it elicits and reinforces faith in Jesus that is already active in the listener, activated by God (1:12–18; 3:6–8, 16–21). Thus the rhetorical style of the Johannine Jesus is no less revelatory than the character of the revelation that he discloses and indeed is.[28] All things considered—the speaker's character, the audience's sympathies, the circumstances of the speech—the convergence of style and substance in John 14–17 could hardly be more apposite or more in keeping with the express counsel of classical rhetoricians, for whom suitability to the matter declaimed was the touchstone of stylistic excellence (Cicero, *Inv.* 1.7.9; Cornificius, *Rhet. ad Her.* 1.2.3).

THE RHETORIC OF A JOHANNINE INTERPRETER

At least as early as the third century, Christian commentators have perceived the stylistic as well as conceptual similarities between John and 1 John (*Hist. eccl.* 7.25.17–26). No less than professional exegetes, many modern readers intuitively recognize that the epistle's author writes in "Johannese": the repetitive, antithetical, and interwoven style so distinctive in the NT yet so typical of Jesus' speech in the Fourth Gospel:[29] "Beloved, let us love one another, because love is from God; everyone who loves is born of God and knows God. Whoever does not love does not know God, for God is love" (1 John 4:7–8; cf. John 17:25–26). Less attention has been paid, however, to the argumentative functions and persuasive import of 1 John's grand style, as compared with its use in John's Gospel.

The Role of Sublimity in the First Epistle of John

1. Already I have noted the Fourth Gospel's use of a metahistorical rhetoric to support its metahistorical presentation of Jesus. A similar though not identical use of sublime style is found in 1 John. The epistle's avowed objectives are the proclamation and assurance, to an earthly community, of an indestructible life that partakes of God's new age (1:2; 5:13, 20). Of related significance are 1 John's

---

28. "Thus the fundamental question or issue of the Gospel can be stated as the nature of revelation. What God is revealed, and how is God revealed?" (D. M. Smith, *Theology of John*, 75). In a similar vein, see Ashton, *Understanding the Fourth Gospel*, 515–53; Cadman, *The Open Heaven*.

29. See esp. Schnackenburg, *Johannine Epistles*, 6–11; Watson, "Amplification Techniques"; C. Black, "First, Second, and Third Letters of John," 371–72.

repeated assertions that believers who act justly, reject sin, and love their fellows are "begotten of God" (3:9; 4:7; 5:1, 4, 18) or are "children of God" (3:1–2, 10; 5:2) or more simply are "of God" (3:10; 4:4, 6; 5:19). The theological dialectic implied by these claims—the encouragement of a community whose character is at once historical and suprahistorical—is crystallized in 1 John's literary form: while avowedly written (1:4; 2:1, 7–8, 12–14, 21, 26; 5:13), the epistle lacks both salutation and conclusion, addressing its readers as though from beyond time and space in a style that, by the conventions of its day, marries the heavens and the earth (Demetrius, *Eloc.* 2.75). When (as is frequent in 1 John) dialectic dissolves into dualism, positing a gulf (2:15; 4:4; 5:4–5, 21) or at least ambivalence (2:2; 4:9, 14) between believers and the world, the medium for this message is antithetical parallelism, itself a dimension of sublimity (2:16–17; 4:5–6a; see also 1:6–10; 2:4–5a, 9–11; 4:6–8; 5:10, 12; cf. Anaximenes, *Rhet. ad Alex.* 26.25–38).[30] Whereas in the Fourth Gospel Jesus personifies the sublime focalization of humanity and divinity, 1 John articulates this convergence with respect to the believing community (3:1–3; 4:4, 6–7, 11–12; 4:16–5:4), whose life flows from God (2:5, 29; 3:1, 24a; 4:13) and whose lodestar is Christ (2:1–6; 3:16, 23; 4:2, 9–10, 14; 5:1, 5, 10–11, 20).

2. Another resemblance between 1 John and John lies in their exercise of grand style to accent the mutuality of love and abidance in God that defines Christian community. Possibly owing to the blow inflicted by schism (1 John 2:19; 4:1, 5), the claim of corporate responsibility (2:12–14; 3:17–18) and demands of love for "the brother" (2:10; 3:10; 4:20–21) or for one another (3:11, 23; 4:7, 11–12) are more thoroughly worked out in 1 John than in the Fourth Gospel (John 13:34–35; 15:12, 17). The means for that development in the epistle are multiple: substantively, a correlation of unrighteous behavior, or "sinning," with failure to love (1 John 3:4–18; cf. John 3:18; 5:24; 8:24; 16:8–9, which associate sin with unbelief); stylistically, the sheer redundancy of "love," noun (ἀγάπη [*agapē*] 18 times) and verb (ἀγαπάω [*agapaō*] 28 times); and the balanced reciprocity of 1 John's formulations, which mirror the believers' experience of "abiding" in God as God abides in them (2:24, 27; 3:24; 4:13, 15–16; so also John 15:4–5, 7, 10).

---

30. For this reason great caution is warranted in reconstructing the position of opponents against whom 1 John inveighs and whose alleged theological profile looms large in R. Brown, *Epistles of John*, 47–68, 762–63. That the epistle's author contrasts his own position with that of unnamed schismatics (2:18–22; 4:1–6) and deceivers (2:26; 3:7a) cannot be doubted. Less certain is the presence of secessionist doctrine behind other instances of 1 John's refutatory style (1:6–7, 8–10; 2:4–5, 9–11; 3:7b–8, 9–10; 4:7–8, 19–21; 5:10–12; cf. Perkins, *Johannine Letters*, xvi–xxiii). If 1 John is as relentlessly contentious as some have suggested, one wonders why the blade of its rebuttals is so dull, given its author's presumed access to a tradition that wields polemic with such devastating effect (John 8:21–59).

3. While the Fourth Gospel's priority to, and presupposition by, the First Epistle has not been established beyond doubt,[31] certainly 1 John draws from a tradition whose most extensive deposit is John's Gospel. A modern reader of both documents might conclude that 1 John's style and substance mimics that of John. Lest that conclusion deteriorate into disparagement of the epistle, we should remember that imitation (μίμησις [mimēsis]) carried an honorable connotation among many rhetorical theorists of the imperial period.[32] Among them, Longinus associates mimēsis with the attainment of sublimity:

> Yet another road to sublimity . . . is the way of imitation and emulation of great writers of the past. . . . In all this process there is no plagiarism. It resembles rather the reproduction of good character in statues and works of art. . . . When we are working on something which needs loftiness of expression and greatness of thought, it is good to imagine how Homer would have said the same thing, or how Plato or Demosthenes or . . . Thucydides would have invested it with sublimity. These great figures, presented to us as objects of emulation and, as it were, shining before our gaze, will somehow elevate our minds to the greatness of which we form a mental image. (*Subl.* 13.2–14.2; see also Quintilian, *Inst.* 10.2.1–28)

I doubt that the author of 1 John aspired to this or to any aesthetic principle, consciously aiming at literary effect for its own sake. Given this ancient rhetorical context, one may reasonably surmise, however, that 1 John's grand style not merely ornaments but also meaningfully complements the epistle's persistent concern for the community's tradition (1:1–3; 2:7, 24; 3:11) and the coherence of its faith with Jesus' sacrificial love (1:5–10; 4:2–3, 7–12). By replicating the linguistic style of Jesus as remembered in the Johannine tradition, 1 John sublimely and subliminally bolsters its exhortation that the church conduct its life in *imitatio Christi* (2:1–6; 3:16). The rhetoric of the epistle abides, as it were, in the rhetoric of the Johannine Jesus, in a manner compatible with the author's

---

31. Some commentaries proceed from the minority position that 1 John was written before, or alongside, the Gospel in its final form: Grayston, *Johannine Epistles*; Talbert, *Reading John*; von Wahlde, *Gospels and Letters*. Equally provocative is M. Martin's recourse to ancient conventions of *synkrisis* (comparison) to argue, "What the elder has done in epistolary discourse, when he polemically associates the secessionists theologically and ethically with Cain (1 Jn 3.11–17), the [fourth] evangelist does in biographical narrative, associating them with Judas" (*Judas and the Rhetoric of Comparison*, 150).

32. The concept of imitation underwent a complicated evolution in antiquity. The term *mimēsis* most commonly refers to an artistic representation of reality, whose epistemological, psychological, and ethical implications are variously assessed by classical theoreticians (cf. Plato's more negative assessments [*Resp.* 10.1.595–7.607; *Soph.* 264a–268d] with the more positive though diverse presentations of Aristotle [*Poetica*, passim], Cicero [*Opt. gen.* 3.8; 5.14], and Augustine [*Doctr. chr.* 4.29.62]). By the late Hellenistic and imperial era, imitation was often understood as emulation of the good and the beautiful, since it was assumed that the orator was a Roman of unimpeachable character (e.g., Quintilian, *Inst.* 1.pr.9 et passim). For further consideration of *mimēsis* in the history of rhetoric, consult Kennedy, *Classical Rhetoric*, 116–19; Russell, *Criticism in Antiquity*, 99–113; and Swearingen, "*Ethos*."

express intention: "This is the message we have heard from him and proclaim to you" (1:5a; cf. John 17:8).[33]

4. Left inexplicit in 1 John is a final impression of its mimetic grandeur, which must remain moot. Elsewhere in the excerpt from *On Sublimity*, quoted above, Longinus muses on the relationship that obtains among *mimēsis*, inspiration, and artistic achievement:

> [Imitation] is an aim to which we must hold fast. Many are possessed by a spirit not their own. It is like what we are told of the Pythia at Delphi. . . . Similarly, the genius of the ancients acts as a kind of oracular cavern, and effluences flow from it into the minds of their imitators. Even those previously not much inclined to prophesy become inspired and share the enthusiasm that comes from the greatness of others. (*Subl.* 13.2; cf. 8.1, 4; Plato, *Ion* 533c–d; *Phaedr.* 245a; Cicero, *De or.* 2.46.194)

Longinus (though to my knowledge neither Plato, Cicero, nor other ancient theorists) believes that an author may be so steeped in a model's style and thought that the sublime spirit of that mentor is reproducible within one's audience. Without ever advancing an equivalent claim, 1 John does affirm (a) that the gift of God's abiding presence in the believing community is proved by the Spirit (3:24; 4:13), (b) that God's Spirit engenders and bears witness to authentic confession of Jesus (4:2–3; 5:6–8), and (c) that Jesus is the standard by which the church knows the "spirit of truth" and confirms that "We are from God" (4:1, 6 AT).

The backdrop supplied by Longinus brings into relief 1 John's stylistic similarity with the Fourth Gospel in a most provocative way. One may pose the matter as an open question: Could the epistle's *mimēsis* of the Johannine Jesus, in sublimity of thought and expression, have been intended or accepted as tacit corroboration of the validity of its author's testimony—a witness whose probative weight was relativized within a church that (a) assumed of every believer an inspired ability to interpret its tradition (2:20, 27) and (b) was riven by the contesting claims of the author and of would-be deceivers (2:26; 3:7; 4:1–6)? Perhaps. The writer of 1 John is no proto-Montanist, for the only Paraclete mentioned in this letter is Jesus (2:1–2).[34] Just as obviously, 1 John chimes with 2 John 7 in emphasizing the salvific importance of Jesus' humanity (most clearly in 1 John 4:2–3; probably also in 1:1–4; 4:15; 5:1, 5–8). Nevertheless, the author's insistence that he and his audience are of God and not of the world (3:1; 4:5–6) is consistent with his adoption of a rhetorical sublimity that constantly reminds the reader of the "transworldly" Jesus of Johannine tradition: "God the only Son," who promised those who abide

33. This suggestion elaborates more theologically D. M. Smith's opinion that, in structuring its comments, 1 John has used John's Gospel as a model (*First, Second, and Third John*, 23–24). See also Berge's meticulous analysis in "The Word and Its Witness."
34. For primary sources on Montanism, see Stevenson, *A New Eusebius*, 103–8.

in him the sending of "the Advocate, the Holy Spirit," who would "remind you of all that I have said to you" (John 14:25–26; cf. 1:13, 18; 8:23; 15:19).[35] Throughout 1 John the author cites no external or authoritative warrants to buttress his claims; a rhetorical appeal, expressed in the glorious diction of Jesus, may have been the strongest suit available to him.[36] The proof for this hypothesis is, however, quite beyond reach since the epistle says surprisingly little about the Spirit and absolutely nothing of the Spirit's relationship to kerygmatic style.[37] Less problematic is a more general conclusion: theologically and rhetorically—doubtless for both the letter's author and its implied antagonists—the Fourth Gospel describes and circumscribes the field on which the First Epistle of John plays.[38]

EPILOGUE AS PROLOGUE

At the level of literary analysis, this chapter challenges the long-standing judgment of Blass and Debrunner: "The absence of rhetorical art in the Johannine discourses is quite clear."[39] Yet I shall have failed my subject and my readers if the symbiosis of style and substance in John goes neglected. For the evangelist, as for the culture in which he wrote, style was not simple adornment, detachable from the ideas it conveyed.[40] Peculiarly sublime, Johannine rhetoric is at least one mode of thought, indigenous to the Gospel, by which Johannine theology can be appropriately investigated.[41] Furthermore, the loftiness of the Fourth Gospel and 1 John corresponds with those aspects of Johannine thought that were evidently intended to consolidate the life of believing communities in the Johannine tradition. Implicit in our results, therefore, is a *constitutive* purpose for John's rhetoric in the ethos of churches within the Johannine circle, a role no less notable than the widely recognized critical and discriminative functions served by John's dualistic language and theology.[42] Put differently: the evangelist's discourse not only distinguishes the Johannine community from a hostile world beyond its borders

35. With von Wahlde I concur that "the author [of 1 John] and the opponents differ in that the author constantly anchors his conception of the Spirit in the ministry of Jesus" (*Johannine Commandments*, 127), while demurring on the amplitude and precision with which we can reconstruct the opponents' position (ibid., 105–98).

36. For a comparable though less speculative estimate, see Lieu, *Johannine Epistles*, 23–27.

37. The equation of Christ's voice, the Spirit's speech, and Christian prophecy is clearer in Revelation (2:1, 7, 11, 17, 29, et passim). See Bauckham, *Theology of Revelation*, 109–25. R. Brown, *Community of the Beloved Disciple*, 138–44, offers an intriguing appraisal of 1 John's pneumatological ambivalence.

38. Likewise, D. M. Smith, *First, Second, and Third John*, 32, 130–32.

39. Blass and Debrunner, *Greek Grammar*, 260.

40. Similarly, Evans, *Theology of Rhetoric*, 3–4.

41. Kysar ("The Fourth Gospel," 2464): "The document itself must yield up to us the modes of thought by which it can be best investigated."

42. Thus Ashton, *Understanding the Fourth Gospel*, 205–37.

(e.g., 3:16–21) but also—and just as significantly—solidifies that community's theological self-understanding.

A final implication of this study bears on modern appropriation of John for preaching, which provides for many of this book's readers a regular experience of modern oratory. Johannine literature is nothing if not expressly kerygmatic (John 16:13–15; 1 John 1:5). What difference does an appreciation of Johannine grandeur make for those whose interpretation of John migrates from the classroom into the pulpit?

An adequate answer to that question would entail yet another chapter. Here it might begin: the sublimity of John's witness both *confronts* and *elevates* the church (whether ancient or modern) with the core of its own kerygma, conjugated in a mode that is unabashedly grand and inescapably compelling. If ever a NT document resisted the homiletical tendencies of liberalized theology—the maceration of biblical myth into moralistic ideals—it is the Fourth Gospel. That is true not because of its dearth of that paraenesis so common in the Synoptics. Rather, Johannine theology and rhetoric are driven by a different engine: the living voice of the incarnate Word, whose glory the church has witnessed and in whose love it abides. Likewise, John gains little from sermon illustrations in the conventionally mundane sense. A modern congregation, however, would benefit incalculably from the homiletical experience of *being* illustrated—irradiated by "the true light, which enlightens everyone" (1:9) and to which John testifies.

An unrelieved diet of Johannine preaching would give any congregation theological dyspepsia. Nevertheless, proclamation of John and 1 John invites, if not mandates, a rhetoric that engages one's listeners with the supernal God who loved the world so much that he gave his only Son for its sins. When the Johannine witness is thus released, "a Bible-shaped word" is communicated "in a Bible-like way."[43] At stake in such preaching is nothing less than the penetration of this world's brutality and banality by a confession most sublime: "And the Word became flesh and lived among us, and we have seen his glory" (John 1:14). Nothing could be more needful for today's church than to be grasped afresh by the grandeur of its own gospel.

---

43. Here my debt to Keck is manifest (*Bible in the Pulpit*, 106; idem, "Toward a Theology"). For further explorations in a pastoral vein, see C. Black, "Christian Ministry."

The Acts of the Apostles

Chapter Six

The Case of the Feckless Ficelle

[32]And Peter was come down out of the ship, and walked on the water, to go to Jesus. But when he saw the wind boisterous, he was afraid; and beginning to sink, he cried, saying, Lord save me. [33]And immediately Jesus stretched forth his hand and caught him, and said unto him, O thou of little faith, if thou hadst merely turned upon thy back and not panicked, thou wouldst have floated, it is simple hydrodynamics, one day all Jews will swim, personally I blame Moses, parting the Red Sea was just molly-coddling people.

Alan Coren, "The Gospel according to St Durham"[1]

Among the colorful dramatis personae on the teeming stage of Acts, John Mark seems a pallid bit player, whose performance gets short shrift among commentators. This chapter is an exercise of exegetical redress. We shall test the hypothesis that some of Luke's religious concerns acquire greater depth and resonance if we attend more closely to the subtle shadings of John Mark's depiction in the second volume of the evangelist's narrative.[2] Latent in this proposal is an assumption congenial with the redaction-critical perspective, as well as with some currents in narrative criticism: namely, that the depiction of John Mark, like that of other figures in Acts, assists Luke in formulating or reinforcing particular theological convictions whose historical interest is not coterminous with strictly historical

---

1. In Coren's *Chocolate and Cuckoo Clocks*, 256.
2. That the Third Gospel and the Acts of the Apostles constitute a narrative unity when read in sequence remains the consensus view among scholars, following Bacon (*Introduction to the New Testament*, esp. 211–21, 280) and Cadbury's influential lead (*Making of Luke–Acts*). For an alternative view, see Parsons and Pervo, *Rethinking the Unity*.

preoccupations.[3] I shall argue that Luke's characterization of John Mark is an especially interesting tile in the Lukan mosaic of Judaism, to which many scholars have directed our attention in recent decades.[4]

THE PORTRAYAL OF JOHN MARK IN ACTS

Acts 12:12

We begin at Acts 12:12,[5] where, in passing, Luke mentions "John, whose other name was Mark," as the son of a certain Mary, in whose house in Jerusalem Peter took refuge after his miraculous release from prison (Acts 12:6–12). Beyond the familial connection, in 12:12 we learn nothing directly about John Mark.[6] Indirectly, we learn that his mother is a Jerusalemite woman of substance: Mary is served by a maid (παιδίσκη [paidiskē], 12:13) and owns a house, access to which is gained by the porch (ὁ πυλών [ho pylōn], 12:13) and large enough to accommodate a congregation of believers who have gathered to pray, presumably for Peter's welfare (12:5, 12). Curiously, in Luke's narrative John Mark is introduced in order to identify his mother, Mary—not the other way around, as we might have expected.[7] Equally intriguing and contrary to expectation is the fact that neither here nor anywhere in Acts is John Mark explicitly associated with Peter. When, after his comical detention at the door (12:13–16), Peter finally gains entry to Mary's house, he stays only long enough to describe his miraculous escape from jail and to ask that the report be relayed to James and the other believers in Jerusalem (12:17). Luke never suggests what has sometimes been assumed: "Presumably Mark was at home in those days, and so found himself in association with early representatives of the new religious movement,"[8] Peter in particular. In fact, the narrator[9] of Acts whisks Peter off the

---

3. See above, chap. 2. With Haenchen's pioneering redaction-critical treatment (*Acts of the Apostles*, 90–116), one might compare the approaches of Tannehill, *Acts of the Apostles*, 1–8; and Darr, *On Character Building*; idem, "Narrator as Character."

4. Exegetes disagree whether the picture of Jews and of Judaism in Luke–Acts is essentially positive (Jervell, *Luke and the People of God*), negative (Sanders, *The Jews in Luke–Acts*), or ambivalent (Tyson, *Images of Judaism*). A helpful guide to the contours of this debate is Tyson, *Luke–Acts and the Jewish People*.

5. Peter's colleague in Acts 3–4 is most likely John the son of Zebedee, not John Mark. See C. Black, *Mark: Images*, 26–27.

6. In particular, no connection is wrought between Mary's house in Acts 12 and the site of the Last Supper in Luke 22 (contra Bruce, *Acts of the Apostles* [1951], 247 and elsewhere).

7. Spencer wonders if "[Mary's] main claim to fame in Acts is as the mother of John Mark": he reappears in the narrative of Acts, while Mary fades away entirely (*Acts*, 127).

8. Case, "John Mark," esp. 372.

9. Modern critics distinguish the "real author" from the author whose ideals are "implied" in a literary work. The "implied author" can be further distinguished from the "narrator," whose voice we hear "telling" the story. Contrary to Dawsey (*Lukan Voice*), I see no difference in Luke–Acts between the values of the "implied author" and its "narrator" (so, too, Darr, "Narrator as Character"); thus I refer interchangeably to "the [implied] author," "the narrator," and "Luke," without specific assumptions about its flesh-and-blood writer.

premises almost as quickly as he arrives: "Then [Peter] left and went to another place" (12:17). In Acts 12:12–17 the name of John Mark is tangentially used to identify Mary, Peter's patron, not to establish any connection between her son and that apostle. On a first reading of Acts, oblivious to other early Christian traditions or literature, a reader would have no reason to expect that John Mark would ever reappear.

Acts 12:25

At Acts 12:25 we are surprised to learn that John Mark has been inducted into an apostolic entourage: "Then Barnabas and Saul returned [to Antioch: see 11:27–30; 13:1], after completing their mission at Jerusalem, taking along with them John, whose other name was Mark" (AT).[10] The reader's expectations are twisted anew: perhaps this John Mark will emerge as a major protagonist in the drama of Acts. After all, he is traveling with Barnabas and Saul, who by now have emerged as chief envoys from significant Christian centers at Jerusalem and Antioch (9:26–30; 11:19–30). Moreover, both of those principals were themselves introduced as minor figures who first appeared, then abruptly disappeared (see 4:36–37; 8:1a) in a manner that fortifies the narrative unification of Acts and seems characteristic of its implied author.[11] On the other hand, one cannot be sure of John Mark's potential influence since he does not appear to be a fully equal partner of those he accompanies: rather than uniformly collocating the three missionaries, Luke completes his update on Barnabas and Saul with a subordinate clause to the effect that John Mark "was taken along [συμπαραλαβόντες (symparalabontes)] with [them]." In this team John Mark is the junior partner, whose character awaits further disclosure.

From among all the Christian faithful in Jerusalem, why was John Mark selected to accompany Barnabas and Saul? Luke never explains. Henry Barclay Swete gave voice to perhaps the most common suggestion: "It was for Barnabas to seek fresh associates in his work, and John was a near relative of Barnabas"[12]—a theory that rests on identifying John Mark in Acts 12–13 with "Mark" in Colossians 4:10. Yet, although Luke identifies Mary as John Mark's mother—as though Mark would have been more widely known than Mary—he never identifies Barnabas and John Mark as cousins. If Luke's intention, in Acts 12:12, was to relate Mary with someone better known to his readers, and if Luke had known of a cousinship of Mark and Barnabas, why would he not have identified Mary as *Barnabas's* kinswoman? Also lacking in narrative foundation is the notion that

---

10. For consideration of this verse's text-critical problems, see Metzger, *Textual Commentary*, 350–52.
11. Tannehill, *Acts of the Apostles*, 78, 99. Note also Philip's introduction and delayed development in Acts 6:5; 8:26–40.
12. Swete, *St Mark*, xvi.

Barnabas and Paul lodged with Mark's mother during their stay in Jerusalem,[13] or that "Mark was taken on Paul's first missionary journey because his eye-witness reminiscences supplied an element in the Gospel-preaching that neither Paul nor Barnabas could supply."[14]

The question stands: Why is John Mark suddenly aligned with Barnabas and Saul in Acts 12:25? Without clear narrative clues, any answer is unavoidably conjectural. One possibility, tradition-critical in orientation, is that Luke learned of this association from one of his sources and simply reported it, without knowing its rationale or without interest in explaining it. Another alternative pays closer attention to the narrative logic of Acts, inquiring into the allusive reverberations between John Mark and other characters and events with which, in 12:25, he is related. Richard Pervo observes that John Mark is a thread stitching together Peter, Barnabas, and Paul.[15] Through his mother, Mark is tacitly associated with both wealth and piety, typified by the Christians gathered at Mary's house in fervent prayer (12:12). In similar terms Luke has previously introduced and sketched Joseph Barnabas: the "son of encouragement"[16] who laid the proceeds from the sale of some real estate at the apostles' feet (4:36–37) and, as a leading delegate of both the Jerusalem and Antiochene churches (11:22, 30),[17] manifested goodness, fidelity, and fullness of the Holy Spirit (11:24a). Moreover, Luke identifies John Mark as a Jerusalemite (12:12; 13:13): his presence at the start of Paul's first major missionary journey into Gentile territory (13:4–14:28) silently represents the reach of Jerusalem Christianity, whose general influence is maintained in Acts yet harmonized with other potent spheres of Christianity beyond Judean boundaries. (Earlier, at 4:35–36, Barnabas, a Cypriot, has subjugated himself to the Jerusalem apostles, who bestow on him a new name; later, at 9:26–30 and 11:25–26, Barnabas accredits and recruits Saul, a Cilician [see 21:39; 22:3; 23:34].) Furthermore, in the light of events to come, it may not be sheer happenstance that the beginning of John Mark's travels with Barnabas and Saul coincides with different narratives of divine intervention and rectification amid human thickheadedness (Rhoda and the Jerusalemite congregation: 12:14–16) or outright hubris (Herod Agrippa: 12:18–23). John Mark seems to be another link in an interlocking chain forged in Acts 11:27–12:25, whereby Luke tightens a transition as Peter exits and Paul assumes his role.[18] While these allusions are not far-fetched, one must concede their attenuation. Luke simply asserts that, on the

---

13. Bruce, *Commentary on Acts* (1954), 258.

14. Paul, *St. John's Gospel*, 16 n. 1. For alerting me to this suggestion and for making available this quotation, I thank Beverly Gaventa.

15. Pervo, *Acts*, 317.

16. *Pace* Luke (Acts 4:36), "Barnabas" means "son of Nebo," not "son of encouragement." Nevertheless, in Acts that characterization holds, even if not its etymological association.

17. Barnabas appears to be the senior member of those delegations: notice Paul's nominal subordination to Barnabas in Acts 9:27; 11:25–26, 30; 12:25; 13:1–2, 7; 14:14. On Barnabas's pivotal role, see Johnson, *Literary Function*, 53, 203–4.

18. Longenecker, "Lukan Aversion."

threshold of a major missionary expedition, Barnabas and Saul take John Mark with them. It is left for the reader to ponder why.

Acts 13:5b

We next meet John Mark in Acts during the mission of Barnabas and Saul (now "Paul," 13:9) in Cyprus, Barnabas's homeland (4:36). "When they arrived at Salamis, they proclaimed the word of God in the synagogues of the Jews; and they had John as a ὑπηρέτης [hypēretēs]" (13:5 AT). This verse presents two problems. The minor question involves Luke's ambiguous reference to "John." As there has been no mention of anyone else by this name in the verses intervening 13:5 and 12:25, which contained the narrator's last mention of "John, whose other name was Mark," surely he is the referent here.

More difficult is Luke's description of John (Mark) as a ὑπηρέτης and how that appositive should best be translated. In classical Greek the root meaning of ὑπηρέτης is that of a galley slave, one who oars in the lower tier of a trireme (a ship with three rows or banks of oars on each side).[19] In Herodotus (Wars 3.63.1; 5.111.4) and Plato (Polit. 289c) the term refers generally to an underling, a servant or attendant. The word comes to denote subordinate relations in domestic, political, or religious spheres; this variegated usage persists in Hellenistic Jewish writings (thus LXX: Prov. 14:35; Wis. 6:4; Isa. 32:5; Ep. Arist. 111; Philo; Josephus). More technically, in the works of Attic historians Thucydides (Hist. 3.17) and Pseudo-Xenophon (Cynegeticus 2.4.4; 6.2.13), ὑπηρέτης is used in military contexts to designate an armed foot soldier's attendant (who carried the warrior's baggage, rations, and shield) or any adjutant, staff officer, or aide-de-camp.

Occurring six times in Luke–Acts, ὑπηρέτης is employed in no single, consistent way. Rather, Luke's usage captures different nuances within the term's semantic field.

1. Subordinate service, albeit within a religious framework, is suggested in the preface to Luke's Gospel (1:2: "those who from the beginning were eyewitnesses and servants of the word") and in Paul's account, before Agrippa, of his appointment by the Lord as Jesus' "servant and witness" (Acts 26:16 AT). The same connotation suits Luke's use of the verbal cognate, ὑπηρετέω (hypēreteō in Acts 13:36; 20:34; 24:23).

2. The particular nuance of a cultic functionary is present in Luke 4:20, with reference to a synagogue president's liturgical assistant.

3. The specifically military use of the term, denoting "officers" who answered to the high priest and Sanhedrin, appears in Acts 5:22 and 26.

---

19. Moulton and Howard, Accidence and Word Formation, 328. This connotation of galley slave may linger in Pauline metaphor (1 Cor. 4:1).

Which of these connotations best describes John Mark in Acts 13:5? Modern scholars have suggested variations of possibilities 1 and 2.

1. Conzelmann and Haenchen opine that only the most general sense of "assistance" fits Acts 13:5.[20] Swete defines Mark's help precisely: "arrangements for travel, the provision of food and lodging, conveying messages, negotiating interviews, and the like."[21]

2. A technical interpretation of Mark as ὑπηρέτης has received wide currency. B. T. Holmes argues that the term implies secretarial responsibility: "Mark handled a written memorandum about Jesus in the course of the first Gentile mission in Cyprus."[22] Attempting even finer etymological precision, R. O. P. Taylor proposes that ὑπηρέτης in Acts 13:5 was functionally equivalent to the priestly assistant in the cultus of Palestinian and later rabbinic Judaism ("ministers of the Temple": *m. Tamid* 5.3; *t. Sukkah* 4.11–12).[23] Thus, for Taylor, John Mark was "the schoolmaster—the person whose duty was to impart elementary education [, which] consisted in teaching the actual wording of the sacred records, the exact and precise statements of the facts and dicta on which their religion was based."[24] It is this kind of image that some scholars presuppose of Acts 13:5 when they speak of Mark as the teacher or catechist authorized by Paul and Barnabas.[25]

The context of Acts 13:5b should guide us to the most reasonable exegesis. First to be noted is the commissioning scene in Acts 13:1–3. Gathered at Antioch, worshiping and fasting, are various "prophets and teachers": Barnabas, Symeon Niger, Lucius of Cyrene, Manaean, and Saul. John Mark is not mentioned as either προφήτης (*prophētēs*, prophet) or διδάσκαλος (*didaskalos*, teacher), even though we have just been informed that he is accompanying Barnabas and Saul (12:25). John Mark is not singled out, as are they, as one set apart for the particular work to which they have been called by the Holy Spirit (13:2). Nor is it even clear, in 13:3, that Mark is among those who, after fasting and prayer, either lay hands upon the Spirit's delegates or have others' hands laid upon him. If the reader of Acts is supposed to regard John Mark as an emissary with prerogatives for teaching or catechesis, then Luke has left unexploited a fitting juncture in the narrative at which that point could have been clearly communicated.

Dispatched by the Holy Spirit, the delegates proceed to Seleucia, the ancient port city of Antioch; from there they sail to Salamis, where they proclaim the word of God in Jewish synagogues (13:4–5a). In a dependent clause (13:5b) Luke

20. Conzelmann, *Acts of the Apostles*, 99; Haenchen, *Acts of the Apostles*, 397.

21. Swete, *St Mark*, xvi.

22. Holmes, "Luke's Description," esp. 64.

23. On this figure, see L. Levine, *Ancient Jewish Synagogues*, 387–428.

24. R. O. P. Taylor, "Ministry of Mark," 136; Chase, "Mark (John)." More recently see Beavis, *Mark's Audience*, 63–67.

25. Thus Blair, "Mark, John"; Barclay, "Comparison of Paul's Missionary Preaching," esp. 169–70.

adds that they have (εἶχον [eichon]) John Mark as a ὑπηρέτης. While proclamation could be included in this "service," the wording and syntax of Acts 13:4–5 mitigate against elevating Mark's role. First, since John is distinguished from those whom he assists, the subject pronoun implied in 13:5b must refer to Barnabas and Saul, which in turn suggests that it is those apostles whom Luke had most prominently in mind in the statement of itinerary at 13:4–5a. Second, almost as an afterthought, Luke informs the reader that Barnabas and Saul are still accompanied by John Mark (13:5b)—a datum that, on an initial reading of Acts, we would have no reason to presume. As in 12:25, Luke's phraseology suggests that John remains subordinate: neither here nor soon afterward (in 13:7) does John stand on equal footing with his patrons, who are very much the narrative's focal missionaries. This remains so throughout the story, immediately following, of confrontation between the apostles and Elymas the magician (13:6–12): again John Mark drops from sight, and Saul steps into the spotlight. Third, and perhaps most telling, Acts 13:5b says that John is present as an *assistant*, neither to the Holy Spirit (cf. 13:2, 4) nor to the Lord (cf. 26:16) nor to the word (cf. Luke 1:2), but rather to Barnabas and Saul. Though not denigrated, John Mark's status is qualified. While indeed a *servus*, he is a *servus servorum Dei* ("servant of the servants of God").

The simplest reading of the narrative favors a neutral interpretation of ὑπηρέτης: John Mark is simply at Barnabas and Saul's disposal. Speculation about the kinds of service he renders probably veers away from Luke's intentions. Of all Lukan references to a ὑπηρέτης, John Mark's attribution as such in Acts 13:5b is the most colorless.

Acts 13:13b

At Acts 13:13 we encounter Luke's most tantalizing reference to John (Mark). Having worked their way from Salamis, on the east coast of Cyprus, through the whole of the island to the western port at Paphos, Paul and his companions (οἱ περὶ Παῦλον [hoi peri Paulon]) set sail northwest for Perga, the principal seaport of Pamphylia, in southern Asia Minor. "John, however, withdrew from them and returned to Jerusalem" (13:13b AT).

In both classical and Hellenistic Greek, the verb ἀποχωρεῖν (apochōrein) means "to go away from" or "to depart," though it can connote dereliction of duty or withdrawal after defeat (as an army in battle: Thucydides, *Hist.* 2.89.8). Scott Spencer notes the verb's nuance of "desertion" or "abandonment of a cause" in 3 Maccabees 2:33.[26] Beyond Acts 13:13 this verb appears only twice in the NT.[27] At Luke 9:39, with reference to a demonic spirit, it may—though need not—suggest capitulation

26. Spencer, *Acts*, 143.
27. I do not include the textual variant in Luke 20:20.

(and probably does not in Matt. 7:23). The other verb in Acts 13:13b, ὑποστρέφειν (*hypostrephein*), may simply be translated "to return," its most common connotation in Luke–Acts (e.g., Luke 1:56; Acts 1:12). Alternatively, it can convey the negative nuance of retreat under fire (Homer, *Iliad* 5.581; 12.71; Herodotus, *Wars* 7.211.3; 9.14; Thucydides, *Hist.* 3.24; cf. Luke 11:24 and 23:48). The precise timing of John Mark's separation from Paul and company is vague. Later, at Acts 15:38, we learn that John has accompanied Paul and Barnabas as far as Pamphylia; without that clarification the wording of 13:13b might have suggested that John withdrew from the others at Paphos, the point of their embarkation in Cyprus. A bit clearer, at 13:13b, is the probably adversative import of the connective particle, δέ (*de*): at the outset of their Pisidian mission, the apostles set out in one direction; John heads in the other. If at the beginning of 13:14 δέ is again taken as an adversative, Luke thus positions all of the characters: at Perga (not Paphos) John Mark withdraws, but Paul and Barnabas continue to Antioch of Pisidia.

Why does John Mark turn away and return to Jerusalem? Guesses proliferate: Mark's missionary commitment, limited from the start, up to but not beyond Syrian Antioch or Cyprus;[28] an unwillingness to participate in Paul's mission to the Gentiles[29] or resentment at Cousin Barnabas's falling into second place behind Paul;[30] his fear of crossing northern Pamphylia's formidable Taurus Mountains;[31] his sense of responsibility to his mother back in Jerusalem;[32] even his preference for Mary's home cooking![33] Many have judged it futile to speculate on reasons left undisclosed by the narrator.[34]

One sympathizes with those who refuse to traffic in uncontrollable conjecture about John Mark's intentions at Acts 13:13. Neither, however, should we succumb to the temptation of dropping the matter without pondering Luke's narrative presentation. John Mark's unexplained return to Jerusalem is like the Philippian magistrates' unexplained about-face regarding the arrest of Paul and Silas (16:35), the ambiguity surrounding the condition of injured Eutychus and the degree of symbolism (if any) that pervades his resuscitation (20:7–12), and the contradiction between Governor Felix's promise to render a verdict on Paul's case and his subsequent failure to do so (24:22–27). In all these cases, the narrator of Acts withholds information from the reader, which permits multiple interpretations. In his illuminating study of Hebrew narrative, Meir Sternberg distinguishes between "gaps," either temporary or permanent omissions of

---

28. F. Jackson and Lake, *Acts of the Apostles*, 147.
29. Culpepper, "Paul's Mission," 488.
30. Bruce, *Acts of the Apostles* (1951), 259. Notice again the assumption of Luke's acquaintance with Col. 4:10.
31. Krodel, *Acts*, 231.
32. Swete, *St Mark*, xvii.
33. Krodel, *Acts*, 231, proposed (one hopes) with tongue in check.
34. Haenchen, *Acts of the Apostles*, 407; Conzelmann, *Acts of the Apostles*, 105.

material that are relevant to interpretation; and "blanks," omissions judged by the narrator to be unimportant or irrelevant.[35] Which kind of omission do we encounter in Acts 13:13b?

At this stage we cannot tell. Luke withholds from the reader any explanation for John's activity. On a first reading of Acts it is not clear that John's return to Jerusalem is inherently problematic. After all, he is a Jerusalemite (12:12); throughout the narrative the Jerusalem church functions as the principal base and collective arbiter of early Christianity's operations (Acts 1:4, 12; 9:26–30; 11:1–18, 27–30; 15:1–35; 16:4; 21:15–26). At this juncture John's withdrawal to Jerusalem is enigmatic but not intrinsically sinister.

On the other hand, Luke leaves clues in the narrative that, while not decisive, do envelope John Mark's conduct in wisps of suspicion. John's standing is not equal to that of Barnabas and Saul/Paul. To this point he has been a passive figure, taken along by two others. Because we as readers have not witnessed his independent assertion of positive Christian values or conduct, we cannot be sure of his character. Although Acts tends to portray relations among believers as remarkably harmonious (2:43–47; 4:32–37), by no means does Luke suppress all Christian malfeasance (5:1–11; 8:9–24). We may recall, and now wonder, that John Mark was neither expressly set apart and dispatched by the Holy Spirit nor confirmed by the Antiochene church for mission (13:1–4). Immediately preceding the notice of John's separation from his patrons, we learn of a Roman proconsul's conversion and Paul's ensuing confrontation with Elymas the magician (13:6–12). From this account emerge some items that may help us interpret Mark's character.

First, the story of Elymas depicts an instance of human obstinacy and corruption, overcome by divine intervention. Luke's first references to John Mark (12:12, 25) bracket different episodes (Peter's reception [12:12–17]; Herod's atrocities [12:18–23]) that convey the same theme.

Second, the two references to John in Acts 13 (his assistance of Barnabas and Saul [v. 5b]; his departure from them [v. 13b]) frame a story whose outcome is a prominent Gentile's conversion to Christianity. While John's response to this event is indiscernible, we know that the Jerusalemite has been associated with missionary activity within Jewish synagogues (v. 5a). Soon we shall learn (in Acts 15) that all qualms about Jewish and Gentile relations were not allayed at the earlier Jerusalem conference (see Acts 11:1–18).

A third point may be noted, though its significance for John Mark is indeterminate. It is with the story of Elymas and Sergius Paulus that the relationship between Barnabas and Saul is reversed (cf. 9:26–30; 11:19–30; 12:25; 13:1–2, 7)

---

35. Sternberg, *Poetics of Biblical Narrative*, 230–40. Tannehill (*Acts of the Apostles*, 199–200, 248–50, 306–7) appropriates Sternberg's concepts without considering their relevance for John Mark in Acts 13:13.

and Paul becomes the "senior partner" of the missionary team. From this point on, Paul's name is usually mentioned first or representatively (13:13, 43, 45, 46, 50; 14:9, 11; 15:2, 35; though cf. 14:14; 15:12, 25), and Paul's authority, preaching, and fortunes assume center stage (13:9–12, 16–41; 14:9–11, 19–20; 15:36). Although Paul and Barnabas are described as jointly acting or preaching (13:43, 46–47, 50–52; 14:1–7, 14–18, 21–28; 15:2–4, 12, 22, 30–35), no specific activity of Barnabas alone is portrayed throughout the first missionary journey, the Jerusalem conference, or its immediate aftermath (Acts 13:1–15:35). Though its import be uncertain, it is interesting that John Mark enters the narrative of Acts at that point where Paul moves into ascendance and Barnabas recedes.

These associations, tensions, and reversals attending John Mark's entry to and exit from the narrative are quite subtle. At 13:13b we cannot determine whether John's disappearance is an inconsequential "blank" or a significant "gap," or if the latter, whether the omission is temporary or permanent. Amid apostolic triumph over adversity (13:42–52; 14:1–28; 15:30–35), Luke's comment about Mark's withdrawal might plant in the reader's mind a seed of suspense. It could as easily pass unnoticed. Having read no farther than 13:13b, one might suppose that John Mark had made his last bow in Acts.

Acts 15:36–40

The narrative in Acts 13–14 offers a sketch of Paul's mission to a Gentile world: bold preaching and miraculous deeds, favorably though not universally received (13:14–43); encounters with pagan polytheism and mostly Jewish persecution in Iconium, Lystra, and Derbe (13:44–14:20); pastoral fidelity to newly organized churches (14:21–25). In a progress report to the congregation in Syrian Antioch, where the Spirit has commissioned them, Paul and Barnabas credit God for opening "a door of faith for the Gentiles" (14:26–28). A potentially catastrophic rupture between Christians in Antioch and Jerusalem is averted in Acts 15:1–35, with the consensus decision that Gentile converts to Christianity need not be circumcised but adhere only to Moses' basic requirements in Leviticus 17:1–18:30 (Acts 15:19–29). At stake in this "apostolic decree" are several Lukan desiderata: the Gentile mission's intrinsic legitimacy, absolution of Gentiles from conversion to Judaism, and a modus vivendi between Jewish and Gentile believers in Christ.

On the eve of a new voyage at Acts 15:36, Paul proposes to Barnabas a return visit with believers in every city that they have previously missionized:

> [37]Now Barnabas was also eager to take with them John, the one called Mark. [38]Paul, however, believed it best not to take with them this one, who had deserted them at Pamphylia and had not gone with them to the work. [39]And so sharp a disagreement arose that they separated from each other: taking Mark with him, Barnabas sailed away to Cyprus. [40]And choosing Silas, Paul set out, having been commended to the grace of the

Lord by the [Antiochene] brothers. [41]And he went through Syria and
Cilicia, bolstering the churches. (Acts 15:37–41 AT)

Unexpectedly, John Mark here returns to the narrative. Now we know that
his absence since Acts 13:13b has been a temporary gap, not an irrelevant blank.
Straightway we also learn how his withdrawal was regarded: Paul was not pleased
by John Mark's return to Jerusalem (see 13:13), thus confirming our worst fears
for Mark's conduct. Supporting that assessment is this little tableau's harsh tone,
apparent from Luke's choice of words.

1. Note the two main predicates in verses 37 and 38: Barnabas "was desirous
of" (ἐβούλετο [ebouleto]) bringing Mark, while Paul "was insisting" (ἠξίου [ēxiou])
that they not do so. Both verbs are conjugated in the imperfect tense, indicating
continuous action in the past: in this case, persistent and deliberate attitudes in
mutual opposition.

2. Luke's vocabulary for his characters' actions is tart. John Mark is described
as the one who in Pamphylia had withdrawn from them: the participle τὸν
ἀποστάντα (ton apostanta) stems from ἀφίστημι (aphistēmi), a verb that typically
connotes desertion, defection, or apostasy (see Luke 8:13; Acts 5:37–38; LXX: Jer.
3:14; 1 Macc. 11:43; and often throughout the LXX with reference to falling away
from God).[36] The term used to portray Paul and Barnabas's "sharp disagreement," παροξυσμός (paroxysmos, v. 39), suggests not only the English derivative,
"paroxysm" (a sudden, violent outburst), but also the more vivid Greek verbal
cognate, παροξίζω (paroxizō, "to have a sharp odor"). An English colloquialism
captures the sense of it: at Antioch, Barnabas and Paul "raised a stink" with each
other over John Mark's inclusion.

3. By placing a demonstrative pronoun at the end of verse 38, Luke empha-
sizes John Mark as a defector: Παῦλος δὲ ἠξίου τὸν ἀποστάντα . . . καὶ μὴ
συνελθόντα αὐτοῖς . . . μὴ συμπαραλαμβάνειν τοῦτον (Paulos de ēxiou ton apostanta . . . kai mē synelthonta autois . . . mē symparalambanein touton: "Him who had
deserted and had not accompanied them, . . . Paul thought it better not to take
along this one"). Observe also the balanced contrast of the missionaries after their
separation: taking Mark, Barnabas sails away to Cyprus; choosing Silas, Paul
departs for Syria and Cilicia (vv. 39–41). With new associates in tow, the erstwhile
partners head out in opposite directions.

The history of this text's exegesis has tended to highlight things neither stated
nor implied. For instance, an elder cousin's affection for his junior has been proposed as motivating Barnabas's intervention for Mark.[37] Others think that Acts

---

36. Used transitively, the verb describes one who misleads others or incites a revolt (Herodotus,
Wars 1.76, 154; Thucydides, *Hist.* 1.81; Josephus, *Ant.* 8.198; 20.102; Deut. 7:4 LXX; Acts 5:37). In
patristic literature ἀφίστημι is used with reference to withdrawal from church communion (Irenaeus,
Adv. haer. 3.4.2) or apostasy (Herm. *Sim.* 8.8.2; Irenaeus, *Adv. haer.* 1.13.7).

37. Krodel, *Acts*, 294; Johnson, *Acts of the Apostles*, 282–83.

15:36–40 bespeaks more than Luke is willing to admit of the controversy narrated in Galatians 2:11–14; thus he shifts the cause of Barnabas and Paul's separation away from missionary substance to colliding personalities: Paul's steadfastness versus John Mark's unreliability.[38]

Acts 15:36–40 bears an underdeveloped quality. That could suggest Luke's discomfiture at airing this portion of early Christianity's dirty linen, particularly as it involves two heroic apostles. Yet Luke's concern for personalities can be misconstrued. He never mentions, and may not have known, the tradition that Barnabas and Mark were cousins (Col. 4:10). Certainly that is never offered to explain Barnabas's judgment in Acts 15:37–39. Nor is it accurate to speak of Luke's account as "neutral."[39] In fact, παροξυσμός is anything but a neutral term for depicting the disagreement between Paul and Barnabas, which is left unresolved and arguably entails more than Paul's pique with Mark's blemish.

However delicate its rendering, Acts 15:36–40 amounts to a disturbing, if not traumatic, rift within Luke's narrative—and John Mark stands at its epicenter. The falling-out between Paul and Barnabas ruptures that common mind and concerted action within the Christian community that Luke has taken great pains to establish in his narrative (2:41–47; 4:32–27).[40] Even more pointedly, as Richard Cassidy notes,[41] the reader of Acts has been encouraged to regard Barnabas with great favor: as magnanimous (4:36–37), insightfully supportive of the newly converted Saul (9:26–27; 11:25–26), and in Luke's own words, "a noble man, full of the Holy Spirit and of faith" (11:24a AT). To the reader of Acts, Barnabas's estrangement from Paul is startling and distressing, especially since their breach is never explicitly repaired: even though Paul functions as an agent of reconciliation elsewhere in the narrative (15:1–31; 16:3–4; 21:18–26), after Acts 15:36–40 no further contact between him and his closest colleague is ever reported.

Within the narrative, we are permitted access neither to Mark's motive for returning to Jerusalem (13:13b) nor to Barnabas's reason for reintegrating him into the missionary team (15:37). We are told what Paul thinks: it was best not to take with them one who had resigned and had not participated with them "in the work" (εἰς τὸ ἔργον [eis to ergon], 15:38). What is "the work" that (the Lukan) Paul has in mind? Used absolutely, τὸ ἔργον occurs six times in Acts. Gamaliel's use in his cautionary speech to the Sanhedrin (5:38) is so vague that the term is variously translated as "undertaking" (NRSV), "movement" (NJB), or "[an idea's] execution" (NEB). Often translated as "deed," the term also appears twice in 13:41, in a quotation from the LXX (Hab. 1:5). The remaining occurrences in Acts of τὸ ἔργον are all proximate to one another: 13:2, in reference to that work for which

38. Conzelmann, *Acts of the Apostles*, 123; Achtemeier, *Quest for Unity*, 41–42.
39. Haenchen, *Acts of the Apostles*, 474.
40. Consult Kee, *Good News*, 86–89.
41. Cassidy, *Society and Politics*, 26, 66–67, 190 n. 38.

Barnabas and Saul were set apart by the Holy Spirit; 14:26, regarding the work
that those two missionaries fulfilled in Cyprus, Pamphylia, Pisidia, and Galatia;
and 15:38, the work from which John Mark recoiled. Evidently the particular
"work" that Luke has in mind is the propagation of faith even among Gentiles,
the door to which God has opened (thus the climax of Paul's first missionary
journey at 14:27; see also 10:1–11:18). If that be the case, this is the same work
that, in Paul's (read Luke's) estimation, John Mark has rebuffed. And if that is how
we should understand Acts 15:38, then its conventional interpretation misses the
bull's-eye by a considerable margin. For Luke the problem with John Mark apparently is not that he simply threw in the towel. Much worse: Mark has given up on
a mission extended to Gentiles as well as to Jews.[42]

Several scraps of circumstantial evidence buttress this conclusion. First, even
though Acts tells us little about Mark, we know he is a Jerusalemite sympathetic
to that city (12:12, 25; 13:13b). Through his civic affiliation, Mark (better known
by his Jewish name, John [13:5b]), is thus associated with the locus for the Juda-
izing party: those who hold the position "Unless you are circumcised according
to the custom of Moses, you cannot be saved" (Acts 15:1; cf. Gal. 2:12). Indeed,
throughout the second half of the narrative in Acts, no little tension is generated
by observant Jews or Jewish Christians who repeatedly oppose Paul's liberal
mission among Gentiles.[43] Second, we have learned of Mark's assisting his apostolic mentors in the context of proclamation in Jewish synagogues (Acts 13:5);
precisely at the point where a Gentile proconsul is converted, John Mark withdraws from their mission and heads back to Jerusalem (13:6–13). Third, immediately preceding Mark's reentry to the narrative is the articulation of a plan of
communion between Christian Jews and Gentiles, endorsed by the apostles in
Jerusalem and confirmed at Antioch (15:1–35). Fourth, immediately following
apostolic estrangement over John Mark in 15:36–39, Paul forms a new missionary team (15:40–16:5). In place of Barnabas, he enlists Silas, a believer from
among the leading Jerusalemites (15:22b, 27, 32). Into the position of assistance
formerly occupied by John Mark steps Timothy (16:1–5), whose mixed parent-
age symbolizes the ethnic alliance of Jews and Gentiles that, in Luke's judgment,
should be the wave of Christianity's future.

No doubt about it: Luke could have been more direct, and much of my analysis
is conjectural. But if this proposal be accepted, then the trouble with John Mark
in Acts 15:35–40 entails something deeper than a character flaw or lapse of judgment. In Acts, Mark may represent an aborted future for Christianity: a religious

42. Gaventa demurs: "Paul's adamancy [may be] not so much [about Mark's] resistance to the
Gentile mission as it is about any departure from the work of witnesses" (*Acts of the Apostles*, 231).
While the extension of God's salvation to Gentiles appears to have triggered John Mark's resignation,
Brawley notes that Paul's mission in Acts is not ethnically restricted: many Jews accept Paul and
Barnabas's preaching (13:42–43; 14:1, 27; *Text to Text*, 169 n. 37).
43. See L. Wills, "Depiction of the Jews," esp. 640–43.

outgrowth of Judaism that stubbornly remains within the confines of old Israel. If so, then Acts suggests a tragedy, not only for an Israel that has largely rejected an announcement of fulfillment of its most cherished hopes,[44] but also for early Christianity—one of whose forms may have been stunted, too closely wedded to an ethnically exclusivist conceptualization of that hope.

But would Luke have us infer that Barnabas, Mark's advocate (15:37–39), supported a position so parochial and ultimately unavailing? Does not Luke persistently present Barnabas as a mediator between Jews and Gentiles, between Jerusalem and Antioch (Acts 11:19–30; 13:1–48; 15:1–35)? That, indeed, is the case and perhaps helps us to appreciate the poignancy of the episode in Acts 15:35–40. From his initial appearances at 4:32–37 and 9:26–27, Luke has portrayed Barnabas as a "son of encouragement": defender of underdogs and standard-bearer of Christian unity and generosity. If, however, we have rightly interpreted John Mark's role, then in Acts 15:35–40 Barnabas is stuck on the horns of a dilemma from which escape is impossible. If he casts his lot with Paul (another Jew with missionary proclivities toward Gentiles) and splits with John Mark (whose sympathies are narrower), then the Christian enterprise will be internally fractured. If he breaks with Paul and sides with Mark (as, for different reasons, he has once stood beside Paul: 9:26–30), the result will be precisely the same. Luke may not have known Paul's account, similar though not identical, of the apostolic row at Antioch over Jewish relations with Gentiles (Gal. 2:11–14). Acts 15:35–40, however, whispers something of the same painful and perhaps unresolved controversy, dramatized in terms of Barnabas's effective ensnarement in a tactically divisive Catch-22.[45] Perhaps for this reason Luke handles the split between Paul and Barnabas over John Mark with such a light touch: in 15:35–40, as in 15:1–5, we encounter one of the few instances in Acts where opposition to Christianity's future is expressed in-house by other, more traditionally observant, Jewish Christians. Unlike the Jerusalem controversy, which ends in a compromise satisfying to all (Acts 15:22–35), here we find a fracture within the Christian movement that proves immediately if not indefinitely irreparable.[46]

For reasons left unexpressed, yet in a manner consistent with his character in Acts, Barnabas separates from Paul and takes Mark back to Cyprus. With the benefit of hindsight, we may now understand why, since chapter 13, Barnabas's

---

44. Tannehill, "Israel in Luke–Acts."

45. Note Spencer (*Acts*, 158): "Barnabas plays true to form by standing up to Paul on Mark's behalf. The one who steps out of line, so to speak, is *Paul*, who is not willing to give Mark the same benefit of the doubt as a reformed deserter that he himself received earlier (from Barnabas) as a reformed persecutor."

46. In private correspondence (March 6, 1991) Gaventa observes a similar contrast between the antagonists in Acts 15 and those in Acts 5:1–11; 8:9–24: "Perhaps Luke treats Mark (and Barnabas) with such care because they are not villains in the blatant sense [that Ananias, Sapphira, and Simon Magus are]. [Mark and Barnabas] are reputable members of the community, whose position (on the Gentile mission) Luke will not endorse."

leadership has been fading. That character is preparing to vanish from the narrative altogether, and Paul will take his place. As commentators regularly observe,[47] a positive outcome may be intimated by these sad circumstances: the division between Barnabas and Paul, and their respective entourages, could imply that the Gentile mission has been effectively doubled. Though such an ironically providential twist would cohere with Luke's theology, evidenced elsewhere,[48] in fact Luke is not clear about that prospect: while considered Gentile territory, Cyprus has been previously missionized (13:4–12), and no itinerary beyond that island is suggested for Barnabas and John Mark. Those two characters fade out of the narrative, without ever being reconciled with the evangelism thereafter associated with Paul. The same could be said, historically and theologically, for the narrower vision with which John Mark appears to have been associated.

CONCLUSIONS

In the book of Acts, John Mark plays a minor but highly suggestive role.

1. Patently he is associated with the early Christian church at Jerusalem (12:12; 13:13), latently aligned with the piety and wealth of those among its number (12:12).

2. He is clearly associated with Barnabas and Paul, at whose invitation he renders general service at the start of their first mission to Cyprus (12:25; 13:5). He is not expressly kin to Barnabas (cf. Col. 4:10), nor is he directly or indirectly linked with Peter (though the latter repairs to the home of Mark's mother, Mary: 12:12; cf. 1 Pet. 5:13).

3. Implicitly he is connected with Christian mission exercised within Jewish synagogues (13:5) and detached from the broader sweep of that mission among Gentiles (13:13; 15:38).

4. In general, John Mark is cast in an obscure (13:5, 13) or downright derogatory light (15:38–39), arguably owing (in Luke's view) to his reticence or refusal to participate in Paul's missionary labors among Gentiles. Evidently for this reason, in Luke's account, he is the cause of a split between Barnabas and Paul (15:39b–40).

5. With his patron, Barnabas, John Mark disappears from Acts after chapter 15.

These results prompt some general reflections. First, although it has long proved tempting to blend elements from Acts and the NT Letters, consolidating them into a unitary image of John Mark—the Jewish-Christian backslider who,

---

47. Bruce, *Commentary on Acts* (1954), 319; Haenchen, *Acts of the Apostles*, 474; Achtemeier, *Quest for Unity*, 42; Pervo, *Acts*, 387.

48. Throughout Acts (4:1–22; 8:1–4; 16:25–34; 26:32–28:31), persecution and imprisonment become vehicles for the gospel's dissemination.

with his cousin's help, returned to the Pauline and Petrine fold[49]—that temptation should be resisted. From this analysis there has emerged no evidence whatever that Luke knew, much less depended on, Pauline (Phlm. 24), Deutero-Pauline (Col. 4:10; 2 Tim. 4:11), or Petrine (1 Pet. 5:13) sources for his portrayal of Mark as an apostolic associate.[50]

Second, although the Lukan Mark lacks sharp definition and the reader of Acts must work hard to discern this character's significance, it can scarcely be doubted that John Mark plays the literary role of a *ficelle*: a representative yet individualized character, whose function is to delineate and to engage the narrative's protagonists, as "foils" in drama traditionally do.[51] Through John Mark's character and conduct, Luke subtly discloses or confirms the values and purposes of Barnabas, Paul, and even God, who through the Holy Spirit initiates and sustains their missionary program.[52]

Finally, if the outcomes of this chapter hold, then an ambivalence toward Judaism is not the only intrareligious tension that pulses within Luke–Acts.[53] John Mark and Paul, with Barnabas caught somewhere betwixt, represent conflicting visions of early Christianity: one so firmly dedicated to the significance of Jesus Christ for the Jewish people that it pulls back from outreach beyond Israel; the other acknowledging an open door of faith for both Jews and Gentiles, in fulfillment of God's restoration of Israel. Although Luke's heart lies with the second, his account remembers John Mark and thus laments, without denying, the existence of the first.

---

49. N.B. the summary in Cross and Livingstone, *Oxford Dictionary of the Christian Church*, 1038b: "Mark is associated with Peter in I Pet. 5:13. He has traditionally been associated with John Mark, the cousin of St. Barnabas (Col. 4:10), a Jew, who set out with St. Barnabas and St. Paul on their first missionary journey, but for reasons which failed to satisfy St. Paul turned back (Acts 12:25, 13:5, and 13, 15:37f.); afterwards he accompanied Barnabas on a mission to Cyprus (Acts 15:39), and he was in Rome with St. Paul (Col. 4:10, Philem. 24, 2 Tim. 4:11). The identification may not be justified." Nevertheless, this view persists: Parker, "Authorship of the Second Gospel"; Jefford, "Mark, John"; Barrett, *Acts of the Apostles*, 200, 243.

50. The NT's various depictions of Mark manifest the superficial similarity and distinctive differences that would be expected of documents that seem to have been literarily independent of each other, yet traditionally interrelated. See C. Black, *Mark: Images*, 50–73.

51. "Ficelle" (cf. *montrer la ficelle*, "to expose the string [that pulls something]") appears to have been coined in English (borrowed from the French) by Henry James in his preface to the New York edition (1908) of *The Portrait of a Lady*: "Maria Gostrey and [Henrietta] Stackpole then are cases, each, of the light *ficelle*, not of the [novel's] true agent; they may run beside the coach 'for all they are worth,' they may cling to it till they are out of breath . . . , but neither, all the while, so much as gets her foot on the step, neither ceases for a moment to tread the dusty road" (13). Acknowledging his indebtedness to James, Harvey popularized the term among twentieth-century literary theorists in *Character and the Novel* (56–58, 62–68).

52. On Lukan subtlety, see Phillips, "Subtlety as a Literary Technique"; note Bass's complementary conclusions in "Narrative and Rhetorical Use."

53. Thus Tyson, *Images of Judaism*, esp. 187–89; R. Thompson, "Believers and Religious Leaders."

Chapter Seven

The Rhetorical Form
of the Early Christian Sermon

We do not make sermons out of air: our creations, poor or brilliant
as they may be, are always variations on someone else's theme. The
main melody is always a given, and even when we launch into our
own bold improvisations we are limited to a scale of eight notes.
Our words are not ends in themselves; they exist to serve other
words, which means that we never work alone. . . . Together we
explore the parameters of our common faith, testing the truth of
one another's discoveries and holding each other accountable so
that what we offer those who listen to us will not aim to dazzle but
to nourish them.

Barbara Brown Taylor[1]

Some years ago[2] Lawrence Wills identified, within a wide range of Hellenistic
Jewish and early Christian literature, a recurring pattern that is occasionally characterized in those sources as a "word of exhortation" (λόγος παρακλήσεως [*logos
parakléseōs*], in Acts 13:15; Heb. 13:22; cf. Acts 2:40; 1 Macc. 10:24; 2 Macc. 7:24;
15:11; *Ap. Const.* 8.5). He opined that the form of this "hortatory word" may define
a point on a larger rhetorical trajectory within Greco-Roman Hellenism, suggesting that "we can perhaps go further and note the actual compositional techniques
that have passed over from Greek rhetoric into Jewish and Christian oratory."[3] In
that assessment Wills is, I believe, quite correct. In this chapter I aim to build on
and to refine his formal analysis of Hellenistic Jewish and early Christian sermons.

---

1. B. Taylor, *The Preaching Life*, 81.
2. L. Wills, "Form of the Sermon" (1984).
3. Ibid., 298.

WILLS'S PROPOSAL REVISITED

We begin by examining the contours of Lawrence Wills's research. Regarding as paradigmatic the structure of Paul's missionary sermon at Pisidian Antioch (Acts 13:13–41), Wills delineates a pattern of argumentation that comprises the following three elements: (a) a presentation of *exempla*, scriptural quotations or other authoritative evidence from past or present (13:16b–37); (b) a *conclusion*, inferred from those examples and pointing up their significance for the audience addressed (13:38–39); (c) an *exhortation* based on that conclusion (13:40–41).[4] Having identified this basic pattern, Wills discerns the impressively frequent recurrence of the same word-of-exhortation form in other early Christian and Jewish writings beyond Acts.[5] In the course of his exploration, Wills observes some corollary phenomena. First, logical or quasi-logical connections between the parts of this homiletical pattern are usually established with the use of inferential particles or phrases.[6] Second, the last element in the pattern, the exhortation, can refer not only backward to its supporting exempla and conclusion but also forward, in anticipation of other exempla and conclusions to come (e.g., Heb. 2:1; 3:1; 4:1, 14b–16; *1 Clem.* 7.2; 13:1a; 40.1b).[7] Third, the word-of-exhortation form can either stand alone (e.g., Acts 2:14–40; 13:13–41; 2 Cor. 6:14–7:1) or be employed repeatedly, in cyclical fashion, within a given document (among others, Heb. 1:5–4:16; 8:1–12:28b; *1 Clem.* 4.1–13:1a; 37.2–40:1b; Ign. *Eph.* 3.1–4.2; 5.1–3b; 7.2–10.1).[8] After marshaling, analyzing, and interpreting the evidence, Wills attempts to determine the provenance of the λόγος παρακλήσεως. Finding no trace of it in the Hebrew Bible, he concludes that this distinctive sermonic form originates in Greek rhetoric.[9]

As used by form critics, the terms "sermon" and "homily" are notoriously ambiguous, so much so that modern scholarship is sharply divided on how much, if anything, can be confidently said about Jewish and Christian preaching before the late second century CE.[10] Within that context, Wills is to be congratulated,

---

4. Ibid., 279.
5. Namely, in Hebrews, *1 Clement*, 1 and 2 Corinthians, 1 and 2 Peter, the Ignatian Epistles, *Barnabas*, the old LXX version of Susanna, the Epistle of Jeremiah, the *Testaments of the Twelve Patriarchs*, Eusebius's *Preparation for the Gospel*, and Josephus's *Jewish War*.
6. L. Wills, "Form of the Sermon," 279 et passim.
7. Ibid., 281–82, 284–85.
8. Ibid., 280–85, 291.
9. Ibid., 296–99.
10. Much of the dispute turns on how true to first-century homiletical reality either NT portrayals or later Jewish midrashim may be accepted. Thyen (*Stil der jüdisch-hellenistischen Homilie*, 1955) is a classic, maximalist reconstruction; more recent and equally expansive is Osborn (*Folly of God*, 1999). Both Thyen (47–58) and Osborn (51–74) devote attention to rhetoric in historically situating their subjects. Less firmly grounded in ancient rhetorical theory is Siegert's argument (in "Homily and Panegyrical Sermon") that early Christians imitated Jewish homiletical practice in Greek-speaking Diaspora synagogues. Considerably more skeptical are the appraisals of Evans, "'Speeches' in

both for having fleshed out a clear and precise pattern of Hellenistic Jewish and early Christian argumentation, and for having displayed its occurrence in so broad a range of primary literature. His presentation is carefully documented and, in the main, convincingly argued. If his is neither the first word nor the last, it seems to me a valid word, cautiously injected into a murky realm of biblical research.

Still, a number of questions remain unanswered. Some of these Wills himself raises.

1. Having established the fundamental exempla-conclusion-exhortation pattern and its sometimes cyclical repetition within a work, Wills notes with interest, but is hard pressed to explain, occasional and lengthy interruptions of the form. Thus the extended exempla or doctrinal exposition of Hebrews 5:1–7:28; *1 Clement* 42.1–44.6; 2 Peter 1:12–3:2; Ignatius, *To the Ephesians* 17.2–20.2; and *Barnabas* 7.3–16.10 constitute temporary cessations of the otherwise firmly entrenched hortatory pattern evidenced by those books.[11] Can the pattern of argumentation proposed by Wills be modified to account for these structural aporias?

2. In his treatment of the sermons in Acts, Wills indicates that at least two short speeches exhibit the word-of-exhortation form, despite the fact that they lack a liturgical or missionary context and cannot properly be classified as sermons: the address of the town clerk to the mob at Ephesus (19:35–40) and the charge given to Paul by the elders in Jerusalem (21:20–25). Wills concedes that these speeches may "[call] into question the supposition that the form was limited to Jewish and Christian sermons."[12] If we grant that the exempla-conclusion-exhortation pattern is characteristic of, yet not confined to, homiletical address, is there a broader rhetorical paradigm within which that pattern may be located and better understood?

3. In Wills's judgment Greek rhetoric ultimately provides the most probable background for the origin of the word of exhortation, especially since "Jews and Christians could have learned something of Greek rhetoric in the Hellenistic schools."[13] However, the Hellenistic Jewish and Christian form does not fit as snugly into that context as Wills might wish:

> Although Greek and Roman rhetoricians indulged in minute analysis of almost every conceivable aspect of the art of speaking, they nowhere . . .

Acts"; L. Levine, *Ancient Jewish Synagogues*; and Stemberger, "Response [to Folker Siegert]." As this chapter unfolds, it should become clear that I stand somewhere between these extremes. As Christian preaching evolves into the patristic era, our critical footing becomes surer, or more slippery for other reasons (Cunningham and Allen, *Preacher and Audience*; Stockhausen, "Christian Perception of Jewish Preaching"). Stewart-Sykes (*From Prophecy to Preaching*) argues that Christian prophecy in house churches gave way to homilies subject to judgment and application in "the house of God."

11. L. Wills, "Form of the Sermon," 282, 285, 291–92.

12. Ibid., 287. L. Wills's study focuses on intramural sermons, in contrast to missionary sermons or speeches directed to outsiders (ibid., 277, 280, 298–99).

13. Ibid., 299. L. Wills's inference is substantiated by Marrou, *History of Education in Antiquity*; Clark, *Rhetoric in Greco-Roman Education*; and Clarke, *Higher Education*.

explicitly described the pattern called here the word of exhortation. . . . The parts into which [forensic, deliberative, and epideictic] speeches are usually divided—prologue, narration, proof, and epilogue for the forensic speech—do not correspond to what we have seen above, nor should we expect popular Jewish and Christian writings to conform in all respects to the canons of Aristotle, Cicero, and Quintilian.[14]

Unable to locate within conventional rhetoric the pattern he has uncovered, Wills tentatively traces it "to the innovations in Greek rhetoric in the fifth century BCE" associated with Thucydides' deliberative speeches and Socrates' epideictic address in Plato's *Menexenus* (236d–248e).[15]

This appraisal is fraught with difficulties. First, it creates for Wills the dilemma of having to argue for familiarity with classical rhetoric among Hellenistic Jews and Christians, only to conclude that the structure of their sermons was essentially anomalous by Greek rhetorical standards. Second, to regard the speeches of Thucydides and Plato as "innovations" seems odd since it is precisely the rhetoric of these earlier figures that such later theorists as Aristotle, Cicero, and Quintilian avowedly attempt to systematize and standardize.[16] In view of these curiosities, one wonders, third, if Wills may have exaggerated the dissimilarities in structure between Greco-Roman addresses and Jewish-Christian sermons.

In my judgment, Wills has indeed overstated the case for a formal divergence of the word of exhortation from classical rhetrorical conventions. Their likenesses, I suggest, far outweigh their differences. Once the form of the Hellenistic Jewish and early Christian sermon is viewed in alignment with the canons of Greco-Roman rhetoric, a number of Wills's intuitions receive primary verification, and the residual problems associated with his treatment are dispelled.

THE WORD OF EXHORTATION'S
SETTING IN CLASSICAL RHETORIC

For Lawrence Wills, two things confirm a deviation of the λόγος παρακλή-σεως from Greco-Roman rhetorical norms. First, he intimates that the *content* of the word of exhortation does not conform to that of the classical species of rhetoric (judicial, deliberative, and epideictic). Second, he argues that the *form*

14. L. Wills, "Form of the Sermon," 296. "I have found no explicit mention [in Greek rhetoric of the Hellenistic schools] of just this division into exempla, conclusion, and exhortation" (299).

15. Ibid., 297–98; see also 293.

16. Later rhetorical theorists admired Thucydides and Plato, not as innovators, but as touchstones of eloquence and argumentation: on Thucydides, see Cicero, *Opt. gen.* 5.15–6.16; Quintilian, *Inst.* 10.1.73; on Plato, see Aristotle, *Rhet.* 1.9.1367b; 2.23.1398a; 3.7.1408b; 3.14.1415b; Cicero, *Opt. gen.* 6.17; Quintilian, *Inst.* 2.15.25–32; 5.7.28; 10.1.8; 12.2.22; et passim; cf. Cornificius, *Rhet. ad Her.* 1.2.3; 3.6.10; 4.37.49; 4.45.58.

of Jewish and Christian sermons diverges from the customary arrangement of Greco-Roman speeches: prologue, narration, proof, and epilogue.[17]

With both of these assessments I disagree. First, consider content. If, with Wills, one defines judicial, deliberative, and epideictic speeches as, respectively, "arguments at a court of law," "arguments of policy, usually before a governing body," and "public, usually honorary speeches," then the word of exhortation seems disqualified from all. Most extant Hellenistic Jewish and early Christian sermons have as their *Sitz im Leben* neither the lawcourt, nor the legislative assembly, nor the ceremonial address. But are not these definitions overly restrictive, even by classical standards? As first formulated by Aristotle and elaborated by subsequent theorists, forensic oratory attempts to elicit positive or negative judgments, based on truth or justice, about a fact or action that has occurred in the past. Deliberative speeches entail consideration of future action, a choice between two or more forms of conduct, based on self-interest or future benefit. Typically, epideictic address praises or blames a person, thing, or quality, based on accepted values (such as what is honorable or just), with the intent to instill or to enhance an audience's present belief.[18] When viewed in a more functional context, the sermons examined by Wills *do* conform to one or another of the types of classical oratory: either a judicial assessment of what has happened in the past ("God has made him both Lord and Christ, this Jesus whom you crucified" [Acts 2:36 RSV]),[19] a deliberative appeal for future action on the basis of future benefit ("Repent, and be baptized every one of you in the name of Jesus Christ for the forgiveness of your sins; and you shall receive the gift of the Holy Spirit" [Acts 2:38 RSV]),[20] or an epideictic attempt to stimulate belief in the present ("Therefore, brothers and sisters, holy partners in a heavenly calling, consider . . . Jesus, the apostle and high priest of our confession" [Heb. 3:1]).[21]

To be sure, Wills grants a similarity between the word of exhortation and Thucydides' deliberative speeches and epideictic speech in the *Menexenus*. He regards these antecedents as "innovations," similar to later Jewish and Christian sermons primarily in their organizing structure. Here one must demur: *pace* Wills, neither these sermons nor their classical precursors are "innovative" in any significant sense, since they exemplify two of the basic species of ancient oratory. Nor is similarity between the word of exhortation and the speeches of Thucydides and Plato confined only to their structural arrangement; *substantively* they are all mutually accordant in their intention

17. L. Wills, "Form of the Sermon," 296.
18. See Aristotle, *Rhet.* 1.2.1358b; Cicero, *Inv.* 2.3.12–13; 2.51.155–58, 176; 2.58.176–77; Cornificius, *Rhet. ad Her.* 1.2.2; 3.2.2–3; 3.6.10–11; Quintilian, *Inst.* 3.4.12–16; 3.7.1–28; 3.8.1–6; 3.9.1.
19. Predictably, the best examples of judicial rhetoric in Acts are Paul's addresses at his trials (Acts 22:1–21 [to Jerusalem's populace]; 24:2b–21 [before Felix]; 26:2–23 [before Agrippa et al.]). On the conformity of these speeches with Quintilian's canons, consult Hogan, "Paul's Defense"; Keener, "Some Rhetorical Techniques."
20. Haraguchi ("A Call for Repentance") carefully examines Acts 3:12–26.
21. Lestang ("À la louange de dieu inconnu") assesses the epideictic character of Acts 17:22–31.

to prescribe some future course of action or to affirm some present point of view.[22] Indeed, for Quintilian (*Inst.* 3.4.15), Jewish and Christian sermons *could not* be regarded as exceptions to the basic genres of oratory, since all kinds of speeches were regarded as necessarily amenable to categorization as either judicial, deliberative, or epideictic.

What of Wills's contention that the structure of the word of exhortation flouts the arrangement of Greco-Roman speeches? He seems to have a point: ancient rhetorical handbooks do not divide the parts of a discourse into exempla, conclusion, and exhortation. Just here, however, at least four cautions should be interposed, which collectively align ancient Jewish and Christian sermons more rather than less closely with Hellenistic rhetorical conventions.

1. We should beware of confusing the absence of a particular nomenclature, used in describing certain phenomena, with absence of the phenomena themselves. To suggest, as does Wills, that ancient rhetoricians speak in terms of prologue, narration, proof, and epilogue—rather than in terms of exempla, conclusion, and exhortation—may indicate nothing more than that classical theorists employ conventional terminology in denoting many of the same elements that Wills abstracts in Jewish and Christian homilies but to which he gives different names.[23]

2. Wills is not entirely accurate in his representation of the arrangement (or *taxis*) of classical discourse. Theoretically, judicial oratory exhibited the most comprehensive structure in the most firmly established order: an introductory exordium or proem, followed in turn by a narration of the facts (background information), the proposition to be proved (often accompanied by its partition into separate headings), the actual demonstration of the thesis, a refutation of opposing positions conjoined (if necessary) with a digressive examination of attendant circumstances, and a concluding epilogue or peroration.[24] It is to this comprehensive arrangement that Wills refers, albeit in condensed form,[25] when comparing early Christian sermons with Hellenistic rhetoric. Wills neglects to mention, however, that this complete arrangement is not evidenced in all species of oratory. Usually it is abbreviated in deliberative address (characterized by a proem, statement of facts [sometimes omitted], proposition, proof, and epilogue) and severely truncated in epideictic discourse (proem, amplified topics, epilogue).[26]

---

22. The distinctions among judicial, deliberative, and epideictic discourse are not hard and fast. Quintilian (*Inst.* 3.4.16) admits that the lines differentiating rhetorical species are often blurred: like judicial rhetoric, deliberative discourse often inquires about the past (3.8.6), and both species are frequently colored by epideictic concerns (3.7.28; 3.8.15). In theory and practice, the identification of the species of rhetoric affords a relative, not an absolute, indication of a speech's primary intentions.

23. Hilgert ("Speeches in Acts") argues that the speeches in Acts adhere to standards enunciated by Dionysius of Halicarnassus (ca. 40–10 BCE) and Lucian of Samosata (ca. 120–180 CE), even though "rhetorical criticism" of those speeches is probably the farthest thing from Luke's own mind.

24. This *taxis* synthesizes presentations found in Aristotle, *Rhet.* 3.13.1414a–18.1420b; Cicero, *Inv.* 1.14.19–56.109; Cornificius, *Rhet. ad Her.* 1.3.4–2.31.50; Quintilian, *Inst.* 4.pr.6–6.5.11.

25. L. Wills ("Form of the Sermon") omits mention of the proposition and the often optional partition, refutation, and digression.

26. On the *taxis* of deliberative and epideictic address, consult Cornificius, *Rhet. ad Her.* 3.2.2–5.9; 3.6.10–8.15; Quintilian, *Inst.* 3.7.1–6; 3.8.6–15.

The organization of a speech varied with respect to its components and their degree of elaboration, depending on the species of rhetoric to which the address belonged and on the particulars of the rhetorical situation.[27] Therefore, the fact that Hellenistic Jewish and early Christian sermons do not exhibit the full-blown arrangement of judicial discourse should kindle no surprise: no species of classical rhetoric, not even judicial oratory itself, was straitjacketed into this comprehensive *taxis*. Within broad constraints, structural mòdification and abridgment were the rule, not the exception.

3. The absence of certain aspects of judicial, deliberative, and epideictic oratory from the structure of the λόγος παρακλήσεως is not as significant as Wills suggests. While a statement of facts, a formal proposition, and a proof are not differentiated in most of the homilies he considers, neither are such clear demarcations always acknowledged or even prescribed by classical rhetoricians.[28] It is equally true that a full-dress proem is missing from the Jewish and Christian sermons surveyed by Wills; yet this is explicable and even defensible on classical grounds. As Quintilian notes,[29] the sole purpose of the exordium is to render one's audience well disposed to the speech that will follow; in cases where such receptivity and goodwill toward the orator have already been secured or may be assumed, the exordium is rendered superfluous and may be deleted. Of course, those are precisely the circumstances that obtain with Wills's examples of the word of exhortation: these sermons do not require a lengthy introduction, since (a) most of them are addressed to coreligionists, in synagogue or church, who constitute an already sympathetic audience, and (b) all of these homilies occur in the context of larger literary works, whose authors have already secured their audiences' attention and benevolent disposition.[30] Interestingly enough, in those addresses of Acts where the speaker *cannot* automatically assume a favorable reception of his words, we find an exordium that ingratiates the speaker to his listeners or otherwise prepares them for the address that follows (see Acts 2:14–15; 3:12; 4:8–10; 7:2a; 10:34–35; 13:16b; 15:13; 17:22; 19:35; 21:20–22; 22:3; 24:2b–4, 10; 26:2–3; 27:21; 28:17).[31]

27. On the need for oratorical flexibility in responding to the demands of a special case or set of circumstances, see Quintilian, *Inst.* 5.10.103; 6.1.4–5; 7.2.22, 51; 7.10.11–13; 8.3.13–14; 9.3.101–2; 10.2.25–27.

28. Quintilian is characteristic of most classical rhetoricians in his willingness to distinguish, theoretically, different parts of a speech while granting that in practice those parts often overlap: see his *Inst.* 4.2.4, 8; 4.2.79; 4.4.1–2; cf. Cicero, *Inv.* 1.24.34; Cornificius, *Rhet. ad Her.* 2.30.47.

29. Quintilian, *Inst.* 4.1.5–6, 25–26; also Aristotle, *Rhet.* 3.14.1414b–15.1416b; Cicero, *Inv.* 1.15.20–18.26; Cornificius, *Rhet. ad Her.* 1.4.6–7.11.

30. See, e.g., Acts 1:1–5; 1 Pet. 1:1–9; 2 Pet. 1:1–4; *1 Clem.* pr.; 1.1–3.4; Ign. *Eph.* pr.; 1.1–3.2; *Barn.* 1.1–8; *T. Reu.* 1:1–10; *T. Levi* 1:1–2; *T. Naph.* 15:7; Josephus, *J.W.* 1.1.1–12.30. Maxwell ("Role of the Audience") is right: Luke tends to encourage his audience to participate more fully in the narrative by omitting some information.

31. Even in those speeches of Acts where the speaker presumes a favorable hearing, good relations are cursorily cemented between him and his audience with the use of introductory address, ἄνδρες ἀδελφοί / Ἰσραηλῖται (*andres adelphoi / Israēlitai,* "Men, Brothers" / "[Fellow] Israelites": 1:16; 5:35; 13:7; cf. 20:18b–21).

4. Such considerations lead to the heart of my disagreement with Wills: in spite of his reservations, the basic form of the λόγος παρακλήσεως agrees with the *taxis* of judicial, deliberative, and epideictic address. To illustrate this, take Paul's homily at Pisidian Antioch (Acts 13:13–41), the form of which is paradigmatic for Wills in establishing the structure of the word of exhortation. This address is, in fact, the only one in Acts that actually claims to be a synagogue sermon (13:14) and seems to bear traces of a homiletic pattern—the preacher's move from Torah (13:15a, 17–19; cf. Deut. 4:37–38) to Prophets (Acts 13:20–22; cf. 1 Sam. 13:14), drawing out scriptural implications (Acts 13:23–41) at the congregation's request (13:15b: *yelammedenu rabbenu*, "Let our teacher instruct us")—a request that becomes more clearly discernible among the rabbis.[32]

According to Wills, the exempla appear in the recounting of Israel's salvation history from Egyptian captivity, the exodus, and the conquest of Canaan to King David, and then the appearance of Jesus and the announcement of the gospel (Acts 13:16b–33a), plus the citations from Scripture and the comparison of the resurrected Messiah to David (vv. 33b–37). The conclusion, inferred from this evidence, is drawn in verses 38–39 (RSV): "Let it be known to you, therefore, brethren, that through this man forgiveness of sins is proclaimed to you, and by him every one that believes is freed from everything from which you could not be freed by the law of Moses." By Wills's reckoning, Paul's sermon ends with a warning against repudiation of his message, at peril of perishing (vv. 40–41). To what extent does Wills's analysis of this sermon's structure—exempla, conclusion, and exhortation—correspond with classical dicta for arranging a discourse?

The section of this sermon identified by Wills as the exempla actually incorporates three different but closely related parts of a classical address. Following a forthright exordium in Acts 13:16b (for which Wills does not account), Paul's recital of God's salvific intervention in Israelite history (vv. 17–25) corresponds to a *narratio*: a statement of the facts of the case, presenting the personages involved as well as the time, place, and causes of pertinent occurrences (Quintilian, *Inst.* 4.2.1–3, 31). Such narration presents necessary background information on which the listener is expected to render a judgment. This is precisely the function of the exempla delineated by Wills in Acts 13:16b–37 and in other Jewish and Christian homilies: "authoritative evidence adduced to commend the points that follow."[33] Acts 13:17–25 displays many qualities that Quintilian recommends for a *narratio*: Paul's statement of facts is lucid, brief, plausible, and vivid (*Inst.* 4.2.31–52, 123; also Cicero, *Inv.* 1.20.28–21.30). Presupposing the audience's attentiveness, it anticipates and

---

32. Commendably, Bowker does not force the evidence: "Unfortunately this [reconstruction] cannot be advanced beyond a guess, since part of the skill of a preacher was to allude to and to imply the readings for the day without necessarily quoting them in direct form; in the absence of direct quotation they have to be inferred from the homily itself. This means that there must always be a considerable element of doubt" ("Speeches in Acts," 103).

33. L. Wills, "Form of the Sermon," 279.

responds to the demands of the occasion (Quintilian, *Inst.* 4.2.64, 76, 119); it obviously intends not only to instruct but also to persuade (*Inst.* 4.2.21, 31).

At first blush the statement of facts in this speech seems to continue through the description of the condemnation, execution, and vindication of Jesus, in fulfillment of prophecy (Acts 13:27–37). Indeed, Wills construes all of the material in verses 16b–37 as constituting the exempla. This analysis is plausible but founders at verse 26: here Paul sums up his narrative of salvation history in verses 17–25 with the assertion that the message of salvation, reaching its climax in Jesus, has been issued both to Jews and to God-fearers. This appears to function, not so much as another datum in a recital of exempla, but as a lucid proposition (*propositio*), the proof (*probatio*) for which is presented in verses 27–37: a demonstration that the significance of Jesus, formerly ignored by the inhabitants of Jerusalem and their rulers, has been vindicated by his resurrection and corroborated by Scripture. *Pace* Wills, in Acts 13:27–37 Luke is doing more than presenting additional, evidential exempla. From the perspective of classical rhetoric, an argument is being carefully constructed: "a process of reasoning that provides proof and enables one thing to be inferred from another and confirms uncertain facts by referring to facts that are certain" (Quintilian, *Inst.* 5.10.11).[34] Moreover, in crafting this argument for maximum persuasive impact, the creator of the *probatio* in Acts 13:27–37 has drawn on all four types of a priori "certainties" that Quintilian would later conceptualize (5.10.12–13): things perceived by the senses (the appearance of the risen Jesus to creditable witnesses, vv. 30–31), things on which there is general agreement (the providence and power of God, vv. 32–33, 37), things established by law (Scripture's fulfillment, vv. 27, 29, 33–35), and things pertaining to the issue that sympathetic members of Paul's audience would admit (Jesus' innocence and execution by Pilate, v. 28; Jesus and David's death and burial, vv. 29, 36).[35]

This brings us to Acts 13:38–41, which in Wills's analysis comprises a conclusion (vv. 38–39) and a final exhortation (vv. 40–41). In the light of classical rhetorical canons, Wills has abstracted and divided two aspects, characteristic of a speech's conclusion, that Greco-Roman rhetoricians conflated into one section known as the epilogue. Aristotle's analysis of the four requisites of an epilogue (*Rhet.* 3.18.1419b–1420b) is apropos of the content of Acts 13:38–41: rendering the audience well disposed to the orator and ill disposed toward his opponents

---

34. In "Hellenistic Rhetoric," Kurz identifies Luke's christological proof as a rhetorical enthymeme.

35. Since the primary impetus for rhetoric's conceptualization was the presentation of cases in lawcourts, classical theoreticians devoted much attention to the crafting of arguments (Aristotle, *Rhet.* 3.17.1417b–1418b; Cicero, *Inv.* 2.4.1–59.177; Cornificius, *Rhet. ad Her.* 2.2–31.50; Quintilian, *Inst.* 5.pr.1–14.35). Aristotle went so far as to generalize the arrangement of any speech as consisting of only two necessary parts, the statement of the case and its proof (*Rhet.* 3.13.1414a–b). Similarly, Quintilian suggested that "any single [part of a speech] other than the proof may on occasion be dispensed with, but there can be no suit in which the proof is not absolutely necessary" (*Inst.* 5.pr.5; cf. 3.6.104). Classical emphasis on argument and demonstration—with style and arrangement as means to these ends—should be borne in mind when considering ancient Judeo-Christian discourse.

("my brothers" [v. 38] vs. "you scoffers" [v. 41]); amplifying the leading facts ("the forgiveness of your sins" [v. 38a AT]); recapitulating the basic argument ("through union with him everyone who believes is cleared of every charge of which the law of Moses could not clear you" [vv. 38b–39 AT]); and exciting the emotions of the hearers ("Beware . . . Look . . . Then wonder and begone!" [vv. 40–41 AT]).[36] Wills is correct that this speech's final appeal, "although somewhat indirect, nevertheless carries an unmistakable hortatory tone."[37] Such indirection suggests that this speech is finally not a direct exhortation to prescribed conduct (as one finds in deliberative address) but rather an epideictic address aimed at stimulating belief. This judgment is confirmed by Luke's description of the response of Paul's audience: instead of adopting a particular course of action, left undefined by Paul, "the people begged that these things might be said to them on the following sabbath" (Acts 13:42 AT).[38] As Luke presents it,[39] the success of Paul's address at Pisidian Antioch reflects favorably, not only upon the sermon's content, but also upon its preacher's powers of persuasion.

To summarize: neither the structure nor the content of Acts 13:13–41 deviates from Greco-Roman rhetorical conventions. On the contrary, to an impressive degree, Paul's oration at Pisidian Antioch hews closely to those norms. The same could probably be argued for the other sermons considered by Wills. Thus his intuition regarding the origin of the so-called "word of exhortation" in Greco-Roman oratory has been validated, though not his judgments concerning innovative departures of that homiletical form from classical standards. The structure of these Hellenistic Jewish and early Christian sermons is altogether intelligible in the light of Aristotle's *Rhetoric*, Quintilian's *Institutio oratoria*, and the *Rhetorica ad Herennium* attributed to Cornificius.

SOME RESIDUAL QUESTIONS AND IMPLICATIONS

There is more is at stake than a pedantry to prove Wills wrong, or deficient, in his assessment of provenance for the λόγος παρακλήσεως. Once we appreciate the striking coherence of this sermonic form with classical conventions, the way is paved for us to understand more fully the function of various phenomena,

---

36. The peroration of this speech exemplifies two other qualities urged by Quintilian: its recapitulation is as brief as possible (Acts 13:38–39; cf. Quintilian, *Inst.* 6.1.2) and invokes the Deity for persuasive effect (Acts 13:40–41, citing the oracle of Yahweh in Hab. 1:5; cf. *Inst.* 6.1.34).
37. L. Wills, "Form of the Sermon," 279.
38. Stimulation of belief can change a course of action, as Acts 13:43 attests: many in Paul's audience followed him and Barnabas. To classify Acts 13:16b–41 as epideictic is to suggest only that it is primarily aimed at belief. Action based on that belief is a by-product of rhetorical effectiveness.
39. Penner reminds us, "Lukan narrative ultimately reflects on the character of the author, as much as it tries to effect elements of that character in the reader" ("Reconfiguring the Rhetorical Study," 438–39). The framework for Penner's analysis is found in idem, *In Praise of Christian Origins*.

exhibited by these homilies, to which Wills calls our attention but for which he is often unable to account.

1. Wills observes that inferential particles or conjunctions (οὖν [*oun*, "thus"], διό [*dio*, "wherefore"], διὰ τοῦτο [*dia touto*, "because"]) are used to connect these sermons' examples, conclusions, and exhortations. Such linkages are sometimes only quasi-logical, conveying an impression of deductive reasoning even though "the exact logical relations between the parts are not dictated absolutely"[40] (e.g., Acts 13:38–39; *1 Clem.* 7.2). Wills's observations are apt, but more to the point is what he omits: such logical and quasi-logical features place Jewish and Christian oratory squarely in the mainstream of classical rhetoric. Regarding style, Quintilian urges the orator to fashion smooth transitions between the various parts of a speech (*Inst.* 4.1.76; 4.4.2; 9.4.32–33). In matters of substance, however, Quintilian is fully aware that a degree of legerdemain characterizes some arguments' "logic";[41] he and other theorists describe the *logos* of a speech as either proof or the *appearance* of proof.[42] It is hardly surprising, therefore, that Hellenistic Jewish and early Christian sermons display the *forms* of logical argument, even though those arguments' *validity* depend on premises that cannot be logically or objectively demonstrated. Those same phenomena are exhibited in other types of NT rhetoric[43] and are consistent with the classical understanding of *logos* as entailing probable argument rather than logical certainty.

2. Of course, practitioners of the word of exhortation did not lack interest in logical argument. Wills has made his case that the form of those sermons evinces a commitment to the persuasiveness of inductive reasoning. What he has not explained is *why* this recurring pattern of argument, based upon exempla, would have been considered convincing by a Hellenistic audience.

Once again, an awareness of classical rhetoric's modus operandi offers us some clues. Aristotle distinguishes two different kinds of proof: external or nonartistic (ἄτεχνοι [*atechnoi*]) proofs, not created by the speaker but already in existence (such as witnesses); and internal or artistic (ἔντεχνοι [*entechnoi*]) proofs, invented by the speaker (such as rhetorical syllogisms, or "enthymemes").[44] In theory both types of proof were acceptable, though both had their drawbacks or limitations, and one type was more effective than the other for use in different spe-

---

40. L. Wills, "Form of the Sermon," 284.

41. Thus he states that the most artful rhetoric conceals its artistry, thereby hoodwinking the listener who sits in judgment (Quintilian, *Inst.* 4.1.57; 4.2.58–59; 4.5.5; 9.4.147). Such sleight of hand does not appear to violate Quintilian's unshakable conviction that the consummate orator must first be a good and honorable man (*Inst.* 1.pr.9–20; 1.2.3; 2.2.1–8; 2.16.11; 2.20.4; 12.1.1–2.10; et passim).

42. Aristotle, *Rhet.* 1.2.1356a–1356b. Note also—in Cornificius, *Rhet. ad Her.* 3.10.18; and Quintilian, *Inst.* 5.12.4; 7.1.17—counsels for careful disposition of the orator's strongest arguments for optimal persuasive effect.

43. As Kennedy has shown, with reference to the Beatitudes in the Matthean Sermon on the Mount (*New Testament Interpretation*, 49–50).

44. Aristotle, *Rhet.* 1.2.1355b–1356b; 2.20.1393ab; Cicero, *Inv.* 1.34.57–41.77; Quintilian, *Inst.* 5.1.1–3; 5.10.1; 5.14.1; 8.5.9.

cies of rhetoric. For instance, Aristotle and Quintilian regarded deductive proof based on enthymemes as more persuasive in forensic oratory, whereas inductive reasoning based on examples was valuable in deliberative speeches (Aristotle, *Rhet.* 1.9.1368a; 3.17.1418a; Quintilian, *Inst.* 3.8.36).

Although enthymematic argument is not absent from the sermons analyzed by Wills,[45] and while the preachers under consideration are by no means hesitant to use intentional proofs of theological or christological exposition,[46] by far the most frequently cited proofs are examples (παραδείγματα [*paradeigmata*], Aristotle; *exempla*, Quintilian). These may be categorized:[47]

    a. *Citations from Scriptures:* Acts 2:17–21, 25–28, 34–35; 13:33–35; 2 Cor. 6:16–18; Heb. 1:5–13; 3:7–11, 15; 8:8–12; 1 Pet. 2:6–8; *1 Clem.* 30.1–8; 53.1–5; *Barnabas* passim

    b. *Historical figures:* Acts 7:2–50; 1 Cor. 10:1–14; Heb. 11:1–40; 2 Pet. 2:4–10; *1 Clem.* 4.1–12.8; 17.1–18.17; 43.1–6; 47.1–7; *Testaments of the Twelve Patriarchs;* Josephus, *J.W.* passim

    c. *Eyewitnesses to crucial events:* Acts 2:32; 3:15b; 13:31; 20:18b, 34; 2 Pet. 2:16–19a; *1 Clem.* 42.1–5; 44.1–6; *T. Jos.* 1–18; *T. Benj.* 2.1–5; 10.1–11:5; *J.W.* 1.1–12

    d. *Appeals to supernatural authority:* Acts 2:33; 3:12, 16; 11:17; 1 Cor. 7:40; Heb. 2:4; 1 Pet. 1:10–12; 2 Pet. 1:3–4; *1 Clem.* 8.1; 9.1; 58.1–2; *T. Levi* 2.6–9.14; *T. Naph.* 5.1–6.10

Judged by classical standards, Hellenistic Jewish and early Christian sermons exhibit nuanced, sophisticated forms of proof.[48] Tacitly conforming to Quintilian's admonitions, their creators draw liberally and creatively from all the material at their disposal (*Inst.* 2.21.4, 20); their arguments are sensitive to the circumstances of the cases in which they are involved (5.10.119–21; 10.2.25–28); their ultimate

---

45. Behind 1 Pet. 1:17–21 lies a logical syllogism: a suppressed major premise ("Those with a proper regard for God and Christ will stand secure in faith, hope, and godly fear"), a stated minor premise ("The Christian exiles in Asia Minor confidently regard God as father and impartial judge, who raised from the dead Christ, who is their predestined, imperishable, and spotless ransom from futility"), and a conclusion ("The faith, hope, and reverence of the exiled Christians are secure and to be expected"). Though the reasoning here is hardly pellucid, I regard this a more plausible reckoning of its argument than that of Wills, who with trepidation parses this sentence into the exhortation of one sermonic cycle and another cycle's exempla and conclusion ("Form of the Sermon," 289–90).

46. Thus *T. Naph.* 2.2–10; Acts 3:12–26; 13:17–33a, 38–39; 17:24–31; 1 Cor. 10:1–14; Heb. 2:14–18; 5:1–10; 6:13–7:28; 8:1–7; 9:1–10:18; 1 Pet. 2:21–25; 3:18–22; 2 Pet. 2:4–10a; *1 Clem.* 16.1–17; 20.1–12.

47. For discussion, consult Aristotle, *Rhet.* 1.15.1375a–1376a; Cornificius, *Rhet. ad Her.* 2.6.9; and Quintilian, *Inst.* 5.7.9–25; 5.11.8, 32–44. Jewish and Christian arguments based on Scripture appear analogous to classical proofs from legal documents (cf. Aristotle, *Rhet.* 1.15.1375ab; Cicero, *Inv.* 1.12.17–18; Quintilian, *Inst.* 5.11.32–33).

48. One is tempted to generalize Evans's comments about Peter's Pentecost address in Acts 2:14–40: "Such close-knit argumentation would seem to put a question mark against the assumption that in view of their brevity the speeches in Acts are to be regarded as summaries only, to be expanded in the mind into a more detailed version of what was said, or filled out with elements of the Christian messages deemed to be missing; as also against the view that they are to be seen primarily as typical examples of Christian preaching and models of how the message was to be proclaimed" ("'Speeches' in Acts," 296).

concern is the confirmation of positions that may be in doubt by reference to evidence that their audiences would admit as certain (5.10–11).

3. Wills notes that the structural element in the Jewish or Christian λόγος παρακλήσεως demarcated as the "exhortation" sometimes provides a link between separable cycles of argument within the sermon: the exhortation can refer backward, forward, or in both directions (thus Heb. 2:1; 3:1; 4:1, 14b–16; *1 Clem.* 7.2; 13.1a; 40.1b). The issue here is that of coherence: the cohesion of different arguments into a single idea. Once more we are confronted with a phenomenon best understood, not as a departure from classical canons, but rather as exemplifying those standards. As early as 370 BCE Plato recognized that "any discourse ought to be constructed like a living creature, with its own body, so to speak; it must not lack either head or feet; it must have a middle and extremities so composed as to fit each other and the whole work" (*Phaedr.* 264c6–9). Quintilian develops this principle (*Inst.* 4.2.55; 7.10.5–9, 16–17; 8.5.34), stressing the importance of coherence among the parts of a speech, achieved by the reflexive interplay between matters recounted in the *narratio* with arguments presented in the *probatio.* When in Jewish and Christian sermons we observe the reflexive character of the exhortations and arguments that surround them, can we doubt their authors' concern for rhetorical coherence?

4. After recognizing repetitive cycles of exhortation within some Hellenistic Jewish and early Christian documents, Wills draws a double-pronged conclusion: "Since the speeches in Greek literature do not repeat the three-part [exempla-conclusion-exhortation] pattern, it is most likely that where we find repeating cycles we have even stronger evidence of specifically sermonic material, and not simply a literary adaptation of Greek rhetorical forms."[49] Again one wonders if Wills attributes greater novelty to these sermons than the evidence demands. Recall, first, that a number of Wills's examples of repeated, cyclical exhortations occur within the broader context of literary genres that do not overtly intend to function as self-contained orations (the various speeches in Acts, a theological history of the church; the biblical interpretations scattered throughout letters like 1 Corinthians and *Barnabas*). Comparing the sermonic cycles in Acts with a unified Greek oration is to confuse peaches with pears. Second, even on Wills's terms, it is fallacious to suggest that "the speeches in Greek literature do not repeat the three-part pattern." Although any number of examples might be cited to rebut this assessment, one selected at random must suffice: the funeral oration delivered by Pericles on behalf of the fallen Athenians, which, as presented by Thucydides (*Hist.* 2.34–46), displays at least three different cycles of (what Wills would classify as) exempla,

49. L. Wills, "Form of the Sermon," 299, referring to *T. Naph.* 8.1–2; 8.9–10; *T. Jos.* 10.1–2; 17.1–2; *T. Benj.* 2.5–3.1; 4.1a–b; 6.7–7.1; 7.5–8.1; 10.2–3; Josephus, *J.W.* 5.362–415; 7.341–80; Heb. 1:5–4:16; 8:1–12:28b; *1 Clem.* 4.1–13.1a; 37.2–40.1b; Ign. *Eph.* 3.1–4.2; 5.1–3b; 7.18a–10.1.

conclusion, and exhortation.[50] Third, such classical orators not only admitted repetition: they also esteemed it. When the authors of Hebrews and *1 Clement* augment complementary ideas with multiple arguments, they are engaged in what classical handbooks call "amplification" or "refinement": "dwelling on the same topic and yet seeming to say something ever new . . . by merely repeating the same idea, or by descanting upon it" (Cornificius, *Rhet. ad Her.* 4.42.54). Such a procedure betokens no verbosity or impoverishment of ideas: one measure of the ideal orator, in Quintilian's opinion, is the talent "[to] cast the same thought into a number of different forms, . . . [to] dwell on one point and linger over the same idea" (*Inst.* 9.1.41; also 4.5.14–17; 8.4.3–29).

5. Finally, the congruence of the word of exhortation with classical oratory offers a perspective from which regular deviations from that argumentative form may be better viewed. When works such as Hebrews (5:1–7:28), 2 Peter (1:12–3:2), *1 Clement* (42.1–44.6), *Barnabas* (7.3–16.10), and Ignatius, *To the Ephesians* (17.2–20.2) depart from established hortatory patterns to present extended exempla or theological expositions, at least two motivations seem at work. First, such departures might be regarded as "digressions," pertinent and sometimes vivid examinations of the circumstances attending major points at issue (Aristotle, *Rhet.* 1.9.1368a; Quintilian, *Inst.* 6.2.29–36; 8.3.61). Second, such digressions reveal concerns that are less than strictly hortatory and more obviously forensic or epideictic in character.[51] If so, then Wills's designation of these sermons as "exhortations" may be overly restrictive, notwithstanding some works' use of the appellation λόγος παρακλήσεως.

In short: there are genuine benefits in regarding Hellenistic Jewish and early Christian sermons in concert with, rather than as innovative departures from, Greco-Roman oratory. From that standpoint we can better understand their use of logical and quasi-logical argument, the rhetorical function of certain exhortations in building transitional bridges between arguments, and the role played by repetitions of, and deviations from, established patterns of argument. Practically all questions

---

50. Cycle #1: praise of Athenian government, games, warfare, and nobility (Thucydides, *Hist.* 2.37–40), followed by a conclusion (Athens is the school of Hellas: 2.41.1–5a) and exhortation (surviving Athenians should willingly suffer for the city's sake: 2.41.5b); cycle #2: praise of the Athenians slain in battle (2.42.1–4), followed by a conclusion (the nobility of their death befitted their city: 2.43.1) and three exhortations to a noble life among their survivors (2.43.1, 4); cycle #3: sympathy with the parents of those who have fallen (2.44.1–2), followed by an exhortation to bear up in the hope of other children (2.44.3), based on the conclusion that new sons will secure the city in the future, dispelling painful memories of old sons lost in war (2.44.3). Notice that multiple exhortations occur in one of these cycles—a phenomenon Wills recognizes in some early Christian λόγοι παρακλήσεως (see "Form of the Sermon," 282, 284, and 287 on Heb. 10:22–25; *1 Clem.* 9.1; and Acts 20:28, 31).

51. For example, the lengthy doctrinal and largely nonhortatory section in Heb. 6:1–10:18 appears anomalous only if one is scrutinizing that document with an eye for "the word of exhortation." That anomaly vanishes once we remember that the author explicitly aims, not only to admonish (6:1), but also to entrench present belief, based on a proper understanding of past events (the superior, once-for-all sacrifice of Christ as heavenly high priest, a sacrifice for the sins of many).

left dangling in Wills's analysis are resolved by locating first-century Jewish and Christian preaching within the mainstream of classical and Hellenistic rhetoric.[52]

CONCLUSIONS AND AVENUES FOR FURTHER INVESTIGATION

Lawrence Wills has rendered considerable service in our understanding of the form of Hellenistic Jewish and early Christian sermons. The point at which this chapter has attempted to build on his work has entailed disagreement with one of his principal conclusions: *pace* Wills, the form of the "word of exhortation" conforms to the standards of ancient oratory. Once we recognize this basic alignment of Judeo-Christian preaching with the prevailing rhetorical norms of its time, most of the ill-fitting phenomena uncovered by Wills fall neatly into place.

Neither Wills's study nor my own has drawn this line of investigation to a close. Much work remains; here are some suggestions.

First, if my findings are valid, we need to dig more deeply into these sermons and inquire, from a classical frame of reference, precisely how they exert persuasive impact. Do the Jewish and Christian sermons cited by Wills presuppose the same *stases*, the same formulations of the basic issue of the case?[53] Are the arguments in those sermons devised in terms of the same rhetorical topics (*topoi*, or *loci*)?[54] How might the *style* of these sermons—their diction and composition, their employment of tropes and figures—be characterized?[55] What modes of persuasion other than logical argument (*logos*) are in play in these sermons? Specifically, how effective are their *ēthos* and *pathos*: the credibility of the preacher's character and the emotional reactions generated among his listeners?[56] Aligning the λόγος παρακλήσεως with classical standards provides the basis for more finely tuned rhetorical discriminations.[57]

---

52. That said, one can push the evidence too far, as does Oporto ("La articulación literaria del Libro de los Hechos") by pressing the whole of Acts into the disposition of a classical speech.

53. Anticipated by Aristotle (*Rhet.* 3.17.1417b), the primary questions at issue in a case—fact, definition, quality, and jurisdiction—were outlined by Cicero (*Inv.* 2.14.12–39.115) and Quintilian (*Inst.* 5.10.53; 8.pr.8) and elaborated by Hermogenes of Tarsus (*Peri ideōn*) in the late second century CE.

54. On "common" and "material" topics, consult Aristotle, *Rhet.* 1.3.1359a–8.1366a; 2.18.1391b–19.1393a; 2.23.1397a–1400b; Cicero, *Inv.* 2.15.48–50; Quintilian, *Inst.* 5.10.20–52.

55. On style, see Aristotle, *Rhet.* 3.2.1404b–7.1408b; Demetrius, *De elocutione*; Cornificius, *Rhet. ad Her.* 4.8.11–55.69; Quintilian, *Inst.* 8.1.1–9.4.147.

56. For discussions of these modes of persuasion and the oratorical duties germane to each, see Aristotle, *Rhet.* 1.2.1356a; 1.15.1377b–2.1.1378a; 3.1.1403b; Cicero, *De or.* 2.27.115; 2.43.183–85; idem, *Or.* 69; Quintilian, *Inst.* 3.5.2; 3.8.15–16; 6.2.9–20; 8.pr.7; 12.10.58–59; Augustine, *Doctr. chr.* 4.27–33.

57. Two recent studies open fresh avenues of research. Forbes ("Comparison, Self-Praise and Irony") demonstrates Paul's sophisticated adaptation of the familiar rhetorical conventions of comparison (σύγκρισις [*synkrisis*]), bragging (ἀλαζονεία [*alazoneia*]), and ironic self-depreciation (εἰρωνεία [*eirōneia*]) in 2 Cor. 10–12. D. L. Smith (*The Rhetoric of Interruption*) argues that Luke's peculiar use of interrupted discourse, esp. in Acts, highlights controversial yet nonnegotiable claims of the gospel: Jesus' exaltation and salvation for the Gentiles (e.g., Acts 4:1; 7:57; 13:48; 22:22; 26:24).

Second, it remains a moot question whether the form isolated by Wills was a distinctive homiletical pattern, characteristic primarily of coreligionists' proclamations and not of sermons preached to outsiders. I find that most of the features to which Wills has alerted us—their persuasive aims, argumentative strategies, stereotyped structure—tend to nudge the "word of exhortation" closer to conventional rhetoric, not farther away. Support for this conclusion is provided, ironically, by Wills himself: though he seeks to define the form of sermons preached to religious "insiders," Wills construes Paul's speech to "outsiders" at Pisidian Antioch (Acts 13:13–41) as paradigmatic of that form; and the equally anomalous speeches of the town clerk at Ephesus (19:35–40) and of the elders at Jerusalem (21:20–25) allegedly exemplify "coreligionists' liturgical address."[58] These, I think, are telling indicators that Wills is in touch with a broader, more basic rhetorical pattern, such as I have presented above, not with a uniquely liturgical product. Once we are clear about this, continued research could delineate precise, creative modifications of Greco-Roman oratory by its Hellenistic Jewish and Christian practitioners.[59]

Finally, the usefulness of rhetorical analysis in assessing some dimensions of the form and content of biblical and intertestamental literature is validated once more. Rhetorical criticism takes seriously the fact that most of these documents were addressed not just to the eye but also to the ear. As Aristotle would have understood (Rhet. 1.2.1355b), all were written with the intent to persuade—although he would not have countenanced the NT's sticking point: that Christian conduct depends on Christian faith in a crucified Messiah. The study of rhetoric helps us better to understand both the pervasiveness and the limits of logic in religious proclamation. The extraordinary degree to which rhetoric was conceptualized enables us better to control and to develop our exegetical intuitions in the reading of ancient texts. Rhetorical criticism is no interpretive panacea; no single method can address all queries lodged by biblical interpreters. Still, in analyzing the sermons to which Lawrence Wills has drawn our attention, rhetorical criticism holds promise, not only in illuminating their form, but also in accounting for their power.

58. L. Wills, "Form of the Sermon," 278–80, 287–88; cf. 277–78.
59. In this connection recall Schweizer's astute observation that while the speeches in Acts evince "a far-reaching identity of structure . . . [,] the christological kerygma is replaced by the theological one wherever a typical Gentile congregation is listening" ("Concerning the Speeches," 210, 214).

Preaching

Chapter Eight

Four Stations en Route to a Parabolic Homiletic

I gave orders for my horse to be brought round from the stable. The servant did not understand me. I myself went to the stable, saddled my horse and mounted. In the distance I heard a bugle call, I asked him what this meant. He knew nothing and had heard nothing. At the gate he stopped me, asking: "Where are you riding to, master?" "I don't know," I said, "only away from here, away from here. Always away from here, only by doing so can I reach my destination." "And so you know your destination?" he asked. "Yes," I answered, "didn't I say so? Away-From-Here, that is my destination." "You have no provisions with you," he said. "I need none," I said, "the journey is so long that I must die of hunger if I don't get anything on the way. No provisions can save me. For it is, fortunately, a truly immense journey."

Franz Kafka[1]

NINEVEH

The word of the LORD came to Jonah son of Amittai: Go at once to Nineveh, that great city, and proclaim judgment upon it; for their wickedness has come before Me.

Jonah, however, started out to flee to Tarshish from the LORD's service. . . . But the LORD cast a mighty wind upon the sea, and such a great tempest came upon the sea that the ship was in danger of breaking up. . . .

Then [the sailors] cried out to the LORD: "Oh, please, LORD, do not let us perish on account of this man's life." . . . And they heaved Jonah overboard, and the sea stopped raging.

---

1. Kafka, *Parables and Paradoxes*, trans. E. Kaiser and E. Wilkins, 189.

The men feared the LORD greatly, and they offered a sacrifice to the LORD and they made vows.

The LORD provided a huge fish to swallow Jonah; and Jonah remained in the fish's belly three days and three nights. Jonah prayed to the LORD his God from the belly of the fish. . . .

The LORD commanded the fish, and it spewed Jonah out upon dry land.

The word of the LORD came to Jonah a second time: "Go at once to Nineveh, that great city, and proclaim to it what I tell you." Jonah went at once to Nineveh in accordance with the LORD's command. . . .

Jonah . . . proclaimed: "Forty days more, and Nineveh shall be overthrown!"

The people of Nineveh believed God. They proclaimed a fast, and great and small alike put on sackcloth. . . .

God saw what they did, how they were turning back from their evil ways. And God renounced the punishment He had planned to bring upon them, and did not carry it out.

This displeased Jonah greatly, and he was grieved. He prayed to the LORD, saying, "O LORD! Isn't this just what I said when I was still in my own country? That is why I fled beforehand to Tarshish. For I know that You are a compassionate and gracious God, slow to anger, abounding in kindness, renouncing punishment. Please, LORD, take my life, for I would rather die than live." The LORD replied, "Are you that deeply grieved? . . . You cared about the plant, which you did not work for and which you did not grow, which appeared overnight and perished overnight. And should not I care about Nineveh, that great city, in which there are more than a hundred and twenty thousand persons who do not know their right hand from their left, and many beasts as well?" (Jonah 1:1–3a, 4, 14a, 15–16; 2:1–2, 11; 3:1–3a, 4b–5, 10; 4:1–4, 10b–11 NJPS)

Hear then the parable. What, then, is a parable? At its simplest a parable is a metaphor: "Judah is a lion's whelp" (Gen. 49:9). Stretch the metaphor into a similitude: "This generation . . . is like children sitting in the marketplaces and calling to one another, 'We piped to you, and you did not dance; we wailed, and you did not mourn'" (Matt. 11:16b–17 RSV/NRSV). Unfold a simile, and you have a parable proper: "The word of the LORD came to Jonah son of Amittai: . . . 'Are you that deeply grieved? . . . Should not I care about Nineveh?'"[2] Among NT scholars, no definition of a parable has enjoyed wider currency than that proposed in 1935 by C. H. Dodd: "At its simplest the parable is a metaphor or simile drawn from nature or common life, arresting the hearer by its vividness or strangeness, and leaving the mind in sufficient doubt about its precise application to tease it into active thought."[3] Admirable as Dodd's definition is, it lacks one vital element.

2. V. Taylor, *Formation of the Gospel Tradition*, 88–118, elaborates this taxonomy.
3. Dodd, *Parables of the Kingdom*, 5.

Literally translated, the term "parable" (ἡ παραβολή [hē parabolē]) refers to something "thrown alongside" something else. It is that "thrown-besideness," that collision of this world with God's word, that accounts for so much in Dodd's definition: the metaphorical quality, the vivid strangeness, the doubtful tease. When everyday reality is pierced by divine revelation, a parabolē has happened: a parable is uttered. That's why, in Mark's Gospel (1:14–15 AT), "the season is filled up, and God's dominion is at hand" when Jesus so much as sets foot in Galilee, before he has said or done a thing. It may also explain Mark's comment that Jesus "did not speak to them without a parable" (4:34b RSV), even though Jesus in that Gospel says many things without an obscure story attached, and some things very "plainly" (8:32a RSV). Mark speaks of Jesus theologically, not form-critically: wherever Jesus treads, God's parable pops. Invariably that occurrence is a jolt to his followers' religious imagination and a shock to their nervous system. "They were amazed, and those who followed were afraid" (Mark 10:32b).

From this proposal follow two corollaries. The first is twinned: A parable may be but is not necessarily an exercise in storytelling; not every story told in a religious setting functions parabolically. When the Johannine Jesus professes, "I am the bread of life; one who comes to me shall never hunger, and one who believes in me shall never thirst" (John 6:35 AT), the Fourth Gospel is trading in parable, albeit one expressed differently from anything we find in the Synoptics.[4] By that announcement of Jesus, our deepest hunger and most profound thirst have been brought into the presence of the true God, more nourishing than any food or drink this world can offer. We may come to Jesus and believe; we may disbelieve and withdraw. Whatever our response, our encounter with reality has been forever transformed. Moreover, not every story recounted in a religious setting functions parabolically, at least in the Christian sense of a parable. For Leonard Bernstein, a narrative taught; for Ronald Reagan, an anecdote won votes; for Garrison Keillor, a story entertains. For a preacher of the gospel, a parable explodes this world with God's power. Absent that theoburst, we may have spun a yarn, but we have not voiced a parable.[5]

A second corollary is positive, though subject to misinterpretation. Authentic Christian preaching may be construed as an intrinsically parabolic activity. So saying, I do not urge that every sermon take as its text a parable. Neither do I suggest that to make its point, all preaching must create or adopt a parable, or be framed as a parabolic story. Nor can Christian preaching be reduced to parables or to a parabolic template for homiletics.[6] My point is neither formal nor tactical, but theological: namely, whatever else it may be, Christian preaching is nothing

---

4. Schweizer, "Johannine 'Parables.'"
5. Similarly, Wilder, *Early Christian Rhetoric*, 71–88.
6. Two studies that take up the parables for practical preaching more directly than I do are Long, *Preaching and the Literary Forms*; and Sensing, "Imitating the Genre of Parable."

less than a life-giving encounter between human hunger and godly nurture. By its very nature preaching is parabolic, because preaching is that jarring-but-exquisite clash of inescapable human need with God's merciful power.[7] Thus we may say of every preacher who faithfully mounts a pulpit precisely what Justin Martyr observed of Christ: "Brief and concise utterances fell from him, for He was no sophist, but His Word was the power of God" (*1 Apol.* 14.5).

GALILEE

And he said to his disciples, "There was a rich man who had a manager, and it was reported to him that this fellow was squandering his property. So he called him in and said to him, 'What's this that I hear about you? Make an accounting for your conduct of my affairs, for you cannot be my manager any longer!' Then the manager said to himself, 'What am I going to do, because my master is going to take my position away from me? Dig? I am not strong enough. Beg? I should be too ashamed. I know what I will do, so that when I am removed from my position people will take me into their homes.' Then he called in each of his master's debtors, and he said to the first one, 'How much do you owe my master?' The fellow said, 'Eight hundred gallons of oil.' And he said to him, 'Here's your agreement; sit right down and write four hundred!' Then he said to another, 'And how much do you owe?' He answered, 'Fifteen hundred bushels of wheat.' He said to him, 'Here's your agreement; write twelve hundred.' And his master praised the dishonest manager, because he had acted shrewdly." (Luke 16:1–8a, GOODSPEED, alt.)

Any view of Jesus' parables as "sermon illustrations," intended to tighten our grasp of exemplary religious or moral verities, must eventually fall afoul of a certain wily estate manager. Practically from the moment this parable found its way into Luke's Gospel, its interpretation has been confounded by deep, possibly incorrigible, ignorance of first-century business practices and social mores, as well as severe uncertainty about the conduct commended in the (probably) first inter-pretations of the parable in Luke 16:8b–13.[8] Some kind of dishonesty surrounds the steward, both before and after the alleged discovery of his embezzlement of funds (16:1). Implicated either by bad judgment in employing a wild charlatan, or charging exorbitant rental fees, or sanctioning illicit loan reductions in order

---

7. The same could be said for some forms of Christian education: see Boys, "Parabolic Ways of Teaching"; Cavalletti, "The Parable Method and Catechesis." N.B. the latter's comment: "The parable—constituted . . . of a relation between an element taken from the everyday level of existence with another taken from the transcendental level—appears as 'Incarnated' and thus as the privileged instrument in the transmission of the Mystery of the Incarnation" (90).

8. Wailes (*Medieval Allegories*, 245–53) summarizes medieval attempts to interpret Luke 16:1–8 tropologically; historical-critical endeavors are reviewed by Hendrickx, *Parables of Jesus*, 170–97.

to save his own face—or possibly some combination of all—the conduct of the plutocrat himself is not beyond reproach (cf. Luke's criticisms of the rich in 6:24; 12:16; 14:12; 16:19–22). Beyond the involvement of these picaresque characters, tainted by "dishonest wealth" (ὁ μαμωνᾶς τῆς ἀδικίας [ho mamōnas tēs adikias], 16:9), there is among contemporary commentators virtually no consensus on just what Luke is driving at.[9]

One may protest that a shady steward is the joker in a pleasantly predictable deck. Yet just how innocuous are the other cards the evangelists deal us? "Good" Samaritans (Luke 10:29–37)? Oh, come now. Day traders rewarded, mattress stuffers punished (cf. Matt. 25:14–30)? Tell it to the chairman of the Federal Reserve. Parties for delinquents who crawl home after treating their parents like dirt, wasting their legacy, and throwing away their lives among pot and pigs' feces (cf. Luke 15:11–32)?[10] Get real! Pastors who exercise Harry Emerson Fosdick's prescribed ratio of one hour of preparation for every minute of delivery yet receive the same salary as Jughead Joe who cobbles up a sermon while cruising to church (cf. Matt. 20:1–16)? Please.

The parable as pedagogical instrument enjoyed a venerable life in ancient Greece, Israel, and Rome. In *The Art of Rhetoric* Aristotle (384–322 BCE) considers *parabolē* an essential tool of logical persuasion, exemplified by a famous Socratic parable: it is as stupid to elect officials by rolling dice as to select athletes or sailors at random, regardless of their ability to compete or navigate (2.20.4). Among the wisdom handed down by Ben Sirach (180 BCE): "In treasuries of wisdom are *parabolai* of knowledge, but godliness is an abomination to a sinner" (1:25).[11] Observing that the Greek *parabolē* was equivalent to the Latin *similitudo*, Quintilian (ca. 35–95 CE) offers a practical example for speechcraft: "If you want to argue that the mind requires cultivation, you would use a comparison drawn from the soil, which if neglected yields thorns and thickets, but if cultivated will bear fruit" (*Inst.* 5.11.1–5, 24).

George Kennedy suggests other reasons for Jesus' use of parables, which Kennedy defines as inductive arguments with unstated conclusions. "Parables could

9. Some representative alternatives: "Christian disciples are also faced with a crisis by the kingdom/judgment preaching of Jesus, and the prudent use of material possessions might be recommended in the light of that crisis" (Fitzmyer, *Luke (X–XXIV)*, 1098); Jesus' disciples ought to be "canceling debts and giving wealth away" (Tannehill, *Luke*, 249); "'Children of this age'... understand how the world works and use it to their benefit; why do 'children of light' not understand the ways of the kingdom of God?" (Joel Green, *Gospel of Luke*, 593); "It is precisely how we handle the difficult and morally ambiguous situations presented to us in real life that we reveal our true character" (Landry and May, "Honor Restored," 308). These and other exegetical conundrums in Luke 16:1–8a are considered in chap. 4 above.

10. With Carroll (*Gospel of Luke*, 322), I agree that Luke teases us to correlate the dubious actions of the prodigal and his father in 15:11–32 with those of the manager and his boss in 16:1–8a.

11. On the porous membranes between sapiential proverb and prophetic figurative speech, see Herbert, "The 'Parable' (*MĀŠĀL*)"; Westermann, *Parables of Jesus*. Schipper (*Parables and Conflict*) notices the blinding quality of parabolic discourse in the OT.

have been useful to Jesus in avoiding confrontation with the Pharisees, but they would have been equally useful in maintaining communication with that part of the wider public who represented Jesus' main hope of a sympathetic audience." In a Gospel like Mark, wherein Jesus' teaching relies almost entirely on parables, we witness "radical Christian rhetoric, a form of 'sacred language' characterized by assertion and absolute claims of authoritative truth without evidence or logical argument."[12]

With Kennedy I concur that the rhetoric of the Gospels is "radical," both "at root" and "hyperbolically." Thus: "If your hand causes you to stumble, chop it off. It is nobler for you to go through life maimed than to depart into the Gehenna of unquenchable fire with two hands" (Mark 9:43 AT). I am struck, nevertheless, by how wide of the mark some of Kennedy's assessments appear when placed alongside the Gospels. Far from evading the religious authorities, Jesus' parables typically provoke their ire. Thus the scribes and chief priests know that Jesus has leveled the parable of the Vineyard against them (Luke 20:19). In Matthew, where the disciples claim to understand the parables, Jesus blatantly insists that his parables punish Israel at the same time that they bless the believing church (13:13–17). In John (6:60, 66 AT) it becomes even worse: so graphic is the parable of Ingesting Christ—"the one who munches my flesh and drinks my blood has eternal life"— that many of Jesus' own disciples confess their inability to swallow language so revulsive, draw back, and refuse to follow him farther.

Perhaps the biggest question generated by Kennedy's view of the parables is his assumption that they are probative for "good rhetoric": namely, discourse that is logically compelling.[13] For all the syllogisms discerned by Kennedy in Jesus' Beatitudes (Matt. 5:3–12 = Luke 6:20–23), I fail to see how they prove anything to those not predisposed by faith to recognize that, in Jesus, a new age has dawned in which the poor and unjustly persecuted already enjoy the kingdom of heaven. A similar problem bedevils homiletical studies that helpfully remind us of those persuasive and performative traditions from which today's preaching emerges, while little recognizing that Jesus' parables have at least as much to do with *blinding* as with illuminating their audience (Mark 4:10–12).[14] Preaching à la Jesus reveals not merely the staggering profusion of a remnant inexplicably responsive to an indiscriminate sower; it also exposes the futility of a word sown among 75 percent of its audience (Mark 4:3–9). Performance? Persuasion? Show me a church that has perceived the gospel in some outrageous cooking of a fat cat's books, and I'll show you a miracle of faith instigated by the Holy Spirit. And that—neither our cogency nor our eloquence—is precisely the point.

---

12. Kennedy, *New Testament Interpretation*, 71, 104.
13. Ibid., 45–63.
14. Among others, see Lowry, *How to Preach*, 19–41; P. Wilson, *Practice of Preaching*, 61–124, 197–284; Childers, *Performing the Word*; Buttrick, *Speaking Parables*.

HIPPO

> Thus the Father is God, the Son is God, the Holy Spirit is God; and the
> Father is good, the Son is good, the Holy Spirit is good; and the Father
> is almighty, the Son is almighty, the Holy Spirit is almighty; yet there are
> not three Gods, or three good ones, or three almighty ones, but one God,
> good and almighty, the Trinity itself. . . . Let [the mind] then remember
> its God to whose image it was made, and understand and love him. To
> put it in a word, let it worship the uncreated God, by whom it was created
> with a capacity for God and able to share in him. In this way it will be
> wise not with its own light but by sharing in that supreme light, and it
> will reign in happiness where it reigns eternal. (Augustine, *Trin.* 8.pr.1;
> 14.4.15)[15]

It is natural to regard Augustine of Hippo (354–430 CE) as a man of letters.
No Christian thinker in the West, before or since, has exerted greater influence
on Christian theology than he. We tend to forget that his prolific, pivotal master-
pieces, like *The Trinity*, were written on the margins of his life as a busy bishop in
the scruffy African harbor town of Hippo Regius (near present-day Annaba, Alge-
ria). There he functioned as parish priest to mostly poor, largely illiterate, brutally
hot-tempered, thoroughly superstitious Christians. His day-to-day work was consumed by pastoral care, arbitrating civil cases, humanizing Rome's judicial and
penal machinery, and trawling a bottomless river of correspondence. His prayer
life suffered; he complained of being sucked into useless, time-wasting duties that
he nevertheless discharged with scrupulous care. Yet among Augustine's daily
responsibilities no activity outstripped preaching.[16] He did it every day, usually
more than once a day, in sermons that, depending on the liturgical circumstances,
ranged in length from ten minutes to two hours. What did he think he was accom-
plishing? On an anniversary of his consecration, he tells us: "To rebuke those who
stir up strife, to comfort those of small courage, to stand beside the weak, to refute
opponents, to be wary in sidestepping traps, to teach the ignorant, to shake the
lazy awake, to discourage those consumed by buying and selling, to put the pre-
sumptuous in their place, to mollify the quarrelsome, to help the poor, to liberate
the oppressed, to encourage the good, to suffer the evil, and to love all people"
(*Serm.* 340.1). Augustine yearned for escape from the rat race. "Yet," he confessed,
"it is the gospel itself that makes me fear that [softer] way of life. Sure, I can say:
'What do I get out of boring people, reproving evil, telling them, Quit this. Stop
doing that. Why should I feel responsible for others?' The gospel. It's the gospel
that reins me in" (339.4).[17]

---

15. E. Hill, trans., *Saint Augustine: The Trinity*, 241, 383.
16. Bright: "Here is his home and his place, his preferred environment" (*Augustine and the Bible*, xv).
17. See also van der Meer, *Augustine the Bishop*, 235–74.

Augustine is responsible for the first and arguably most influential handbook for preachers in the Western Church: *De doctrina christiana*, or *Christian Instruction* (written in 396–426).[18] Because Augustine was a professional rhetorician before his conversion to Christianity (*Conf.* 4.2), and because *Christian Instruction* is a mature work containing nearly everything he ever wrote on the art of preaching and teaching, its contents and angle of vision commend our inspection. Yet the world of this work is very strange for those who experience themselves so alienated even from modernity that they consider themselves postmodern. Into the teeth of common sense, however, I choose to fling aspects of Augustine's views on biblical interpretation and preaching that extend the parabolic challenge of Scripture itself.

Augustine enters the interpretive process by a door quite different from those of most academicians in our day. Unlike exegetes who "objectively" ground exegesis in the historical or literary specifics of pericopes, and at odds with ideological critics who "subjectively" locate interpretation within their subcultures' particular experiences, Augustine begins with a passionately theological conviction so outré that its *kairos* may have arrived: "Scripture teaches nothing but charity" (*Doctr. chr.* 3.10.36). *Caritas*, for Augustine, is a love properly ordered and conformed to the way things really are: love for the triune God, in whom alone genuine fulfillment is found; love for the neighbor, with whom this love for God is shared in common (1.22.20–1.35.39). This indivisibly double love is *the* epistemological principle of all exegesis and preaching that are set to rights. Hence, Augustine's audacious claims: "Some may think that they have understood Scripture, but if their views fail to build up this double love of God and neighbor, they have not yet succeeded in understanding" (1.36.40). Conversely, those whose views edify that double love will escape serious interpretive error even if they mistake what the biblical authors actually had in mind.[19] "Therefore, a person strengthened by faith, hope, and love, and who steadfastly holds on to them, *has no need of the Scriptures* except to instruct others" (1.39.43).[20] When was the last time that I began and concluded my lectures or sermons by underscoring their anchorage in love, then declaring their ultimate dispensability? When in our classrooms have we followed Augustine's lead in declaring with Paul: "If there are prophecies, they will lose their meaning; if there are tongues, they will cease; if there is knowledge, that too will lose its meaning" (1 Cor. 13:8 AT; cf. *Doctr. chr.* 1.39.43)?

Accept Augustine's starting point for Scripture's treatment—the twin love of God and of neighbor—and still more of our pedagogical dominoes tumble away.

---

18. On this work's influence across the Middle Ages to the Renaissance, consult English, *Reading and Wisdom*.

19. For much in this compressed paraphrase of *Doctr. chr.* 1.36.40–41, and for the translation in the preceding sentence, I am indebted to Babcock, "*Caritas* and Signification."

20. R. Green, trans., *Augustine*, 53, emphasis added.

Take, for instance, our seemingly bottomless fascination with method. More than most topics, methodological multiplication drives the Society of Biblical Literature, the Academy of Homiletics, and other professional organizations within North American theological circles. No surprise there. What accredits a guild—wherein lie its bona fides as a scholarly organization—if not the philosophy, explication, and refinement of its disciplinary methods? So conditioned, many leave *De doctrina christiana* disappointed by its dearth of strategies for preaching. Why, one could sum up Augustine's "methods" in a few pieces of practical advice: Know your listeners. Expound the Scriptures. People must understand, so be clear. Pray for clarity. If good preaching is beyond your ability, don't fret: it is better to say wisely what you cannot say well than to say well what you cannot say wisely (4.4.6–5.7; 4.8.22–10.25). "Abundantly eloquent is the preacher whose life can speak" (4:27.59).

Augustine forgot more about rhetoric than any of us will ever learn. No wonder we are affronted by his stubborn refusal to be spellbound by technique. If we are willing to hear him out, however, the bishop gives us purchase on our own predicament. Recall Augustine's critical differentiation between things to be enjoyed and things to be used. What we *enjoy*, we cling to with love for its own sake. What we *use* should aid us in attaining what we love. God, and the neighbor who is capable of enjoying God with us, are the only proper objects of love for their own sake. Where we go radically wrong is in asking that an object intended for use should supply us the fulfillment that only an object for enjoyment can provide (1.3.3–1.27.28). Just there Augustine exposes the self-delusion in all human projects whose love is radically disordered. We professionals may be overdue for examining the degree to which disordered love has tainted our theological enterprises, whose exponents find their eponym in *Dr. Strange-use: Or, How I Learned to Stop Enjoying and Love the Skill.*

Even more: Augustine had the naïveté, or temerity, to propose that Christian doctrine frames the context within which Scripture should be interpreted and preached. "Once close consideration has revealed that it is uncertain how a passage should be punctuated and articulated, we must consult the rule of faith [*regula fidei*], as it is perceived through the plainer passages of the Scriptures and the authority of the church [*ecclesiae auctoritate*]" (*Doctr. chr.* 3.2.2). Here, compressed into a single sentence, is nearly everything that historical criticism was designed to combat: an interpretive magisterium and a foisting of dogma upon the biblical word. Purged of that tyrannous mumbo jumbo by historical critics, the biblical text could be delivered, pristine, to preachers for its homiletical disposition. Or so we were promised.

Doubtless there have been times when the church and its doctrine wielded dangerously excessive influence over biblical interpretation. In my view, however, that day has been overtaken by a new era in which the prescription's side effects have vitiated its remedy. Let me be clear: as I hope this book attests, I am no defender of an ahistorical criticism.[21] Neither was Hippo's bishop.[22] But he had less patience than we with a theologically anemic historical criticism, of the sort challenged by C. K. Barrett: "History is not a matter of the past only, but an organic process in which past and present are inseparably related, and the way in which New Testament history is presented compels the student of it to ask questions about God's purpose, and his own place, in history."[23] Forgetting or rejecting such a view has eventuated in miserable consequences for preaching; if Protestants had not been so nervous about our Catholic heritage, Augustine could have helped us to see those consequences coming. First, by slicing away the Bible's doctrinal crust and stripping Scripture from its ecclesial platter, too many biblical critics have offered a famished church meatless turkey on paper plates. Even worse, we have convinced homileticians and preachers that they ought to do the same. Too often this estimate has produced sermons that were heady lectures in biblical explanation, lacking the convicting grace of scriptural interpretation. For preachers and congregations whose liturgy, hymns, creeds, and rites have not yet been so cleverly eviscerated, Sundays in many Christian congregations have become carefully orchestrated occasions for theological schizophrenia.[24]

A second outcome of Scripture's divorce from historical and practical theology should by now be obvious. Theologically dyspeptic historians and their randy, ideological offspring have not disentangled from the biblical witness a later intellectual construct—the rule of faith—without implanting puny, secularized alternatives in its place. Christians in fifth-century Hippo were invited to follow their preacher into the depths of the triune God, into whose merciful likeness they believed they were being transformed alongside mulish Jonah, Luke's cunning steward, and other rogues whose lives were invaded by weird grace.[25] To twenty-first-century Christians who share Augustine's conviction that scriptural truth is warranted by the church's authority (*Util. cred.* 14.31), that invitation is still issued. But we all know too many parishes whose preachers have guzzled from wells, deep or shallow, of socionarrative analysis, critical theory, and pop

---

21. In wrestling with texts as difficult as Luke 16:1–8a, we would be pauperized without such perceptive historical and sociological studies as cited in chap. 4 above. Yet even *with* their benefit, in this chapter we have observed how Lukan exegetes remain unable to agree on pinning down this parable's intent.

22. Without completely abandoning allegorization, Augustine's later scriptural exegesis diminishes the text's spiritual sense in favor of its literal meaning. See G. Bonner, "Augustine as Biblical Scholar."

23. Barrett, *Biblical Problems*, 3.

24. The tide may be turning: see Yeago, "The New Testament and the Nicene Dogma"; Wainwright, "Towards an Ecumenical Hermeneutic"; Braaten, "Scripture, Church, and Dogma"; C. Black, "Trinity and Exegesis."

25. I have developed this proposal in "Serving the Food."

psychotherapy that we now face a generation of piteously backward Anselmians whose understanding desperately seeks faith.[26]

The upshot of our willingness to stint on parabolic preaching—a word that nestles Scripture and human need within the mysteries of the apostolic confession—is a timid church too frightened not to two-step to whatever ditty its ambient culture pipes. The Nicene and Post-Nicene Fathers receive another coat of dust, while today's sermon pilfers fodder from tomorrow's remaindered paperbacks. Pastors who would never dream of warning their listeners away from the seven deadly sins will, without second thought, trumpet a sermon series on the "Seven Habits of Highly Effective Churches." Say what you will about the abuses of monasticism, and the record goes unchanged: "the Word in the Desert" was finally not assimilated into that diseased world. The monks proved, rather, to be agents of their culture's Christianization.[27] They kept Christian faith alive. Will our children's grandchildren be able to say the same of us?

GOLGOTHA

> For to those who are on the way to destruction, the story of the cross is sheer nonsense, but to us who are to be saved, it means the power of God. For scripture says,
> "I shall destroy the wisdom of the wise,
> And I shall thwart the shrewdness of the shrewd!"
> Where now is your philosopher? Your scholar? Today's critic? Has not God made a fool of this world's wisdom? For since in God's wisdom the world with all its wisdom did not come to know God, God resolved to save believers through the folly of the gospel message. For Jews insist upon miracles, and Greeks demand philosophy; but we proclaim Christ the crucified: a stumbling block for Jews, absurdity for Greeks, but for those whom God has called—be they Jews or Greeks—a Christ who is God's power and God's wisdom. For God's folly is beyond human wisdom, and God's weakness is beyond mortal strength. . . . God has chosen what the world calls foolish to put the wise to shame. God has chosen what the world calls weak to put the strong to shame. God has chosen what the world calls bastard and despicable, the nothings, to overthrow the world's somethings, so that no mortal may preen in God's presence. (1 Cor. 1:18–25, 27–29 AT)

In the Christian West the dominant mode of theological conversation is kataphatic: the affirmation of positive claims about God. When among ourselves we

---

26. Augustinian theology underlies Saint Anselm's, as Hoitenga ("Faith Seeks Understanding") reminds us. Witten's sociological analysis (*All Is Forgiven*) exposes the tension that stretches contemporary Christian preaching between traditional piety and secularity's individualism and ideological relativism.

27. Consult Dawson, *Allegorical Readers*; Burton-Christie, *Word in the Desert*; Young, *Biblical Exegesis*.

write and read theological essays, we travel this *via affirmativa*. By contrast, the *via negativa* has long held prime position in the Christian East and among some exceptional Western theologians, such as Meister Eckhart. Such Christians are uncomfortable with positive assertions about God and prefer, instead, apophatic claims, nicely epitomized in the fourteenth century by Gregory Palamas: "For God is not only beyond knowledge, but also beyond unknowing."[28] Along that *via negativa*, still more golden is silence: "Don't just say something. Listen." Each approach is valid. When mortals approach God, there is a time to be silent; there is a time to speak. Kataphasis ("accordant speech") and apophasis ("turning from speech") are complementary and mutually corrective.

This chapter's principal claim—presented all too kataphatically, since old habits die hard—is that Christian preaching lies in that middle ground between sheer kataphrasis and pure apophrasis, at the intersection of Affirmation Avenue and Disavowal Drive. Call it, if you will, a peculiar *via analogia*.[29] When, at that crossroads, two realities collide—when this world's stubborn facts clash with the gospel's irresistible force—a parable erupts, revelation strikes, the Word is proclaimed. The fundamental reason for this, I think, is not because parables are clever and ear-catching, not because our neural circuitry is hardwired for narrative, not because parabolic preaching is convenient license for indolent fuzziness and stupidity from the pulpit.[30] The real reason Christian preachers cannot long sidestep parabolism is that the Christian gospel—"the word of the cross"—is intrinsically, devastatingly parabolic: "We proclaim Christ the crucified." With every sure-footed return to the pulpit, we announce the nonsense of God that stupefies this world's wisdom, the weakness of God that overpowers this world's strength. As with hyberbole, so too with parable: "We are first disoriented before being reoriented."[31]

For so long we have handled holy things that we may, God help us, have become nearly inured to their wondrousness. At the heart of every proclamation of the gospel lies a mystery that can be neither explained nor explained away: God's shrouded wisdom, which has embraced us from before the world's foundation and transvalues everything in this world, without exception. Rarely have I encountered the apostle Paul's thought rephrased with greater acuity than in Paul

---

28. Palamas, *The Triads*, trans. N. Gendle, 32. Meyendorff (*St. Gregory Palamas*) offers a superb treatment of Byzantine Hesychasm.
29. Though peculiar to Christianity, *via analogia* is not unique to it. As Stern notes ("Rabbinic Parable," 80), most rabbinic *mĕšālîm* (parables) fall "somewhere between the two extreme poles of open illustration and secret speech."
30. See Lischer, "Limits of Story"; idem, *Theology of Preaching*, esp. 37–40.
31. Ricoeur, "Listening to the Parables," 243; "We immediately surmise that . . . an indiscreet zeal quickly transposes the Parables into trivial advice, into moral platitudes. And we kill them more surely by trivial moralizing than by transcendent theologizing" (ibid.).

Meyer's inaugural address as professor at Princeton Theological Seminary over
thirty years ago:

> Other religious communities celebrate their New Years, commemorate
> the births of their founders or the founding of their institutions, recall
> to consciousness past alienation and its reconciling, present guilt with its
> atoning, and clothe with religious solemnities the high points and the low
> in the cycles of human life, individual and corporate. *But only Christians
> have a Good Friday.* Only they recall in text and liturgy a public historical
> event that once made, and still makes, a mockery of their most central
> claim, and yet return to it as their most central truth: the coming of the
> Messiah in an unredeemed world.[32]

Stand beside Augustine and shiver: "Wondrous is the profundity of your utterances. We see their surface before us, enticing us as children. But wondrous is their
profundity—my God, wondrous their profundity! To look into them is to experience a shudder, the shudder of awe and the trembling of love" (*Conf.* 12.14.17).[33]

> So shall my word be that goes out of my mouth—
>   it shall not return to me barren,
> without having done the thing that I pleased,
>   and accomplishing the purpose for which I sent it. (Isa. 55:11 AT)

The kerygmatic arc is consistent, from Isaiah through Paul to Augustine and
beyond. The "Word of the LORD" is not rhetoric invoked only pragmatically,
for a church's consolation and consolidation. Nor is it indignant harangue of this
world's ignorance, lovelessness, and abuse of power. The Word released in the
preached word, the Word expressed through the sacrament, really changes us,
our listeners, and our world—sometimes patently, often secretly, but always actually, blessedly, stunningly. Through the word of the cross, God has not merely
exposed human wisdom as a fraud. God has made nonsensical (ἐμώρανεν ὁ θεός
[*emōranen ho theos*], 1 Cor. 1:20) everything in this world we ever thought wise—
about power, prestige, wealth, church growth, biblical scholarship, homiletics,
everything. No word could be more witheringly and healthily parabolic than Christ
the crucified. To preach that parable is to administer God's relief for this world's
cardiac sclerosis with grace-full explosions that heal diseased hearts.

Yet it remains God's relief, God's power, God's wisdom, God's mysterious
Word. Of all these we are but stewards (1 Cor. 4:1): trustworthy in our best
moments, at our worst conniving. Without fail, God's parabolic wisdom will pros-
per—perhaps never more evidently so than when revealed to prophets whose persuasiveness irritates the life out of them, whose most memorable performance is a

---

32. Meyer, "This-Worldliness of the New Testament," 223, emphasis added.
33. Trans. Finan, "St Augustine on the 'mira profunditas,'" 173.

beachhead in fish vomit. Whether we hail from Gath-hepher or Nineveh (2 Kgs. 14:25; Jonah 3:5–9), in Scripture we meet the God who will not leave us where we are. The God revealed by Jesus Christ is a God of saving eloquence, the very Word made flesh, whose sweetness is creating in us a new character stamped with faith, hope, and *caritas*.[34] "In the sign of the cross every Christian act is inscribed" (Augustine, *Doctr. chr.* 2.41.62). Why? Because we ourselves are parables of God's love. We have died, and our life now lies hidden with Christ in God (Col. 3:3).

34. "What we have in [Augustine's *De doctrina christiana*] is less a theory of rhetoric per se than a theory of conversion" (Cavadini, "Sweetness of the Word," 164).

Chapter Nine

For the Preacher:
Counsel from an Old Lawyer

As a superior court judge, I always asked an accused who was without an attorney if he wished the court to assign a lawyer to defend
him. . . . A young man appeared before me without a lawyer in the
superior court of Lenoir County. When I put my customary question to him, he replied, "No, Your Honor, I don't need a lawyer.
I'm going to plead guilty and throw myself on the ignorance of the
court."

Sam. J. Ervin Jr.[1]

A young contemporary of Peter and Paul, Marcus Fabius Quintilianus (ca. 30–
ca. 96 CE) was a celebrated orator, advocate, and educator who spent most
of his career in Rome under the emperors Vespasian (69–79), Titus (79–81),
and Domitian (81–96).[2] A Spaniard by birth but educated in Rome (57–59),
he practiced law in provincial Spanish courts until Galba (68–69) called him
to Rome as an imperial litigant. Galba soon died. Probably around 71, while
still trying cases, "Quintilian . . . was the first person to conduct a publicly
established school at Rome and receive a salary from the state treasury, and
he grew famous."[3] There, taking as his touchstone the more illustrious orator
and advocate Cicero (Quintilian, *Inst.* 3.1.20; 7.3.8; 9.1.25–36; 10.1.105, 112),
he gave courses of instruction in rhetoric to adolescent boys, including Pliny

---

1. Ervin, *Humor of a Country Lawyer*, 111.
2. For a useful overview of our subject's life and thought, see Kennedy, *Quintilian*.
3. As reported in St. Jerome's *Chronicle* (ca. 380), which places the start of Quintilian's state
professorship seventeen years later. Kennedy (*Quintilian*, 19) argues that this dating is likely erroneous.

the Younger,[4] burnishing a considerable reputation.[5] After retiring from both the bar and the lectern around 90, he compiled his lectures as *Insitutio oratoria* (*Education of the Orator*), which was published four or five years later. Though not immediately influential, this work in twelve books received renewed attention in late antiquity[6] and, much later, by Petrarch (1304–1374; see *Letters to the Famous* [*Familiares*] 24.7) and other Italian humanists of the Renaissance.[7] In the modern era Quintilian's "summing up" stands as the most comprehensive account of all dimensions of classical rhetoric.

Without intending to do so, the *Institutio oratoria* offers today's preacher meat to chew on. Unlike Aristotle, Quintilian was no theorist: he was a practical man, whose convictions about public speaking were forged in the rough-and-tumble of Roman courts.[8] As an educator, he was something like today's prominent pulpiteer who, employed by a seminary, "brings it home" to students needing to learn a craft.[9] More than that: Quintilian was dedicated to the education, not simply of technicians, but of the whole person. He was interested in forming an ideal orator, "none who actually exists or has ever lived, yet perfect down to the tiniest detail" (1.10.4), whose skill would be maintained in tip-top condition throughout life: "from the very cradle of speech through all stages of education . . . until we have reached the very summit of the art" (1.pr.6; see also 12.1.25). The lawyer's responsibility, then and now, is to plead the strongest case for the plaintiff or the defendant (12.9.7). Similarly, the preacher's duty is to advocate the gospel in a manner that others may be convinced of its truth.[10] While the power of speech was more overtly honored (alongside war) as the fundamental human activity in

---

4. Gaius Plinius Caecilius Secundus (ca. 61–ca. 112 CE) was a notable advocate, imperial executive, and man of letters. His correspondence with Emperor Trajan (ca. 98–112) offers the earliest external account of Christian worship and the reasons for Roman persecution of Christians. His uncle, Gaius Plinius Secundus (Pliny the Elder, 23–79), is remembered for having prescribed ingestion of raw owl's eggs or fried canaries as a remedy for hangovers (*Natural History* 14.142–43). You may remember him for other things, but I can't get that out of my head.

5. "Quintilian, greatest director of straying youth, / You are an honor, Quintilian, to the Roman toga" (in a poem published in 86 by Martial [ca. 40–ca. 103]; quoted in Kennedy, *Quintilian*, 25).

6. Jerome's program for a Christian girl's education (*Epistles* 108) is a manifest (though unattributed) adaptation of Quintilian's work. Cassiodorus Senator (ca. 485–ca. 585) and Isidore of Seville (ca. 560–636) explicitly mediated Quintilian to medieval students.

7. Hugh Blair (1718–1800), Church of Scotland pastor and Regius Professor of Rhetoric and Belles Lettres at the University of Edinburgh, popularized Quintilian during the Scottish Enlightenment.

8. "I am not a stickler for exact terminology, so long as the sense is clear to any serious student" (Quintilian, *Inst.* 8.4.15). Here and throughout, translations are by H. E. Butler (LCL), which I have modified.

9. "My object is to illuminate the secret principles of this art, opening up the subject's innermost recesses, offering the result, not of teaching I have received from others, but of my own experience and the guidance of nature itself" (ibid., 6.2.25).

10. I confess that this chapter's most glaring weakness is its thin coverage of God's good news, which is the suppressed premise of all my remarks from the perspective of a contemporary Christian preacher. This chapter has, instead, a more practical orientation, consonant with Quintilian's own project. For ruminations more scriptural and theological, see chap. 8 above.

imperial Rome[11] than in twenty-first-century America, preaching is the church's oldest profession and retains its importance, especially within Protestantism, as one of the few acts of oratory that many people encounter on a regular basis. Everyone who stands in a pulpit knows that the word delivered there must compete for the listener's attention in a world filled with words, supplied by talk radio or other popular media. My aim in this chapter is not to twist an ancient orator to fit today's homiletical needs. Instead, I wish only to highlight some aspects of *Education of the Orator* that, properly baptized, may still be useful for the contemporary preacher.

THE INESCAPABLE TRIAD

Early in his lectures Quintilian sounds a keynote that resonates throughout: "I insist that no one can be a true orator unless he is also a good man [*bonum virum*] and, even if he could be, I would not have it so" (*Inst.* 1.2.3; see also 1.pr.9; 8.4; 12.1.1–45). This was a controversial position. At least as early as Cicero,[12] and especially during the era of the so-called second Sophistic,[13] professional oratory had been tainted as word-mongering bereft of virtue and driven by profit. Conceding such squalor, Quintilian "trust[s] that not one of my readers would think of calculating the monetary value" of rhetorical study, undertaking it for "mercenary ends and the acquisition of filthy lucre" (1.12.16–17). Quintilian is in search of the orator who is a truly good citizen, "qualified for the administration of both public and private affairs, who can steer cities by [wise] counsel, give them a solid legal basis, and purge their vices by judicial decisions" with "courage, justice, and self-control" (1.pr.10–11). Focused on the imperial state, these are Stoic virtues, though no more so than those expected of overseers, deacons, widows, and elders in local Christian congregations by 1 Timothy (3:1–13; 5:1–22) and Titus (1:7–9; 2:2–15). Quintilian insists, "Without [such] natural gifts, technical rules are useless," and philosophy becomes sterile (1.pr.26). Though pragmatic by disposition, Quintilian would likely have advised today's preachers that neither technique nor theology could transform those whose character is warped. A sermon cannot be good unless preached by a good man or woman: one who, in Christian terms, operates in accordance with "the mind of Christ" (1 Cor. 2:16). "In our day the name of philosopher has too often served as a mask for the worst vices" (1.pr.15). The same could be said of some theology. In Quintilian's view, true rhetoric (or

---

11. See Quintilian's own hymn to speech: "In the beginning God, the parent of all things and architect of the world, distinguished human beings from all other living creatures subject to death by just this: the faculty of speech" (ibid., 2.16.12).
12. Cicero lays the blame on Socrates (*De or.* 3.60; idem, *Brutus* 31).
13. See Kennedy, *Art of Rhetoric*, 553–613.

preaching), the only kind worthy of the name, is virtuous because it is the product of a virtuous speaker (2.20.4; cf. Jas. 3:1–18).[14]

The finest orator, or preacher, is born, not made. (The fourth evangelist would stipulate, "born from above" [John 3:3].) Yet that is not sufficient. Natural talent (in Pauline terms, "gifts of the Spirit" [Rom. 12:3–8; 1 Cor. 12:1–11]) must be educated. "There is absolutely no basis for the complaint that few have the power to accept the knowledge imparted to them, and that the majority are so dim-witted that education is a waste of time and energy" (*Inst.* 1.1.27). Children, especially, are quick to reason and eager to learn (1.1.27). Here three implications are noteworthy for today's pastors. First, whatever one's aptitude for preaching, one dare not coast without rigorous study and deep reading. Quintilian was an educator, dedicated to what we would call lifelong learning (1.pr.22). "The love of letters and the value of reading are not confined to one's schooldays but end only with life" (1.8.12); "unless education in literature well and firmly lays the foundations of oratory, the superstructure will collapse" (1.4.5; see also 10.1).

Second, Quintilian's view of education is spacious: all the arts—which in his day encompassed grammar, rhetoric, logic, arithmetic, geometry, music, and astronomy—are grist for the orator's mill (*Inst.* 1.10).[15] "The material for rhetoric is composed of everything that may be placed before it as a subject for speech" (2.21.4). Precedence in study should be awarded to the morally excellent (1.8.4), those subjects that "enlarge the mind and nourish the intellect to the highest degree" (1.8.8; see also 12.2–3). Third, because his own pupils were quite young, he is dedicated to their education. The quality that sets him apart from many Romans is his gentle sympathy for the child (cf. Mark 9:36–37; 10:13–15).[16] When detailing how an instructor should teach, he radically adopts the child's point of view. Children readily respond to geniality, inquisitiveness, affection, reasonable demands, moderated discipline, appropriate praise, and hope for improvement (2.2.5–8; 2.4.13). "When correcting faults, [the teacher] must avoid sarcasm and above all abuse, for many [pupils] are frightened away from their study by someone who finds fault with them as though he despises them" (2.2.7). "Though it is customary, I disapprove of whipping" (1.3.13); "children are helpless and easily

14. In modern homiletical theory, one finds the equivalent of Quintilian's emphasis on the orator's character in Phillips Brooks: "Truth through Personality is our description of real preaching. The truth must come really though the person, not merely over his lips, not merely through his understanding and out through his pen. It must come through his character, his affections, his whole intellectual and modern being. It must come genuinely through him" (*On Preaching*, 8). A product of liberal Protestantism, the traits extolled by Brooks—gravity, courage, honor, "manliness"—are closer to classical Roman virtues than to anything intrinsic to Christian formation and practice.

15. Education in Quintilian's time tended toward narrower concentration on *controversiae*, judicial declamation, and *suasoriae*, simpler deliberative exercises: see Clarke, *Rhetoric at Rome*, 85–129. Preparatory to those studies were the *progymnasmata*, exercises preliminary to rhetorical study, which boys usually began between the ages of twelve and fifteen (see Kennedy, *Progymnasmata*).

16. "I call these young [children] mine, because the young pupil is always dear to me" (Quintilian, *Inst.* 7.3.30).

victimized; no one should be given unlimited power over them" (1.3.17). Consistent with Quintilian's earlier assessment of the good orator, the good teacher displays goodness: "the highest personal self-control" (2.2.4); "freedom from vice, refusing to tolerate it in others" (2.2.5); "discourse continually turning on what is good and honorable" (2.2.5). Most important, the best teachers practice what they teach: "However many examples for imitation you may assign them in their reading, still, the living voice, as we call it, is far more nourishing—especially the voice of a teacher whom pupils both love and respect if they have been rightly educated. One can hardly exaggerate how much more enthusiastically we imitate those whom we favor" (2.2.8).

Translated into today's church: If you would instill in young people a love of the gospel, enact the gospel yourself in the way you teach and preach. And if you hope to inspire others to be preachers, catch them as early in life as possible: "Don't waste the earliest years; . . . the mind is all the easier to mold before it has hardened. . . . Assume that Alexander [himself] has been entrusted to your care, that the infant placed in our lap deserves no less attention than [the greatest]—though for that matter every mother's child deserves equal attention" (1.1.19, 24; 1.13.8).[17] Not every child can be the next Martin Luther King Jr.; thus the sensitive teacher will not force a child into an unnatural mold but rather will "nudge the pupil into that sphere for which his talents seem specially designed" (2.8.4).[18] "If only we ourselves did not so often ruin our children's character!" (1.2.6).

Rhetoric is a natural gift that education perfects as an art (2.17.1–12). One indispensable quality remains: practice. "Of all schools, experience is the best" (2.17.12), because "rhetoric, by and large, has to do with practical action" (2.17.25). Quintilian paints a bright line between the cloistered philosopher and the public orator: "The character of the one I am seeking to mold should be wise in the Roman sense: that is, a genuine statesman who is so revealed, not in studious disputations, but in the actual practice and experience of life" (12.2.7). His quarrel is not with philosophy as such, from which the orator should learn (10.1.35–36); it is with those philosophers who have abandoned their true sphere of action, "the broad daylight of the forum" (12.2.8), and have retreated into recessively smaller circles of empty conversation. Not so for Quintilian: "Only when theory and practice are perfectly coordinated does the orator reap the harvest

17. Alexander III of Macedon (356 323 BCE), Cuppy notes (*Decline and Fall*, 38, 40 41, 44), "is known as Alexander the Great because he killed more people of more different kinds than any other man of his time. . . . As soon as he finished reading [Aristotle's] *Nicomachean Ethics*, Alexander began killing right and left[:] . . . Thebans, Thracians, Illyrians, Medes, Persians, Pisidians, Cappadocians, Paphlagonians, miscellaneous Mesopotamians, Galatians, Armenians, Bactarians, Sogdians, Arachosians, and some rare Uxians. . . . He might have lived longer if he had not crucified his physician for failing to cure [his friend] Hephaestion. Well, it was fun while it lasted."

18. Though an inductive approach to sermon creation might have offended a first-century sensibility, Quintilian and Fred Craddock (*As One without Authority*) are brothers in one respect: both are sensitive to the organic growth of human beings and the ways they learn to communicate.

of all study" (12.6.7).[19] The final book of his magnum opus concentrates on the career of the practicing advocate: the best age at which to begin litigating (12.6), the principles by which one learns to select cases worth trying and the fees that should be charged (12.7), how to prepare a case (12.8) and then plead it (12.9), the art of selecting the most effective style (12.10), when to retire and how to spend one's retirement (12.11). Repeatedly the emphasis falls on honest practice and practical common sense. No responsible advocate will try cases on the fly, sans deep study and preparation, though the irresponsible do it all the time (12.8.2–6; compare the pastor's "Saturday night special," pilfered from the Internet). No matter how diligent the conscientious lawyer (or preacher) may be, sometimes things come unglued; then the best we can do is, "as the old saying goes, 'Stand on your own two feet'" (12.9.18). Don't let yourself fall in a rut; as you age into your vocation, keep your mind supple with new knowledge and fresh exercises (12.11.16). Don't carp that you haven't time to stay abreast in your field. Remind yourself of how much of life you fritter away (12.11.18–19): "We ourselves cut short the time for study; look how little time we spend on it!" (12.11.18). Keep learning; "the rest depends entirely on practice, which simultaneously develops our powers and keeps them fit" (12.11.16).

To sum up: If you want to speak well, you need talent, study, and practice. When all cylinders are firing, perfection may not be attainable, but it can be increasingly approximated. Without all three, in place and in tune, the orator—lawyer or preacher—goes nowhere.

OLD-FASHIONED TECHNIQUES
FOR NEW-FASHIONED PREACHERS

Once we are as clear as was he on its coordination with talent and practice, we may turn to some of Quintilian's recommendations about the craft of rhetoric, to which the *Education of the Orator* is chiefly devoted.[20] The bulk of the work presents, in great detail, the different kinds of argument (forensic, deliberative, and epideictic) and the various bases on which cases of each kind may be argued (book 3), the parts and respective aims of forensic address in particular (book 4), construction of oral proofs and use of evidence (book 5), discerning and responding to a judge's temperament (book 6), logic and ambiguity in interpreting the law (book 7), style (book 8), figures of thought and of speech (book 9), an excursion into literary

---

19. "Wide is the difference between juridical disputes and philosophical discussions, between the law-court and the lecture-hall, between theoretical precepts and the perils of the bar" (Quintilian, *Inst.* 10.1.36).

20. The closest equivalent in homiletical scholarship I know to Quintilian's *Institutio* is the rhetoric of preaching presented by Davis, *Design for Preaching*, originally published in 1958 and reprinted many times.

criticism (book 10), and the importance of tailoring a speech to the circumstances (book 11). In this single chapter we cannot develop all of this material's exegetical and homiletical implications. Attempts at such analysis have been undertaken in chapters 3, 5, and 7 (above); much of Quintilian's discussion, so narrowly trained on the exigencies of first-century Roman lawcourts, does not apply to the quite different circumstances of twenty-first-century Christian preaching.[21] Still, from these books arise various issues that today's preachers would find practically useful because "teachers more often than not pass over in silence what is necessary" (*Inst.* 5.12.23), and "careless speakers are prone to commit a host of errors" (5.13.34).

In the Study

1. *What is rhetoric?* "The definition that best suits its character" is *bene dicendi scientia* [alternatively, *ars*]: "the science [or 'art'] of speaking well" (*Inst.* 2:15.34; 2.17:37; see also 2.14.5; 3.3.12; 8.pr.6). Fundamentally rhetoric aims to accomplish three things: *docendi, movendi, delectandi*—teaching, moving, and charming an audience (3.5.2; 8.pr.7). Although accepting the first two objectives, contemporary preachers might grow apprehensive over the third: "charm" registers a dubious nuance. While his *Institutio* is quite clear that Quintilian wants to win over a judge, we should interpret *delectatio* in its more positive sense: something delightful, satisfying, or interesting. True, the Latin term also connotes "allure" or "entertainment"; as we shall see, however, Quintilian's ideal advocate intends, not merely to amuse, but also to attract a magistrate to a specific point of view and course of action. The same applies to preachers and their listeners.

2. Before going further, let us orient ourselves in a manner faithful to this author, who reiterates the need for *a flexible practice* of rhetoric, shorn of mindless obedience to regulation for its own sake (*Inst.* 4.1.72–73; 4.2.4, 8; 5.10.110). Quintilian is impatient with pedantry (5.11.30); "only a lunatic would allow superstitious observance of rules to lead him counter to the best interests of his case" (4.2.85). Cases are infinite in their variety (7.pr.4); "in all cases common sense must decide, and common sense cannot be taught" (6.5.2). Over time the orator learns wisdom (6.5.3–5) and, when necessary, to bend the rules to accommodate special circumstances (7.1.12). "Let no one demand from me a rigid code of rules . . . or ask me to impose on students of rhetoric a system of laws as immutable as fate" (2.13.1). What follows, therefore, are general guidelines, which should be adjusted to suit particular circumstances (7.2.51).

3. *What's the point?* Stasis theory was one of the most complicated aspects of classical rhetoric. (Quintilian presents his view of the subject in *Inst.* 3.6–104.) The

---

21. For instance: There is small transfer value in Quintilian's consideration of evidence extracted by torture (*Inst.* 5.4), unless the preacher's technique has itself proved torturous for the congregation.

point of such elaborate analysis was identifying the primary matter that a speech was designed to address. What is at issue? What kind of thing is it? Did something happen? What happened? Why did it happen? Was the cause justifiable, or not? In the courtroom Quintilian had to make a decision: "What is it that [I want] most to impress upon the judge's mind?" (3.6.12), "the most important point on which the whole matter rests?" (3.6.21). To this concern the *Institutio* constantly returns (3.6.9, 15, 80, 85, 104; 3.8.2, 22, 51; 3.11.9, 19, 24–26; 4.2.21, 31, 35, 40, 43, 45; 5.10.11, 103). "There is scarcely anyone, unless he is a born fool lacking the least acquaintance with the practice of speaking, who does not know what is *the main issue* of a dispute (its cause or central argument); what is *the question disputed* by the parties; what is *the point the judge must decide*—and these three are identical" (3.11.24, emphasis added). The relevance for preachers should be obvious: What is the point of *this Sunday's* sermon, for *this congregation*, based on *this biblical text*? If the preacher cannot clearly answer these questions, which also resolve into one, then the listeners cannot be expected to figure it out.

What strategies may the preacher use for determining a sermon's kernel? Quintilian offers several that remain valuable. (a) One criterion to be satisfied is identifying *pertinence*, viewed from differing yet convergent angles. "On every occasion we speak, it is of prime importance that we identify the requirements of its time, place, and character" (*Inst.* 9.3.102; see also 10.2.27; 11.1.46). From that decision of substance, decisions about presentation will follow: "One single style of oratory is never suited to every case, nor every audience, nor every speaker, nor every occasion" (11.1.4). (b) In scriptural exegesis or sermon formulation, while mulling what the precise point is, consider a range of interpretive possibilities. As that point condenses and crystallizes, do not address objections to it as though an idiot had lodged them (5.13.42; 7.1.29). In fact, to test your point's soundness, reason it out from the perspective opposite to that which you will finally adopt (5.13.44, 52; 7.1.31). (You may be sure that some in the congregation will do this.) Don't be obstinate in defending a faulty line of thought (6.4.16). (c) Exercise care in interpreting ambiguous or self-contradictory aspects of the law (or for our purposes, Scripture: 5.10.106–7; 7.6–7); sometimes the intent of the text must be discriminated from its letter (7.10.3; cf. 2 Cor. 3:4–18).[22] (d) After such thorough consideration, decide the heart of what you intend to say, formulate it, and stick with it (*Inst.* 7.1.37). Once you have fixed your point, ideally your sermon will "cast it in a number of different forms, sometimes dwelling on one point and lingering over the same idea" (9.1.41). (e) When interpreting both text and congregation, keep firmly in mind their particular circumstances (5.10.44–52, 94). As

---

22. "A common question is which of two [contesting] laws is the oldest, but the most important question is which of the two laws will suffer less by its contravention" (ibid., 7.7.8). This characterizes Jesus' scriptural hermeneutic in the Synoptics (e.g., Mark 7:1–23//; Mark 10:2–9//).

circumstances change, even our similes change: "while a new ship is more useful than an old one, the same does not apply to friendship" (5.11.26).

4. Once the point is fixed, sensibly organize how you intend to unfold it (3.9.1; 4.1.35, 51, 53; 4.2.51). *Oral organization* should have a firm structure with smooth transitions, coherence, and a sense of proportion among its parts (4.1.76; 4.2.79; 4.4.2; 4.5.17, 28; 7.pr.1; 7.1.1; 7.2.57; 7.10.8).[23]

> It is not enough to arrange the various parts. Each constituent part has its own internal economy, by which one thought comes first, another second, and another third. We must work, not merely to place thoughts in their proper order, but rather to link them together, giving them such cohesion that there will be no trace of any suture. The parts [of the speech] must form a body, not a hodgepodge of limbs. (7.10.16)

A sermon so tightly constructed will create for both preacher and congregation a sense of inevitability (cf. 7.1.35).[24] One caution: Beware of confusing the order in which you have thought things through with the material sequence of your presentation. "As a rule, what occurs to us *first* is just that which ought to come *last* in our speech" (7.1.25, emphasis added).

5. Though operating in a predominately oral culture, Quintilian devotes much attention to *the art of writing*. Doubtless this is because he spent two decades teaching at what North Americans consider junior and senior high school levels; yet he expected even professionals like himself to write out their speeches in the order in which they would be delivered (3.9.9). For Quintilian there is no difference between writing well and speaking well; indeed, continued practice in the former assures the latter's refinement. "Eloquence will never attain its full development or robust health unless it acquires strength by frequent practice in writing" (10.1.2). "Assiduous practice in writing enables us to produce similar rhythmical effects when speaking extemporaneously" (9.4.114). "It is in writing that eloquence has its roots and foundations; writing opens that holy of holies where oratorical wealth is stored and from which we may draw to meet the demands of sudden emergencies" (10.3.3). The *Education of the Orator* offers sensible tips for the writer/speaker: "We must write as much as possible and with the utmost care" (10.3.2). "The sum of the matter: write quickly, and you will never write well; write well, and you will soon write quickly" (10.3.10). Write, then correct what you have written (10.4.1), but do not be fussy. Get things down on your tablet, however less than perfect it seems to you; then, refreshed after a good night's sleep, return to your writing, ready to polish (10.4.4).

---

23. Substitute insights from literary criticism for the classical parts of an oration, and you find kindred proposals in Lowry, *Homiletical Plot*; Long, *Witness of Preaching*, 106–55.

24. The contemporary preacher should not feel constrained by the rules of classical rhetoric in arranging a sermon. The *external* coherence of a sermon's presentation mirrors an *internal* congruence of the sermon's shape with the form of the biblical text being preached. See Craddock, *Preaching*, 155–222.

6. Like speech, writing depends on words. How does one warehouse words? By *reading*, widely and selectively (8.pr.28; 10.15). "Reading provides us a rich storehouse of expressions; we need to learn to use them, not merely when they occur to us, but when they are appropriate" (10.1.13; also 10.7.7). "Read the best writers; listen to the finest orators" (10.1.8). Reading develops a more reliable critical faculty than listening, because "a listener's judgment is often swept away by favor for a particular speaker or by the applause of an enthusiastic audience" (10.1.17). Use good judgment in deciding what you will read; as you read, keep in mind the case (or sermon) now before you (10.3.15). "By constant exercise develop strength in verbal acquisition so that every word is ready at hand and under your very eyes; do that, and you will never be at loss for a single word" (8.pr.28). In particular, poetry "inspires us by the sublimity of language and the power to excite every kind of emotion"—necessary when "[our] minds have become jaded by daily wear and tear at court, and we need the refreshment of pleasurable study" (10.1.27). Finally, however, words are tools: "nothing should be done for the sake of words alone; words were invented only to give expression to things" (8.pr.32). "There is no genuine virtue in words save in their power to represent facts" (8.pr.26).

7. Quintilian assumes of his contemporaries what remains customary for trial lawyers. Barristers need to speak fast on their feet, remembering precedents and facts; consulting brief memoranda (10.7.31), they address those seated in judgment from *memory* (11.2.1). We need not resolve the arguments for preaching with or without notes to appreciate what the *Institutio* says on a practical subject.[25] "Like everything else, memory may be improved by cultivation" (11.2.1). Citing Simonides of Ceos (ca. 556–468 BCE), the father of memory techniques (11.2.11), Quintilian reports that some speakers imagine localities (*imagines*) as an aide-mémoire: associating parts of a speech with stops along the way of a long journey (11.2.21) or with the rooms of a spacious house (11.2.18).[26] The main idea is to lay down mental markers leading you from one stage to the next (11.2.29–30). Beyond that, Quintilian recommends learning the parts piecemeal before tying everything together (11.2.27), with the confidence that something logically written will support memory in following a logical track (11.2.36). Verbalize as you memorize, "keeping the mind alert by the sound of the voice" (11.2.33). Should one memorize word for word, or thought for thought (11.2.44)? "Given a reliable memory and plenty of time, and I would prefer that a single syllable did not escape me" (11.2.45). A good night's rest strengthens memory (11.2.43). A "fast

---

25. See, e.g., Fant, *Preaching for Today*, 112–26; and Webb, *Preaching without Notes*.
26. I have known preachers who swear by such a technique; I myself swear at it. I become so preoccupied by whether I should be headed next to the kitchen or the living room that I forget where I am in my sermon. Recognizing the double burden imposed on the mind by this technique (*Inst.* 11.2.25–26), Quintilian is sympathetic to my plight. On the other hand, our ancient forebears operated very differently than we. In "John's Memory Theater," Thatcher advances a bold argument that the fourth evangelist "wrote" stories of Jesus with the use of the mnemonic techniques of his day.

study," able to memorize quickly, usually will not retain very long what has been memorized (11.2.44). If our memory has grown a bit dull, then it is better to speak freely, with a good grasp of our facts, than to tie our tongues anxiously (11.2.48). If even that is beyond our powers, maybe it is time for us to retire—"but such a misfortune will be only a rare occurrence" (11.2.49). "The one supreme method for memorization: daily practice and industry. For nothing is more enhanced by practice or impaired by neglect than memory" (11.2.40).

From the Pulpit

1. If the lion's share of preparation is concentrated on *logos*, delivery is the moment at which *ēthos* (the speaker's character) and *pathos* (emotions of the audience being addressed) converge (*Inst.* 3.8.15; 4.1.5, 14, 17, 26; 6.2.12). In education Quintilian sides with the student; in the courtroom he is focused on the listener. Practically one expects this: lose the judge and you've lost your case. Yet the *Institutio* suggests a genuine *sympathy and respect for one's audience*, which makes the work beneficial for today's preacher.[27] Anyone who has occupied a pew across the years can appreciate Quintilian's fear of boring an audience through tedium (4.2.49, 111; 4.3.8) or monotony (5.14.30; 8.3.52; 9.4.143). Attentive listening is hard work, and the best orator will relax congregational strain (4.2.118–19). Prepare your audience for what is to come (4.2.115); along the way remind them of where you are headed (4.5.3). Because listeners are in a hurry to grasp your point (4.5.10), reassure them (4.5.18). Don't lose them; keep them listening (4.2.71, 80). Under normal conditions people prefer sense to nonsense, so speak clearly and logically (5.10.1–19; 5.14). If you digress from the main topic (4.3.8, 17; 5.25) or have readied them for a conclusion (6.1.2), be brief (4.2.64, 68, 108; 4.3.3)—though not so curt that listeners are confused (4.2.44; 8.2.19). Build to a strong conclusion (5.12.14; 6.1.11, 29); even "sentences should rise and grow in force" (9.4.23). At the end don't be afraid "to cut loose" (6.1.51) but never sacrifice good taste (6.2.19). Neither should you fear moving your listeners (6.2.3–4), but remember that *you* control the emotion, not vice versa: "The life and soul of oratory is found in its power over the emotions" (6.2.7). The conclusion should seem natural, not forced (6.2.13). Your strongest points should be the first and last things your listeners hear (6.4.22; 7.1.17–18).

2. "*Style* can be corrupted in the very same number of ways it can be adorned" (8.3.58); "mediocre language is beneath the dignity of the subject or the station of the speaker" (8.2.2; also 5.12.20–21). Ever biased toward moderation (5.14.35), Quintilian counsels a style that is elegant but not fancy

---

27. Van der Geest is unusually sensitive to the sermon's listener. The original German title of his work *Presence in the Pulpit* is *Du hast mich angesprochen* [*You Have Spoken to Me*].

(8.3.42), restrained and tasteful (3.8.59, 62, 65; 4.1.28; 4.5.26; 8.pr.17), natural and unaffected (8.pr.19), genuine and simple (8.pr.23), graceful and lucid
(4.5.22, 26; 8.1.1).

"The first essential of a good style is clarity [*perspecuitas*]" (8.2.22). So repeatedly does he return to this topic that Quintilian seems acutely concerned that
his students and colleagues be clear. "For myself, I regard as useless words that
tax the hearer's ingenuity" (8.2.19). "A sentence should never be so long that
it is impossible to follow its drift" (8.2.14). "At bottom, every word that serves
neither the sense or the style is faulty" (8.3.56). He is death on those, "eager to
avoid ordinary modes of expression and enamored of false ideals of beauty,"
who "clot everything with a glut of words solely because they are unwilling to
state the facts directly and simply" (8.2.17). That may be the worst of all stylistic
crimes: "other faults are due to carelessness, but this one is deliberate" (8.3.56).
"Obscurity is produced by the use of words more familiar in certain regions than
in others" (8.2.13), whether geographic or cultural (8.1.3). No congregation uses
suasoria or "soteriology" in everyday conversation; spew such from the pulpit,
lose your listeners, and you may not get them back. "If we say not more and not
less than is required, and if all our words are clear and well placed, the whole
matter will be plain and obvious even to an audience that is not paying much
attention" (8.2.23).

Quintilian commends vivid discourse (4.2.123; 8.3.51–60), sometimes achieved
by "an actual word picture of a scene" (*vision*; 8.3.63; also 7.2.29–36) that attracts
the mind's eye as much as its ear (9.2.40).[28] By definition, an illustration should
throw light: "Anything selected for the purpose of illuminating something else
must be clearer than that which it is designed to illustrate" (8.3.73). Embellish
your speech with strong words that excite, intensify, and invigorate the imagination (3.8.86–89). There's no excuse for delivery so wooden that a congregation
wants to spray the preacher with Liquid Pledge.

Beyond clarity and vivacity, Quintilian offers some tips. (a) Pay attention to the
sound of words. Usually we should strive for elegance and flee from coarseness (8.3.17;
9.4.58). On the other hand, marry the style with the thought (3.8.64; 4.2.62; 8.1.1;
8.3.13–14): when trying to elevate our listeners, use lofty words (8.3.11); when speaking of mean matters, pick base words to put your point across (8.3.21). (b) Old words
"give our style a venerable and majestic air, . . . but we mustn't overdo it, dragging
such words from the deepest, darkest reaches of the past" (8.3.24–25). (c) Verbal
ornament should catch the ear, not bludgeon it (8.3.5; 8.5.34). (d) Season your style

---

28. I cannot recall the sermon, but I can never forget a *vision* I heard while in seminary over thirty
years ago: dozens of rows of uninterrupted, straight white lines, painted onto the empty parking lot of
a nursing home.

with figures,[29] but don't let your discourse become cloying (9.3.4–5). The special merit of figures of speech is that they relieve the tedium of everyday, banal discourse and save us from humdrum language (9.3.3). Figurative speech "attracts the listeners' attention, not allowing it to flag, rousing it from time to time by something especially striking" (9.3.27).[30] (e) Choose your metaphors judiciously (8.6.18), do not mix them (8.6.50),[31] and use them with a light touch, "lest you obscure your speech and wear out your audience" (8.6.14). (f) Irony is a tricky business. If the nature of the subject, the character of the speaker, or the mode of delivery is unclear, the audience may miss the speaker's intention entirely (8.6.54). (g) "Consult [your] own ears" (9.4.93) and change up your style: "Eloquence delights in variety, affording a continuous series of novelties to rivet the mind's attention" (9.2.63). Likewise, vary your pace: "Long syllables carry greater dignity and weight; short syllables create an impression of speed. If short syllables are mixed in with some long ones, the gait of your speech will be a run; take out the long syllables, and you gallop" (9.4.91). "The best judge of rhythm is the ear" (9.4.116). (h) The demands of clarity do not forbid carefully wrought *controversiae*, "hidden meanings left for the audience to discover" (9.2.65). When successfully accomplished, "listeners delight in detecting the speaker's concealed meaning, applaud their own perceptiveness, and regard his eloquence as a compliment to themselves" (9.2.78). (i) Similarly, "we may lend charm to our speech by mentioning some points but deferring their discussion, thereby depositing them in the safekeeping of the [hearer's] memory and later reclaiming our deposit" (9.2.63).

Quintilian seems torn between simplicity and eloquence. "*Eloquentia* aims for a style that is rich, beautiful, and commanding" (5.14.30; see also 4.5.6). "The task of eloquence is to demonstrate quality: there lies its kingdom, there its power, there its unique victory" (7.4.24). On the other hand, strained eloquence is grating and theatrical (6.1.49); to pause for applause is appalling (4.2.126–27; 8.5.14). Thus a tasteful style, which Quintilian certainly approves, must finally serve the substance: "The orator should be careful in choosing words but even more concerned about the subject matter" (7.pr.20). "Good grammar, words brimming with meaning, elegant and well-placed—why should we labor for more than that?" (8.pr.31).

---

29. Today's preachers may think little of figures of thought and speech; it was not always so. The earliest treatise on rhetorical style published in England is that of a Northumbrian monk, the Venerable Bede (ca. 673–735). The construction of *De schematibus et tropis* has an apologetic aim: "I have chosen to demonstrate by means of examples collected from Holy Writ that teachers of secular eloquence in any age have not been able to furnish us with these figures and tropes which did not appear first in Holy Writ" (Venerable Bede, "Concerning Figures and Tropes," trans. G. H. Tannenhaus, 97).

30. In the twentieth century Perelman and Olbrechts-Tyteca challenged Quintilian's position that figures are only stylistic. "For us, . . . the important thing . . . [is] to show how and in what respects the use of particular figures is explained by the requirements of argumentation—in short, their value for proof" (*New Rhetoric*, 168, italicized in the original).

31. No earlier prohibition of mixed metaphors has surfaced from antiquity's rhetorical texts.

3. *Humor* is a thing used delicately (4.1.49; 6.2.3, 6), with exquisite moderation (6.4.10).[32] There is no way to teach it (6.3.14). Like figurative speech, wit is
a seasoning, not the meal itself (6.3.19), whose tastefulness depends on the occasion (6.3.28). The best humor is a casual jest (6.3.30, 45, 57, 107), easily digested
(6.3.93), and often based on a surprise (6.3.61, 84). Forced puns rarely work
(6.3.48). Thou shalt not mug, nor do anything obscene (6.3.29, 46–47), nor slide
into insolence (6.3.33), nor play the buffoon (6.3.82). "We pay too dearly for the
laugh if it is raised at the cost of our own integrity" (6.3.50). Above all, don't allow
humor to obscure the point you are trying to make (6.4.13).

4. No rhetorician of antiquity tells us more about the actual *delivery* of its speeches
than Quintilian. Because it appeals to the ear, delivery depends on voice; because
it attracts the eye, it depends also on gesture (11.3.1, 14). Like it or not, a mediocre
speech delivered with brilliance will be more impressive than the finest material
delivered flatly (11.3.5). Demosthenes is quoted as claiming, "In oratory, delivery
is of first importance—and also second and third" (11.3.6). The best voice has an
even and agreeable tone, strong and durable (11.3.16, 23, 43–44). One develops
such a tone by daily practice, modulating one's inflections and dynamic range
(11.3.24–25, 29) and exercising the breathing capacity (11.3.54). "The greatest,
indeed the sole model of oratory" (10.1.76), Demosthenes did more than roll peb-
bles under his tongue to overcome a speech impediment; "[he] used to recite as
many lines as possible while climbing a hill" (11.3.54). As for style, so also for vocal
delivery: it should be correct, clear, and "suited to the quality of the various subjects on which we speak and the moods they summon" (11.3.45; see also 11.3.30,
61, 174). Lacking video recording and playback amenities, Quintilian offers its
equivalent by articulating the anatomy of gesture: the position of the head, hands,
eyes, shoulders, and feet (11.3.65–138), right down to the eyebrow and finger
(11.3.78, 92), with further attention to posture and carriage (11.3.158–59). "Tailor
your gestures to suit the sections" of your speech (11.3.110; also 11.3.161–74),
but never ham it up (11.3.123–24, 184): "avoid staginess and all extravagance
of facial expression, gesture, and gait" (1.11.3). Dress with dignity (11.3.137–49).
Strive for four touchstones: *conciliatio, persuasio, moveat, delectatio* (11.3.154): conciliation, convincing, moving, giving delight. Nature and nurture—talent, study, and
practice—conspire to produce perfection (11.3.11).

5. *The best artistry is hidden*, never drawing attention to the labor behind it (4.1.57,
60; 4.2.57–58, 117; 9.4.45–147). The best delivery is one "creating the impression
that our words have not been rehearsed in the study but spring from the inspiration of the moment" (11.2.46).[33] Quintilian would have admired Fred Astaire,

---

32. Rendered theologically: "Humor, properly joined to the matter of the sermon, feels at home
and is thus free to frolic, laugh, and celebrate the grace of God" (Craddock, *Preaching*, 219).
33. Thielicke, *The Waiting Father*, exerts on me much of this power.

who rehearsed his dances for months before filming them in precious minutes of seemingly spontaneous, effortless perfection.

6. After thorough preparation, *open yourself to genuine inspiration* in the moment: "we must not cling superstitiously to our premeditated scheme" (10.6.5). Cultivate the power of improvisation (10.7) by paying attention to circumstances right in front of you (6.1.4–5; 7.2.32). Don't miss unexpected opportunities, even those that seem to challenge your point (6.4.8).

7. By nature and by craft, *ēthos* and *pathos* are married. Carefully tune your words to convey whatever you feel and hope to inspire in your audience, be it happiness, anger, fear, wonder, grief, indignation, or desire (9.2.26). Do you yourself experience what you ask others to feel (6.2.25–31)? Are you grasped by the truth of your own position (4.2.38, 108; 5.13.51–52)?

Exit

The colloquy nears its end. We grow tired. Having come from afar, our guest has before him a long return. Quintilian stands to leave, adjusting the fold of his toga so that it falls to a point just above the lower edge of his tunic (11.3.140). We ask him, *Any final thoughts?*

Every case is different. No matter how often you preach, there is no substitute for careful preparation *every time* (7.1.4). Know your subject inside and out (7.1.16). Don't be ashamed to change your mind and revise your opinions (3.6.63). Stay open to new possibilities that require fresh research (5.11.44).

Seek the middle ground between "excessive admiration of antiquity" and "the pernicious allure" of cheap fads (2.5.21–22). Never enslave yourself to something new if it is meretricious (8.pr.26); "future ages shall tell us more fully of things [present]" (10.1.92). Mastery of any craft demands that we be, up to a point, somewhat of a copycat: children naturally learn by imitation, and "it is expedient to imitate whatever has been successfully invented" (10.2.1).[34] Never forfeit the chance to hear others who practice your profession, and learn from them (10.5.19), but choose your guides wisely (5.10.119–20; 7.10.10–11); be sure to imitate *the best* (10.2.18). "Keep before your eyes an array of different kinds of excellence" (10.2.26) but "press toward the mark of supreme excellence rather than contenting yourself to follow in the tracks made by others" (10.2.19).

Confess your ignorance and amend your faults. In detailing figures of speech, Cicero once referred to *relationem*, reference; "just what he meant by that is still a mystery to me" (9.3.97). "My address in the trial [of Nevius of Arpinum] is the

---

34. On the use of *mimēsis* in classical education, consult Clark, *Rhetoric in Greco-Roman Education*, 144–76. In chap. 5 above, also see the discussion of 1 John's *mimēsis* of John's Gospel.

only one of my pleadings that I have so far published; I admit that only a youthful craving for glory led me to do so" (7.2.24).

Be modest in your accomplishments (5.12.17). No one likes a braggart (11.1.15). "As a rule you will find that arrogance implies a spurious self-esteem; those with true merit are amply satisfied by their consciousness of its possession" (11.1.17). The things that most commend an orator are courtesy, kindness, moderation, and generosity (11.1.42).[35]

Play to your personal strengths and natural talent (4.2.88); techniques of delivery must always be adapted to the individual's peculiarities (11.3.181). David could not fight in Saul's armor (1 Sam. 17:38–40); "different kinds of eloquence suit different speakers" (*Inst.* 11.1.31). Judge for yourself when to hold back or pour it on (6.1.45). Concentrate your thoughts (10.3.28): "whether we be in a crowd, on a journey, or at some festive gathering, our thoughts should always have some inner sanctuary of their own to which they may retire" (10.3.30).

Aim high. "Even if we fail, those whose aspirations are highest will reach greater heights than those who give up prematurely, so despairing of ever reaching the summit that they halt at the very foot of the ascent" (1.pr.20). "It is cowardly to despair of anything within the realm of possibility" (1.10.8).

Until the day you retire, never quit practicing. "The best form of exercise is to speak daily before an audience of several persons" (10.7.24). If you cannot manage that, then at least rehearse your subjects entirely in silent concentration (10.7.25). To stay limber, speakers must speak. If you cannot speak, write whenever possible. If you cannot write, then meditate. Never allow yourself to be caught out or left in the lurch (10.7.29).

"Not merely in oratory, but in all of life's tasks, there is nothing more important than seasoned wisdom [*prudentia*]. Without it, all formal instruction is in vain. Good sense, unsupported by learning, will accomplish more than learning unsupported by good sense" (6.5.11).

"Let no one hope to acquire eloquence merely by the labor of others. One must burn the midnight oil, persevere to the end, and grow pale with study. One must form one's own powers, one's own experience, one's own methods. . . . Someone else may point out to us the road, but our speed must be our own" (7.10.14–15).

Turning, Quintilian recedes with dignity, and then he is gone.

---

35. For a measured consideration of a touchy subject, see Arthurs and Gurevich, "Theological and Rhetorical Perspectives on Self-Disclosure in Preaching."

Conclusion

Chapter Ten

Peroration

For I am not ashamed of the good news, for it is God's power for everyone who has faith, of the Jew first and then of the Greek.

The apostle Paul[1]

Any coherent understanding of what language is and how language performs, . . . any coherent account of the capacity of human speech to communicate meaning and feeling is, in the final analysis, underwritten by the assumption of God's presence. . . . It is a theology, explicit or suppressed, masked or avowed, substantive or imaged, which underwrites the presumption of creativity, of signification in our encounters with text, with music, with art. The meaning of meaning is a transcendent postulate.

George Steiner[2]

In the beginning was the Logos. . . . What came to be in him was life, and this life was the light of mortals.

John the Evangelist[3]

In his hilarious memoirs *My Life and Hard Times*, James Thurber recalls passing every course at Ohio State University except botany. "This was because all botany students had to spend several hours a week in a laboratory looking through a microscope at plant cells, and I could never see through a microscope." (A childhood accident had robbed Thurber's vision in one eye; by the time he died at

---

1. Rom. 1:16a, GOODSPEED.
2. Steiner, *Real Presences*, 3, 216.
3. John 1:1a, 3b–4 AT.

sixty-six, he was totally blind.) His professor was convinced that the problem lay in a student's inability to adjust the microscope properly. "Try it just once again," he'd say. The best Thurber could see was "a nebulous milky substance." Most of the time he saw nothing at all.

> So we tried it with every adjustment of the microscope known to man. With only one of them did I see anything but blackness or the familiar lacteal opacity, and that time I saw, to my pleasure and amazement, a variegated constellation of flecks, specks, and dots. These I hastily drew. The instructor, noting my activity, came back from an adjoining desk, a smile on his lips and his eyebrows high in hope. He looked at my cell drawing. "What's that?" he demanded, with a hint of a squeal in his voice. "That's what I saw," I said. "You didn't, you didn't, you *did*n't!" he screamed, losing control of his temper instantly, and he bent over and squinted into the microscope. His head snapped up. "That's your eye!" he shouted. "You've fixed the lens so that it reflects! You've drawn your eye!"[4]

Show me the attitude toward biblical interpretation that a critic adopts, and I'll show you that critic's conception of life and art, of woman and man and God. Whoever revels in life's wondrous patterns will discover in Scripture tropes so apt, *narratio* of such intricacy, as to move stout orators to tears. Whoever is stabbed by life's jagged edges will recognize in the Bible aporias abounding, chaos crouching at every corner. Ignorance should be vanquished; justice must be done. When James speaks of the law as a mirror in which the superficial forgetfully glance and the thoughtful blessedly gaze (1:22–25), he posits a scriptural hermeneutic that holds up remarkably well. In the deepest chambers of humanity and divinity, none of us enjoys an acuity of 20/20 this side of paradise (1 Cor. 13:12). Students and professors alike suffer myopia—at times so advanced that no adjustment of the critical lens may dispel "the familiar lacteal opacity."

Three threads have run through this book's chapters, disparate as they may seem. First, rhetorical study is not one lens but a collection of several. The same may be safely said of all other critical approaches to NT exegesis. Scripture is inexhaustibly complex; the history of its interpretation is our continuing endeavor to polish, then pose, the best and broadest array of questions designed to elicit apt replies from the text. When no replies are forthcoming—better, when Scripture's replies are questions leveled at us—that is a sure sign that our imagination needs expanding and our questions need finer grinding. Through practices of discernment, we can train our eyes to see better.

Interwoven with the first is my second thread. To rephrase Gertrude Stein's cynical appraisal of Oakland, California, there *is* a "there" there in scriptural

---

4. Thurber, *The Thurber Carnival*, 221, 223.

meaning. A single meaning? A determinative original meaning? An invariable meaning decided once for all by a magisterium of one or of many? No. Of those constructions we've nothing to fear: they are Theophrastian *caricatures* of positions, adopted (at times, no doubt clumsily) by academy or church, later respun from thin air by every dogma that wants its day.

Even within the precincts of postmodern departments of literature, the blush is off the ideological rose. Hear this letter to the editor of *The New York Times Book Review*:

> I disagree . . . that "literary study in America has never been in better shape." As a graduate student at N.Y.U., I felt anything but liberated. Although the literary criticism of the "old boys" excluded the perspectives of women, minorities and poor people, the [current] revolutionaries . . . have become as smug as the people they overthrew. The latest wave of criticism has robbed texts of meaning while reducing masterpieces to abstract asides in articles that posit ridiculous theories. By denying the importance of the author or the possibility of intentional meaning, the discussion surrounding literature has turned into a roomful of critics dancing by themselves, imposing their intellectual constructs onto innocent Shakespearean sonnets.[5]

The *sensus plenior*, or deeper meaning, of Scripture can never be reduced to historical investigation. Yet, contrary to some fashions in rhetorical study,[6] I fail to see how a full appreciation of Scripture will ever bypass a deepened historical sensibility among its readers. The evangelists who composed the Gospels were children of history. In time others among history's children accorded their works scriptural authority in response to historical movements. No reader of these works, before or since their canonization, has ever approached them from outside time and space. Accordingly, the methods of rhetorical analysis I have plied in this book are historically grounded. My reasons are attributable, not merely to taste, but also to particular moral obligations: among them, a responsibility to the church that its charter documents be heard for what they have to say and how they say it—not for what I wish they would say in my own manner. Other interpreters claim different allegiances; as stated in chapter 1, it's not for me to dictate how others construe their interpretive labors. They have their reward. I write for those whose approach to Scripture is of another sort: those who join with me in squinting at biblical cells to understand them better, instead of spending precious time or money on the flecks and specks and dots of my own eye.[7]

5. Griffith, "Death of the Critic," 2.
6. See, e.g., Amador, *Academic Constraints*.
7. Similarly, Vanhoozer (*Meaning in This Text?*, 29): "My thesis is that ethical interpretation is a spiritual exercise and that the spirit of understanding is not a spirit of power, nor of play, but the Holy Spirit."

Third and finally, the artistry this book has tried to illumine is neither aes-
thetically inspired nor blandly humanitarian nor politically motivated. At root
it is *theological*. Why? Because, if we take the Gospels at face value, their authors
believed that, in Jesus Christ, ὁ θεός (*ho theos*, "God") was and remains personally
at work for the redemption of all humanity—including its artistry and politics—
and all creation. In believing that, the evangelists may have been fools, as those
scandalized by "the word of the cross" (1 Cor. 1:18 AT) have always reckoned
them, but they were not knaves. They baptized their day's rhetorical conventions
into preaching for the masses, they plumbed faith's fathoms and shallows among
both outsiders and their own number, they strained to hear sublimity and to bear
disappointment, because in all those things they were convinced that the true God
was truly speaking to them and mandating a truthful witness to what they were
hearing. By rhetoric's "re-invention" or "release from restraint" or consolidation
as "power," neither Paul nor John was remotely smitten, even less seduced. They
understood that self-lordship is a delusion; power, aside from the good news of the
cross, is a sham. In Christ, they believed, God's wisdom was not sprucing up their
speech but radically re-creating their very selves (John 1:12–13; Rom. 12:1–2).

What, then, is the critic's duty? There's no single answer; "the Spirit bloweth
where it listeth" (cf. John 3:8 KJV). Years ago Helen Gardner reminded us of
Samuel Johnson's allegory of Criticism, eldest daughter of Labour and Truth,
who at birth was consecrated for Justice, reared in Wisdom's palace, "appointed
the governess of Fancy, and empowered to beat time to the chorus of the Muses."
Before descending with the Muses to earth, Justice bestowed on Criticism a scepter for her right hand, with which she could confer immortality or oblivion. "In
her left hand, she bore an unextinguishable torch, manufactured by Labour and
lighted by Truth, of which it was the particular quality immediately to show everything in its true form, however it might be disguised to common eyes." But in this
world she was confronted by works so equally compounded of beauties and flaws
that, "for fear of using improperly the sceptre of Justice, [she] referred the cause
to be considered by Time," whose proceedings, "though very dilatory, were, some
few caprices excepted, conformable to justice." Before returning to heaven, she
broke her sceptre. One end was seized by Flattery, the other by Malevolence.[8]

Like Gardner, I choose the torch over the scepter for the business of criticism. She feared an inhibited appreciation: "[a] mind . . . concerned with being
right, which is nervously anxious not to be taken in, which sits in judgement, and
approaches works of passion and imagination with neatly formulated demands."[9]
Gardner has a point, which invites theological sharpening: those entrusted
with NT interpretation do well to wield their scepters lightly and take up their

8. Gardner, *The Business of Criticism*, 11–12.
9. Ibid., 13.

cudgels slowly, in the Spirit of the Messiah whose crown was thorn-plaited. When properly directed, the torch throws light on Scripture, be it only a flickering, derivative reflection of the One who is Light (John 1:8). When conformed to the truth of the gospel, scriptural criticism, rhetorical and otherwise, is disciplined by *caritas*, productive of love. If not, why should anyone bother?

Bibliography

INTRODUCTORY ESSAY

George A. Kennedy, *Classical Rhetoric and Its Christian and Secular Tradition from Ancient to Modern Times* (Chapel Hill: University of North Carolina Press, 1980), offers a superb survey of the rhetorical landscape in Western culture. *A New History of Classical Rhetoric* (Princeton: Princeton University Press, 1994) condenses the same author's three-volume history of rhetoric (Princeton: Princeton University Press, 1963–1983), covering the fifth century BCE through the early Middle Ages. Stanley E. Porter, ed., *Handbook of Classical Rhetoric in the Hellenistic Period, 330 B.C.– A.D. 400* (Leiden, New York, and Cologne: E. J. Brill, 1997), explores important dimensions of rhetorical practice during the centuries surrounding the NT.

Aristotle marks the pinnacle of classical rhetoric, philosophically considered. George A. Kennedy, *Aristotle: On Rhetoric; A Theory of Civic Discourse* (New York and Oxford: Oxford University Press, 1991), is a fine translation of this treatise. Donald A. Russell and Michael Winterbottom, eds., *Ancient Literary Criticism: The Principal Texts in New Translations* (Oxford and New York: Oxford University Press, 1972), provide a valuable collection of works by many rhetoricians whose insights have graced this book: Demetrius, Cicero, Dionysius of Halicarnassus, Quintilian, "Longinus," Hermogenes, Menander. The twentieth century's most formidable exponent of the philosophical stream within classical rhetoric was Heinrich Lausberg (1912–1992), whose magnum opus has been translated into English by Matthew T. Bliss, Annemiek Jansen, and David E. Orton: *Handbook of Literary Rhetoric: A Foundation for Literary Study*, ed. David E. Orton and R. Dean Anderson (Leiden, Boston, and Cologne: E. J. Brill, 1998). David E. Aune, ed., *The Westminster Dictionary of New Testament and Early Christian Literature and Rhetoric* (Louisville, KY: Westminster

John Knox Press, 2003), is useful in navigating this formidable work. Less intimidat-
ing than Lausberg is Edward P. J. Corbett and Robert J. Connors, *Classical Rhetoric
for the Modern Student*, 4th ed. (New York: Oxford University Press, 1998).

Reliable translations of Augustine's inestimable *De doctrina christiana* are readily
available: *On Christian Doctrine*, trans. D. W. Robertson Jr., LLA 80 (New York:
Liberal Arts Press, 1958); and John E. Rotelle, ed., *Teaching Christianity: De doctrina
christiana*, trans. Edmund Hill, WSA 1.11 (Hyde Park, NY: New City Press, 1996).
The rhetorical tradition also underlies the approaches of such modern philosophers as I. A. Richards, Richard M. Weaver, Stephen Toulmin, Chaïm Perelman,
Ernesto Grassi, Kenneth Burke, Michel Foucault, and Jürgen Habermas. They,
alongside multicultural challenges to that tradition, are studied by Sonja K. Foss,
Karen A. Foss, and Robert Trapp, eds., *Contemporary Perspectives on Rhetoric*, 2nd
ed. (Prospect Heights, IL: Waveland Press, 1991). Among those theorists, none
has influenced recent NT interpretation more heavily than Perelman; his volume
coauthored with Lucie Olbrechts-Tyteca, *The New Rhetoric: A Treatise on Argumentation*, trans. John Wilkinson and Purcell Weaver (Notre Dame and London: University of Notre Dame Press, 1969), is a modern classic. A simpler introduction
to Perelman's approach is offered in *The Realm of Rhetoric*, trans. William Kluback
(Notre Dame, IN, and London: University of Notre Dame Press, 1982).

Studies in narrative and literary characterization abound; those attuned to
classical theories are harder to come by. An important exception is Erich Auerbach, *Mimesis: The Representation of Reality in Western Literature* (Princeton: Princeton University Press, 1953). For the Oxford World's Classics, D. A. Russell and
Michael Winterbottom have compiled a compendium of *Classical Literary Criticism*
(Oxford and New York: Oxford University Press, 1989). In *The Nature of Narrative*
(London: Oxford University Press, 1966), Robert Scholes and Robert Kellogg
frame an account that draws from narratives both modern and ancient, including
biblical narratives. In spite of the seemingly narrow purview suggested by its title,
I find myself returning to W. J. Harvey's *Character and the Novel* (London: Chatto &
Windus, 1965) for perceptive comments on characterization in creative literature,
including the Gospels.

The breadth of NT rhetorical criticism was captured in a series of seven bien-
nial international conferences, principally sponsored by Pepperdine University.
Sheffield Academic Press has published most of their proceedings (see the volumes
listed below, edited by Stanley E. Porter and Thomas H. Olbricht, plus Porter
and Dennis L. Stamps). Papers delivered at the sixth conference are collected
in Anders Eriksson, Thomas H. Olbricht, and Walter Übelacker, eds., *Rhetorical
Argumentation in Biblical Texts: Essays from the Lund 2000 Conference* (Harrisburg, PA:
Trinity Press International, 2002); those of the seventh in Thomas H. Olbricht
and Anders Eriksson, eds., *Rhetoric, Ethic, and Moral Persuasion in Biblical Discourse:
Essays from the 2002 Heidelberg Conference* (New York: T&T Clark, 2005). In the latter

volume (335–77) Vernon K. Robbins offers a comprehensive assessment: "From Heidelberg to Heidelberg: Rhetorical Interpretation of the Bible at Seven 'Pepperdine' Conferences from 1991–2002."

All works cited in the preceding chapters appear in the following list.

WORKS CITED

Abrams, M. H. *A Glossary of Literary Terms*. 3d ed. New York: Holt, Rinehart, & Winston, 1971.

Achtemeier, Paul J. "*Omne verbum sonat*: The New Testament and the Oral Environment of Late Western Antiquity." *JBL* 109 (1990): 3–27.

———. *The Quest for Unity in the New Testament Church: A Study in Paul and Acts*. Philadelphia: Fortress Press, 1987.

Ackroyd, P. R., and C. F. Evans, eds. *From the Beginnings to Jerome*. Vol. 1 of *The Cambridge History of the Bible*. Cambridge: Cambridge University Press, 1970.

Allen, Fred. *"all the sincerity in hollywood . . .": Selections from the Writings of Radio's Legendary Comedian*. Edited by Stuart Hample. Golden, CO: Fulcrum, 2001.

Allison, Dale C., Jr. *The New Moses: A Matthean Typology*. Minneapolis: Fortress Press, 1993.

Alter, Robert. *The Art of Biblical Narrative*. New York: Basic Books, 1981.

Amador, J. David Hester. *Academic Constraints in Rhetorical Criticism of the New Testament: An Introduction to a Rhetoric of Power*. JSNTSup 174. Sheffield: Sheffield Academic Press, 1999.

Anderson, Graham. *The Second Sophistic: A Cultural Phenomenon in the Roman Empire*. London and New York: Routledge, 1993.

Anderson, R. Dean, Jr. *Ancient Rhetorical Theory and Paul*. Kampen: Kok Pharos, 1996. Rev. ed. Leuven: Peeters, 1999.

Arnold, Duane W. H., and Pamela Bright, eds. *De doctrina christiana: A Classic of Western Culture*. Notre Dame and London: University of Notre Dame Press, 1995.

Arthurs, Jeffrey, and Andrew Gurevich. "Theological and Rhetorical Perspectives on Self-Disclosure in Preaching." *BSac* 157 (2000): 215–26.

Ashton, John. *Studying John: Approaches to the Fourth Gospel*. Oxford: Clarendon Press, 1994.

———. *Understanding the Fourth Gospel*. Oxford: Clarendon Press, 1991.

Auerbach, Erich. *Mimesis: The Representation of Reality in Western Literature*. Princeton: Princeton University Press, 1953.

Aune, David E. *The Blackwell Companion to the New Testament*. Malden, MA, and Oxford: Wiley-Blackwell, 2010.

———, ed. "Literary Criticism." Pages 116–39 in *The Blackwell Companion to the New Testament*. Malden, MA, and Oxford: Wiley-Blackwell, 2010.

———. "Oral Tradition and the Aphorisms of Jesus." Pages 211–65 in *Jesus and the Oral Gospel Tradition*. Edited by Henry Wansbrough. JSNTSup 64. Sheffield: Sheffield Academic Press, 1991.

———. *Prophecy in Early Christianity and the Ancient Mediterranean World*. Grand Rapids: Wm. B. Eerdmans Publishing Co., 1983.

———. *The Westminster Dictionary of New Testament and Early Christian Literature and Rhetoric*. Louisville, KY: Westminster John Knox Press, 2003.

Babcock, William S. "*Caritas* and Signification in *De doctrina christiana* 1–3." Pages 145–63 in *De doctrina christiana: A Classic of Western Culture*. Edited by Duane W. H. Arnold and Pamela Bright. Notre Dame and London: University of Notre Dame Press, 1995.

Bacon, Benjamin W. *An Introduction to the New Testament.* NTH. New York: Macmillan, 1900.

Bailey, Kenneth E. *Poet and Peasant: A Literary-Cultural Approach to the Parables in Luke.* Grand Rapids: Wm. B. Eerdmans Publishing Co., 1976.

Balabanski, Vicky. *Eschatology in the Making: Mark, Matthew and the Didache.* SNTSMS 97. Cambridge: Cambridge University Press, 1997.

Balch, David L. "Two Apologetic Encomia: Dionysius on Rome and Josephus on the Jews." *JSJ* 13 (1982): 102–22.

Barclay, William. "A Comparison of Paul's Missionary Preaching and Preaching to the Church." Pages 165–75 in *Apostolic History and the Gospel: Biblical and Historical Essays Presented to F. F. Bruce on His Sixtieth Birthday.* Edited by W. Ward Gasque and Ralph P. Martin. Grand Rapids: Wm. B. Eerdmans Publishing Co., 1970.

Barnet, John A. *Not the Righteous but Sinners: M. M. Bakhtin's Theory of Aesthetics and the Problem of Reader-Character Interaction in Matthew's Gospel.* JSNTSup 246. London and New York: T&T Clark, 2003.

Barrett, C. K. *The Acts of the Apostles: A Shorter Commentary.* London and New York: T&T Clark, 2002.

———. *Biblical Problems and Biblical Preaching.* FBBS 6. Philadelphia: Fortress Press, 1964.

———. "Christocentric or Theocentric? Observations on the Theological Method of the Fourth Gospel." Pages 1–18 in *Essays in John.* Philadelphia: Westminster Press, 1982.

———. *Essays in John.* Philadelphia: Westminster Press, 1982.

———. *The Gospel according to St. John: An Introduction with Commentary and Notes on the Greek Text.* 2nd ed. Philadelphia: Westminster Press, 1978.

———. "Paradox and Dualism." Pages 98–115 in *Essays on John.* Philadelphia: Westminster Press, 1982.

Barth, Gerhard. "Matthew's Understanding of the Law." Pages 58–164 in *Tradition and Interpretation in Matthew.* By Günther Bornkamm, Gerhard Barth, and Heinz Joachim Held. Philadelphia: Westminster Press, 1963.

Bass, Kenneth. "The Narrative and Rhetorical Use of Divine Necessity in Luke–Acts." *JBPR* 1 (2009): 48–68.

Bauckham, Richard. *The Theology of the Book of Revelation.* NTT. Cambridge: Cambridge University Press, 1993.

Bauer, David R., and Mark Allan Powell, eds. *Treasures New and Old: Recent Contributions to Matthean Studies.* SBLSymS 1. Atlanta: Scholars Press, 1996.

Baumlin, James S., and Tita French Baumlin, eds. *Ethos: New Essays in Rhetorical and Critical Theory.* Dallas: Southern Methodist University Press, 1994.

Beasley-Murray, George R. *Jesus and the Last Days: The Interpretation of the Olivet Discourse.* Peabody, MA: Hendrickson Publishers, 1993.

Beavis, Mary Ann. *Mark's Audience: The Literary and Social Setting of Mark 4.11–12.* JSNTSup 33. Sheffield: Sheffield Academic Press, 1989.

Beck, Brian K. *Christian Character in the Gospel of Luke.* London: Epworth, 1989.

Bede, the Venerable. "*De schematibus et tropis*: A Translation." Translated by G. H. Tannenhaus. *QJS* 48 (1962): 237–53. Repr. as "Concerning Figures and Tropes." Pages 96–122 in *Readings in Medieval Rhetoric.* Edited by Joseph M. Miller, Michael H. Proser, and Thomas W. Benson. Bloomington and London: Indiana University Press, 1973.

Bennema, Cornelis. "A Theory of Character in the Fourth Gospel with Reference to Ancient and Modern Literature." *BibInt* 17 (2009): 375–421.

Berge, Paul S. "The Word and Its Witness in John and 1 John: A Literary and Rhetorical Study." *WWSup* 3 (1997): 143–62.

Berger, Klaus. *Formgeschichte des Neuen Testaments.* Heidelberg: Quelle & Meyer, 1984.

Betz, Hans Dieter. *Galatians: A Commentary on Paul's Letter to the Churches in Galatia.* Hermeneia. Philadelphia: Fortress Press, 1979.

Bitzer, Lloyd F. "The Rhetorical Situation." *PR* 1 (1968): 1–14.
Black, C. Clifton. "Christian Ministry in Johannine Perspective." *Int* 44 (1990): 29–41.
———. *The Disciples according to Mark: Markan Redaction in Current Debate*. 2nd ed. Grand Rapids: Wm. B. Eerdmans Publishing Co., 2012.
———. "The First, Second, and Third Letters of John: Introduction, Commentary, and Reflections." Pages 363–469 in vol. 12 of *NIB*. Nashville: Abingdon Press, 1998.
———. *Mark*. ANTC. Nashville: Abingdon Press, 2011.
———. *Mark: Images of an Apostolic Interpreter*. SPNT. Columbia: University of South Carolina Press, 1994. Reissued, Minneapolis: Fortress Press; Edinburgh: T&T Clark, 2001.
———. "Ministry in Mystery: One Evangelist's Vision." *ChrMin* 22 (1991): 15–18.
———. Review of R. Dean Anderson Jr., *Ancient Rhetorical Theory and Paul*. *BMCR* 8 (1997): 408–11.
———. Review of *Sowing the Gospel: Mark's World in Literary-Historical Perspective*, by Mary Ann Tolbert. *CBQ* 54 (1992): 382–84.
———. "Rhetorical Questions: The New Testament, Classical Rhetoric, and Current Interpretations." *Di* 29 (1990): 62–70.
———. "Serving the Food of Full-Grown Adults: Augustine's Interpretation of Scripture and the Nurture of Christians." *Int* 52 (1998) 341–53.
———. "Trinity and Exegesis," *ProEcc* 10 (2010): 151–80.
———. "Was Mark a Roman Gospel?" *ExpTim* 104 (1993): 36–40.
Black, C. Clifton, and Duane F. Watson, eds. *Words Well Spoken: George Kennedy's Rhetoric of the New Testament*. SRR 8. Waco: Baylor University Press, 2008.
Black, Matthew. *An Aramaic Approach to the Gospels and Acts*. 2nd ed. Oxford: Clarendon Press, 1954.
Blair, E. P. "Mark, John." *IDB* 3 (1962): 277–78.
Blass, Friedrich Wilhelm, and Albert Debrunner. *A Greek Grammar of the New Testament*. Translated and edited by Robert W. Funk. Chicago and London: University of Chicago Press, 1961.
Bloomquist, L. Gregory. "Rhetoric, Culture, and Ideology: Socio-rhetorical Analysis in the Reading of New Testament Texts." Pages 115–46 in *Rhetorics in the New Millennium: Promise and Fulfillment*. Edited by James D. Hester and J. David Hester. SAC. New York and London: T&T Clark, 2010.
Blount, Brian K. "Preaching the Kingdom: Mark's Call for Prophetic Engagement." PSB-Sup 3 (1994): 33–56.
Boer, Martinus C. de. "Narrative Criticism, Historical Criticism, and the Gospel of John." *JSNT* 47 (1992): 35–48.
Bonner, Gerald. "Augustine as Biblical Scholar." Pages 541–63 in *From the Beginnings to Jerome*. Vol. 1 of *The Cambridge History of the Bible*. Edited by P. R. Ackroyd and C. F. Evans. Cambridge: Cambridge University Press, 1970.
Bonner, Stanley F. *Education in Ancient Rome: From the Elder Cato to the Younger Pliny*. Berkeley and Los Angeles: University of California Press, 1977.
Booth, Wayne C. *The Rhetoric of Fiction*. 2nd ed. Chicago and London: University of Chicago Press, 1983.
Bornkamm, Günther, Gerhard Barth, and Heinz Joachim Held. *Tradition and Interpretation in Matthew*. Philadelphia: Westminster Press, 1963.
Botha, Jan. "On the 'Reinvention' of Rhetoric." *Scriptura* 31 (1989): 14–31.
Bowker, J. W. "Speeches in Acts: A Study in Proem and *Yelammedenu* Form." *NTS* 14 (1967): 96–111.
Boys, Mary C. "Parabolic Ways of Teaching." *BTB* 13 (1983): 82–89
Braaten, Carl E. "Scripture, Church, and Dogma." *Int* 50 (1996): 142–55.

Brandenburger, Egon. *Markus 13 und die Apokalyptik*. FRLANT 134. Göttingen: Vanden-
hoeck & Ruprecht, 1984.
Brawley, Robert L. *Text to Text Pours Forth Speech: Voices of Scripture in Luke–Acts*. Bloomington
and Indianapolis: Indiana University Press, 1995.
Bright, Pamela, ed. and trans. *Augustine and the Bible*. Notre Dame, IN: University of Notre
Dame Press, 1999.
Brinton, Alan. "Situation in the Theory of Rhetoric." *PR* 14 (1981): 234–48.
Brodie, Thomas L. *The Gospel according to John: A Literary and Theological Commentary*. New
York and Oxford: Oxford University Press, 1993.
Brooks, Phillips. *On Preaching*. New York: Seabury Press, 1964.
Brown, Raymond E. *The Community of the Beloved Disciple*. New York and Ramsey, NJ: Paulist
Press, 1979.
———. *The Epistles of John: Translated with Introduction, Notes, and Commentary*. AB 30. Garden
City, NY: Doubleday, 1982.
———. *The Gospel according to John (xiii–xxi)*. AB 29A. Garden City, NY: Doubleday, 1970.
Brown, Schuyler. "The Mission to Israel in Matthew's Central Section (Mt. 9:35–11:1)."
ZNW 69 (1978): 73–90.
Browning, Don, ed. *Practical Theology*. San Francisco: Harper & Row, 1983.
Bruce, F. F. *The Acts of the Apostles: The Greek Text with Introduction and Commentary*. Grand
Rapids: Wm. B. Eerdmans Publishing Co., 1951.
———. *Commentary on the Book of Acts*. NICNT. Grand Rapids: Wm. B. Eerdmans Publish-
ing Co., 1954.
Bultmann, Rudolf. *Das Evangelium des Johannes*. Göttingen: Vandenhoeck & Ruprecht, 1966.
———. *Die Geschichte der synoptischen Tradition*. Göttingen: Vandenhoeck & Ruprecht, 1921.
ET, *History of the Synoptic Tradition*. Translated by John Marsh. New York: Harper &
Row, 1963.
———. *Der Stil der paulinischen Predigt und die kynisch-stoische Diatribe*. FRLANT 13. Göttingen:
Vandenhoeck & Ruprecht, 1910.
Burke, Kenneth. *A Rhetoric of Motives*. New York: Prentice-Hall, 1950.
———. *The Rhetoric of Religion: Studies in Logology*. Berkeley, Los Angeles, and London: Uni-
versity of California Press, 1970.
Burnett, Fred W. "Characterization and Reader Construction of Characters in the Gos-
pels." *Sem* 63 (1993): 3–28.
———. "Exposing the Anti-Jewish Ideology of Matthew's Implied Author: The Charac-
terization of God as Father." *Sem* 59 (1992): 155–91.
Burney, C. F. *The Aramaic Origin of the Fourth Gospel*. London: Clarendon Press, 1922.
Burton-Christie, Douglas. *The Word in the Desert: Scripture and the Quest for Holiness in Early
Christian Monasticism*. New York: Oxford University Press, 1993.
Buttrick, David. *Speaking Parables: A Homiletic Guide*. Louisville, KY: Westminster John Knox
Press, 2000.
Cadbury, Henry Joel. *The Making of Luke–Acts*. New York: Macmillan, 1927.
Cadman, W. H. *The Open Heaven: The Revelation of God in the Johannine Sayings of Jesus*. Edited
by G. B. Caird. New York: Herder & Herder, 1969.
Caird, G. B. *The Language and Imagery of the Bible*. Philadelphia: Westminster Press, 1980.
Carroll, John T. *The Gospel of Luke: A Commentary*. NTL. Louisville, KY: Westminster John
Knox Press, 2012.
Case, Shirley Jackson. "John Mark." *ExpTim* 26 (1914–1915): 372–76.
Cassidy, Richard J. *Society and Politics in the Acts of the Apostles*. Maryknoll, NY: Orbis Books, 1987.
Cassiodorus Senator. *An Introduction to Divine and Human Readings*. Edited and translated by
Leslie Webber Jones. New York: W. W. Norton, 1946. Repr. 1969.

Cavadini, John C. "The Sweetness of the Word: Salvation and Rhetoric in Augustine's *De doctrina christiana*." Pages 164–81 in *De doctrina christiana: A Classic of Western Culture*. Edited by Duane W. H. Arnold and Pamela Bright. Notre Dame, IN, and London: University of Notre Dame Press, 1995.

Cavalletti, Sofia. "The Parable Method and Catechesis." *AfER* 26 (1984): 88–91.

Charlesworth, James H., ed. *John and Qumran*. London: Chapman, 1972.

Chase, F. H. "Mark (John)." Pages 245–46 in vol. 3 of *Dictionary of the Bible*. Edited by James Hastings. Edinburgh: T&T Clark, 1909.

Chatman, Seymour. *Story and Discourse: Narrative Structure in Fiction and Film*. Ithaca, NY, and London: Cornell University Press, 1978.

Childers, Jana. *Performing the Word: Preaching as Theatre*. Nashville: Abingdon Press, 1998.

Clark, Donald L. *Rhetoric in Greco-Roman Education*. New York: Columbia University Press, 1957.

Clarke, M. L. *Higher Education in the Ancient World*. London: Routledge & Kegan Paul, 1971.

———. *Rhetoric at Rome: A Historical Survey*. Revised by D. H. Berry. London and New York: Routledge, 1996.

Cohen, Ralph, ed. "Changing Views of Character." Special issue, *New Literary History* 5, no. 2 (1974).

Colani, Timothy. *Jésus Christ et les croyances messianiques de son temps*. 2nd ed. Strasbourg: Treuttel & Wurtz, 1864.

Collins, Adela Yarbro. "The Apocalyptic Rhetoric of Mark 13 in Historical Context." *BR* 41 (1996): 5–36.

———. *The Beginning of the Gospel: Probings of Mark in Context*. Minneapolis: Fortress Press, 1992.

Collins, John J. "Towards a Morphology of Genre." *Sem* 14 (1979): 2–20.

Conley, Thomas M. *Philo's Rhetoric: Studies in Style, Composition and Exegesis*. CHS 1. Berkeley: Center for Hermeneutical Studies, 1987.

Connor, W. Robert, ed. *Greek Orations, 4th Century B.C.: Lysias, Isocrates, Demosthenes, Aeschines, Hyperides, and Letter of Philip*. Prospect Heights, IL: Waveland Press, 1987.

Conzelmann, Hans. *Acts of the Apostles: A Commentary on the Acts of the Apostles*. Hermeneia. Philadelphia: Fortress Press, 1987.

Corbett, Edward P. J., and Robert J. Connors. *Classical Rhetoric for the Modern Student*. 4th ed. New York: Oxford University Press, 1998.

Coren, Alan. *Chocolate and Cuckoo Clocks: The Essential Alan Coren*. Edited by Giles Coren and Victoria Coren. Edinburgh and London: Canongate, 2008.

Cotter, Wendy J. *The Christ of the Miracle Stories: Portrait through Encounter*. Grand Rapids: Baker Academic, 2010.

Craddock, Fred B. *As One without Authority*. 3rd ed. Nashville: Abingdon Press, 1978.

———. *Preaching*. Nashville: Abingdon Press, 1985.

Crafton, Jeffrey A. "The Dancing of an Attitude: Burkean Rhetorical Criticism and the Biblical Interpreter." Pages 429–42 in *Rhetoric and the New Testament: Essays from the 1992 Heidelberg Conference*. Edited by Stanley E. Porter and Thomas H. Olbricht. JSNTSup 90. Sheffield: Sheffield Academic Press, 1993.

Cross, F. L., and E. A. Livingstone, eds. *The Oxford Dictionary of the Christian Church*. 3rd ed. Oxford: Oxford University Press, 1997.

Culpepper, R. Alan. *Anatomy of the Fourth Gospel: A Study in Literary Design*. FF. Philadelphia: Fortress Press, 1983.

———. "Paul's Mission to the Gentile World: Acts 13–19." *RevExp* 71 (1974): 487–97.

Culpepper, R. Alan, and C. Clifton Black, eds. *Exploring the Gospel of John in Honor of D. Moody Smith*. Louisville, KY: Westminster John Knox Press, 1996.

Culpepper, R. Alan, and Fernando F. Segovia, eds. *The Fourth Gospel from a Literary Perspective.* SemeiaSt 53. Atlanta: Society of Biblical Literature, 1991.

Cunningham, Mary B., and Pauline Allen, eds. *Preacher and Audience: Studies in Early Christian and Byzantine Homiletics.* NHS 1. Leiden, Boston, and Cologne: E. J. Brill, 1998.

Cuppy, Will. *The Decline and Fall of Practically Everybody.* New York: Dorset Press, 1992.

Darr, John A. "Narrator as Character: Mapping a Reader-Oriented Approach to Narration in Luke–Acts." *Sem* 63 (1993): 43–60.

———. *On Character Building: The Reader and the Rhetoric of Characterization in Luke–Acts.* Louisville, KY: Westminster/John Knox Press, 1992.

Daube, David. *The New Testament and Rabbinic Judaism.* Salem, NH: Ayer, 1984.

———. "Rabbinic Methods of Interpretation and Hellenistic Rhetoric." *HUCA* 22 (1949): 239–64.

Davis, H. Grady. *Design for Preaching.* Philadelphia: Fortress Press, 1958.

Dawsey, James M. *The Lukan Voice: Confusion and Irony in the Gospel of Luke.* Macon, GA: Mercer University Press, 1986.

Dawson, David. *Allegorical Readers and Cultural Revision in Ancient Alexandria.* Berkeley: University of California Press, 1992.

Deed, Alexander, Walter Homolka, and Heinz-Günther Schöttler, eds. *Preaching in Judaism and Christianity: Encounters and Developments from Biblical Times to Modernity.* Berlin: W. de Gruyter, 2008.

Derrett, J. Duncan M. *Law in the New Testament.* London: Darton, Longman & Todd, 1970.

Descamps, Albert, and André de Halleux, eds. *Mélanges bibliques en hommage au R. P. Béda Rigaux.* Duculot: Gembloux, 1970.

Dewey, Joanna. *Markan Public Debate: Literary Technique, Concentric Structure, and Theology in Mark 2:1–3:6.* SBLDS 48. Chico, CA: Scholars Press, 1980.

Diggel, James, ed. *Theophrastus: Characters.* Cambridge: Cambridge University Press, 2004.

Docherty, Thomas. *Reading (Absent) Character: Towards a Theory of Characterization in Fiction.* Oxford: Clarendon Press, 1983.

Dodd, C. H. "The First Epistle of John and the Fourth Gospel." *BJRL* 21 (1937): 129–56.

———. *The Interpretation of the Fourth Gospel.* Cambridge: Cambridge University Press, 1953.

———. *The Parables of the Kingdom.* Rev. ed. New York: Charles Scribner's Sons, 1961.

Donahue, John R. *The Gospel in Parable: Metaphor, Narrative, and Theology in the Synoptic Gospels.* Philadelphia: Fortress Press, 1988.

———. "Windows and Mirrors: The Setting of Mark's Gospel." *CBQ* 57 (1995): 1–26.

Edwards, Richard A. "Characterization of the Disciples as a Feature of Matthew's Narrative." Pages 1305–23 in vol. 2 of *The Four Gospels, 1992: Festschrift Frans Neirynck.* Edited by F. van Segbroeck, C. M. Tuckett, G. van Belle, and J. Verheyden. BETL 100. Leuven: Leuven University Press / Peeters, 1992.

———. "Uncertain Faith: Matthew's Portrait of the Disciples." Pages 47–61 in *Discipleship in the New Testament.* Edited by Fernando F. Segovia. Philadelphia: Fortress Press, 1985.

Einstein, Albert. *Mein Weltbild.* 2nd ed. Amsterdam: Querido, 1934.

English, E. E., ed. *Reading and Wisdom: The "De doctrina christiana" of Augustine in the Middle Ages.* Notre Dame, IN, and London: University of Notre Dame Press, 1995.

Epstein, E. L. *Language and Style.* London: Methuen, 1978.

Eriksson, Anders, Thomas H. Olbricht, and Walter Übelacker, eds. *Rhetorical Argumentation in Biblical Texts: Essays from the Lund 2000 Conference.* Harrisburg, PA: Trinity Press International, 2002.

Ervin, Sam. J., Jr. *Humor of a Country Lawyer.* Chapel Hill and London: University of North Carolina Press, 1983.

Evans, C. F. "'Speeches' in Acts." Pages 287–302 in *Mélanges bibliques en hommage au R. P. Béda Rigaux.* Edited by Albert Descamps and André de Halleux. Duculot: Gembloux, 1970.

————. *The Theology of Rhetoric: The Epistle to the Hebrews*. London: Dr. Williams's Trust, 1988.

Fant, Clyde E. *Preaching for Today*. New York: Harper & Row, 1975.

Festugière, A.-J. *Observations stylistiques sur l'Évangile de S. Jean*. ÉC 84. Paris: Éditions Klincksieck, 1974.

Finan, Thomas. "St Augustine on the 'mira profunditas' of Scripture: Texts and Contexts." Pages 163–99 in *Scriptural Interpretation in the Fathers: Letter and Spirit*. Edited by Thomas Finan and Vincent Twomey. Dublin: Four Courts Press, 1995.

Finan, Thomas, and Vincent Twomey, eds. *Scriptural Interpretation in the Fathers: Letter and Spirit*. Dublin: Four Courts Press, 1995.

Fishbane, Michael, ed. *The Midrashic Imagination: Jewish Exegesis, Thought, and History*. New York: State University of New York Press, 1993.

Fitzmyer, Joseph A. *The Gospel according to Luke (X–XXIV)*. AB 28A. Garden City, NY: Doubleday, 1985.

Flexner, Stuart Berg, et al., eds. *The Random House Dictionary of the English Language*. 2nd ed., unabridged. New York: Random House, 1987.

Forbes, Christopher. "Comparison, Self-Praise and Irony: Paul's Boasting and the Conventions of Hellenistic Rhetoric." *NTS* 32 (1986): 1–30.

Forster, E. M. *Aspects of the Novel*. San Diego, New York, and London: Harcourt Brace Jovanovich, 1955.

Foss, Sonja K., Karen A. Foss, and Robert Trapp, eds. *Contemporary Perspectives on Rhetoric*. 2nd ed. Prospect Heights, IL: Waveland Press, 1991.

Fowl, Stephen E., ed. *The Theological Interpretation of Scripture: Classic and Contemporary Texts*. Malden, MA, and Oxford: Blackwell, 1997.

Frye, Northrop. *The Great Code: The Bible and Literature*. New York and London: Harcourt Brace Jovanovich, 1982.

Funk, Robert W. *Language, Hermeneutic, and Word of God: The Problem of Language in the New Testament and Contemporary Theology*. New York: Harper & Row, 1966.

Gardner, Helen. *The Business of Criticism*. Oxford: Clarendon Press, 1959.

Garland, David E. *The Intention of Matthew 23*. NovTSup 52. Leiden: E. J. Brill, 1979.

Gasque, W. Ward, and Ralph P. Martin, eds. *Apostolic History and the Gospel: Biblical and Historical Essays Presented to F. F. Bruce on His Sixtieth Birthday*. Grand Rapids: Wm. B. Eerdmans Publishing Co., 1970.

Gaventa, Beverly R. *The Acts of the Apostles*. ANTC. Nashville: Abingdon Press, 2003.

Geest, Hans van der. *Presence in the Pulpit: The Impact of Personality in Preaching*. Atlanta: John Knox Press, 1981.

Gerhardsson, Birger. "Illuminating the Kingdom: Narrative *Meshalim* in the Synoptic Gospels." Pages 266–309 in *Jesus and the Oral Gospel Tradition*. Edited by Henry Wansbrough. JSNTSup 64. Sheffield: Sheffield Academic Press, 1991.

Gitay, Yehoshua. *Prophecy and Persuasion: A Study of Isaiah 40–48*. Bonn: Linguistica Biblica, 1981.

Goosen, D. P. "The Rhetoric of the Scapegoat: A Deconstructive View on Postmodern Hermeneutics." Pages 383–92 in *Rhetoric, Scripture and Theology: Essays from the 1994 Pretoria Conference*. Edited by Stanley E. Porter and Thomas H. Olbricht. JSNTSup 131. Sheffield: Sheffield Academic Press, 1996.

Grant, Robert M. *The Earliest Lives of Jesus*. New York: Harper & Brothers, 1961.

Grayston, Kenneth. *The Johannine Epistles*. NCB. Grand Rapids: Wm. B. Eerdmans Publishing Co.; London: Marshall, Morgan & Scott, 1984.

————. "The Study of Mark XIII." *BJRL* 56 (1974): 371–87.

Green, Joel B. *The Gospel of Luke*. NICNT. Grand Rapids: Wm. B. Eerdmans Publishing Co., 1997.

Green, Jonathan, ed. *The Book of Political Quotes*. New York: McGraw Hill, 1982.

Green, R. P. H., ed. and trans. *Augustine: De doctrina christiana*. Oxford: Clarendon Press, 1995.

Greimas, A.-J. *Semantique structurale: Recherche de methode*. Paris: Larousse, 1966.

Griffith, Jennifer D. "The Death of the Critic." Page 2 of *The New York Times Book Review*. June 25, 2000.

Haenchen, Ernst. *The Acts of the Apostles: A Commentary*. Philadelphia: Westminster Press, 1971.

Haraguchi, Takaaki. "A Call for Repentance to the Whole Israel: A Rhetorical Study of Acts 3:12–26." *AsJT* 18 (2004): 267–82.

Harner, Philip B. *The "I Am" of the Fourth Gospel: A Study in Johannine Usage and Thought*. FBBS 26. Philadelphia: Fortress Press, 1970.

Harris, Edward M. "Law and Oratory." Pages 130–50 in *Persuasion: Greek Rhetoric in Action*. Edited by Ian Worthington. London and New York: Routledge, 1994.

Hartman, Lars. *Prophecy Interpreted: The Formation of Some Jewish Apocalyptic Texts and of the Eschatological Discourse Mark 13 Par*. ConBNT 1. Lund: Gleerup, 1966.

Harvey, W. J. *Character and the Novel*. London: Chatto & Windus, 1965.

Hastings, James, ed. *Dictionary of the Bible*. Edinburgh: T&T Clark, 1909.

Hatina, Thomas R., ed. *The Gospel of Matthew*. Vol. 2 of *Biblical Interpretation in Early Christian Gospels*. London: T&T Clark, 2008.

Hauerwas, Stanley. *A Community of Character: Toward a Constructive Christian Social Ethic*. Notre Dame and London: University of Notre Dame Press, 1981.

Hellholm, David, ed. *Apocalypticism in the Mediterranean World and the Near East*. 2nd ed. Tübingen: Mohr (Siebeck), 1989.

Hendrickx, Herman. *The Parables of Jesus*. Rev. ed. London: Geoffrey Chapman; San Francisco: Harper & Row, 1986.

Herbert, A. S. "The 'Parable' (*MĀŠĀL*) in the Old Testament." *SJT* 7 (1954): 180–96.

Herrick, James A. *The History and Theory of Rhetoric: An Introduction*. Boston: Allyn & Bacon, 1998.

Hester, James D., and J. David Hester (Amador), eds. *Rhetorics and Hermeneutics: Wilhelm Wuellner and His Influence*. ESEC 9. New York: T&T Clark International, 2004.

Hilgert, Earle. "Speeches in Acts and Hellenistic Canons of Historiography and Rhetoric." Pages 83–109 in *Good News in History: Essays in Honor of Bo Reicke* [†]. Edited by Ed. L. Miller. Atlanta: Scholars Press, 1993.

Hill, David. "The Figure of Jesus in Matthew's Story: A Response to Professor Kingsbury's Literary-Critical Probe." *JSNT* 21 (1984): 37–52.

―――. "Son and Servant: An Essay on Matthean Christology." *JSNT* 6 (1980): 2–16.

Hill, Edmund, trans. *Saint Augustine: The Trinity*. Edited by John E. Rotelle. WSA. Brooklyn: New City, 1991.

Hochman, Baruch. *Character in Literature*. Ithaca, NY, and London: Cornell University Press, 1985.

Hock, Ronald F., and Edward N. O'Neil, eds. *The Chreia and Ancient Rhetoric: Classroom Exercises*. WGRW 2. Leiden: E. J. Brill, 2002.

Hogan, Derek. "Paul's Defense: A Comparison of the Forensic Speeches in Acts, [*Chaereas and*] *Callirhoe*, and *Leucippe and Clitophon*." *PRSt* 29 (2002): 73–87.

Hoitenga, Dewey J., Jr. "Faith Seeks Understanding: Augustine's Alternative to Natural Theology." Pages 295–304 in *Augustine: Presbyter Factus Sum*. Edited by Joseph T. Lienhard, Earl C. Muller, and Roland J. Teske. Collectanea Augustiniana. New York: Peter Lang, 1993.

Holland, Glenn S. *The Tradition That You Received from Us: 2 Thessalonians in the Pauline Tradition*. HUT 24. Tübingen: Mohr (Siebeck), 1988.

Holmes, B. T. "Luke's Description of John Mark." *JBL* 54 (1935): 63–72.

Hooker, Morna D. "Trial and Tribulation in Mark XIII." *BJRL* 65 (1982): 78–99.

Horn, Friedrich Wilhelm, and Ruben Zimmermann, eds. *Jenseits von Indikativ und Imperativ: Kontexte und Normen neutestamentlicher Ethik.* Vol. 1. Tübingen: Mohr Siebeck, 2009.

Howard, Wilbert Francis. *The Fourth Gospel in Recent Criticism and Interpretation.* 4th ed. Revised by C. K. Barrett. London: Epworth, 1955.

Hultgren, Arland. *The Parables of Jesus: A Commentary.* Grand Rapids and Cambridge: Wm. B. Eerdmans Publishing Co., 2000.

Hyde, Michael J., and Craig R. Smith. "Hermeneutics and Rhetoric: A Seen but Unobserved Relationship." *QJS* 65 (1979): 347–63.

Irwin, Terence, ed. *Aristotle: Nicomachean Ethics.* Indianapolis: Hackett Publishing Co., 1985.

Jackson, F. J. Foakes, and Kirsopp Lake, eds. *The Acts of the Apostles.* Part 1 of vol. 4 of *The Beginnings of Christianity.* London: Macmillan, 1922.

Jackson, Jared J., and Martin Kessler, eds. *Rhetorical Criticism: Essays in Honor of James Muilenburg.* PTMS 1. Pittsburgh: Pickwick Press, 1974.

James, Henry. "The Art of Fiction." *Longman's Magazine* 4 (September 1884). Repr. in *Partial Portraits.* London: Macmillan, 1888. http://public.wsu.edu/~campbelld/amlit/artfiction.html.

———. *The Portrait of a Lady.* New York: Scribner, 1908. 2nd ed. Edited by Robert D. Bamberg. NCE. New York and London: W. W. Norton, 1995.

Jebb, R. C., ed. *The Characters of Theophrastus: An English Translation from a Revised Text, with Introduction and Notes.* London and Cambridge: Macmillan, 1870.

Jefford, Clayton N. "Mark, John." *ABD* 4 (1992): 557–58.

Jeremias, Joachim. *The Parables of Jesus.* 2nd rev. ed. New York: Charles Scribner's Sons, 1972.

Jervell, Jacob. *Luke and the People of God.* Minneapolis: Augsburg, 1972.

Jewett, Robert. *Romans: A Commentary.* Hermeneia. Minneapolis: Fortress Press, 2007.

———. *The Thessalonian Correspondence: Pauline Rhetoric and Millenarian Piety.* FF. Philadelphia: Fortress Press, 1986.

Johnson, Luke Timothy. *The Acts of the Apostles.* SP 5. Collegeville, MN: Liturgical Press, 1992.

———. *The Gospel of Luke.* SP 3. Collegeville, MN: Liturgical Press, 1991.

———. *The Literary Function of Possessions in Luke–Acts.* SBLDS 37. Missoula, MT: Scholars Press, 1977.

Jones, Leslie Webber, ed. and trans. *Cassiodorus Senator: An Introduction to Divine and Human Readings.* New York: W. W. Norton, 1969.

Juel, Donald H. *A Master of Surprise: Mark Interpreted.* Minneapolis: Fortress Press, 1994.

Jülicher, Adolf. *Die Gleichnisreden Jesu.* 2nd ed. 2 vols. Tübingen: Mohr (Siebeck) 1899. Repr. Darmstadt: Wissenchaftliche Buchgesellschaft, 1963.

Kafka, Franz. *Parables and Paradoxes: In German and English.* Translated by E. Kaiser and E. Wilkins. New York: Schocken Books, 1961.

Käsemann, Ernst. *The Testament of Jesus: A Study of the Gospel of John in the Light of Chapter 17.* London: SCM; Philadelphia: Fortress Press, 1968.

Keck, Leander E. *The Bible in the Pulpit: The Renewal of Biblical Preaching.* Nashville: Abingdon Press, 1978.

———. "Toward a Theology of Rhetoric/Preaching." Pages 126–47 in *Practical Theology.* Edited by Don Browning. San Francisco: Harper & Row, 1983.

Keck, Leander E., and J. Louis Martyn, eds. *Studies in Luke–Acts: Essays Presented in Honor of Paul Schubert.* Nashville: Abingdon Press, 1966.

Kee, Howard Clark. *Good News to the Ends of the Earth: The Theology of Acts.* London: SCM; Philadelphia: Trinity Press International, 1990.

Keener, Craig S. "Some Rhetorical Techniques in Acts 24:2–21." Pages 221–51 in *Paul's World*. Edited by Stanley E. Porter. PS 4. Leiden and Boston: E. J. Brill, 2008.

Kellum, L. Scott. *The Unity of the Farewell Discourse: The Literary Technique of John 13:31–16:33*. JSNTSup 256. London and New York: T&T Clark, 2004.

Kennedy, George A. *Aristotle: On Rhetoric; A Theory of Civic Discourse*. New York and Oxford: Oxford University Press, 1991.

———. *The Art of Persuasion in Greece*. Princeton: Princeton University Press, 1963.

———. *The Art of Rhetoric in the Roman World, 300 B.C.–A.D. 300*. Princeton: Princeton University Press, 1972.

———. *Classical Rhetoric and Its Christian and Secular Tradition from Ancient to Modern Times*. Chapel Hill: University of North Carolina Press, 1980.

———. *Greek Rhetoric under Christian Emperors*. Princeton: Princeton University Press, 1983.

———. *A History of Rhetoric*. Princeton: Princeton University Press, 1963–83.

———, ed. *Invention and Method: Two Rhetorical Treatises from the Hermogenic Corpus*. WGRW 15. Atlanta: Society of Biblical Literature, 2005.

———. *A New History of Classical Rhetoric*. Princeton: Princeton University Press, 1994.

———. *New Testament Interpretation through Rhetorical Criticism*. Chapel Hill and London: University of North Carolina Press, 1984.

———, trans. *Progymnasmata: Greek Textbooks of Prose Composition and Rhetoric*. WGRW 10. Atlanta: Society of Biblical Literature, 2003.

———. *Quintilian*. TWAS. New York: Twayne Publishers, 1969.

———. "Theophrastus and Stylistic Distinctions." *HSCP* 62 (1957): 93–104.

Kingsbury, Jack Dean. "The Developing Conflict between Jesus and the Jewish Leaders in Matthew's Gospel: A Literary-Critical Study." *CBQ* 49 (1987): 57–73.

———. "The Figure of Jesus in Matthew's Story: A Literary-Critical Probe." *JSNT* 21 (1984): 3–36.

———. *Matthew*. 2nd rev. ed. PC. Philadelphia: Fortress Press, 1986.

———. *Matthew as Story*. 2nd rev. ed. Philadelphia: Fortress Press, 1988.

———. "On Following Jesus: The 'Eager' Scribe and the 'Reluctant' Disciple (Matthew 8.18–22)." *NTS* 34 (1988): 45–59.

———. "The Verb *Akolouthein* ('To Follow') as an Index of Matthew's View of His Community." *JBL* 97 (1978): 56–73.

Kinneavy, James L. *Greek Rhetorical Origins of Christian Faith: An Inquiry*. New York and Oxford: Oxford University Press, 1987.

Kloppenborg, John S. "The Dishonoured Master (Luke 16,1–8a)." *Bib* 70 (1989): 479–95.

Knowles, Michael P. "Plotting Jesus: Characterization, Identity and the Voice of God in Matthew's Gospel." Pages 119–32 in *The Gospel of Matthew*. Vol. 2 of *Biblical Interpretation in Early Christian Gospels*. Edited by Thomas R. Hatina. London: T&T Clark, 2008.

Kort, Wesley A. *Story, Text, and Scripture: Literary Interests in Biblical Narrative*. University Park and London: Pennsylvania State University Press, 1988.

Krentz, Edgar. "Community and Character: Matthew's Vision of the Church." *SBLSP* 26 (1987): 565–73.

Krodel, Gerhard A. *Acts*. ACNT. Minneapolis: Augsburg Publishing House, 1986.

Kurz, William S. *Farewell Addresses in the New Testament*. Collegeville, MN: Liturgical Press, 1990.

———. "Hellenistic Rhetoric in the Christological Proof of Luke–Acts." *CBQ* 42 (1980): 171–95.

Kustas, George L. *Studies in Byzantine Rhetoric*. AnVlad 17. Thessaloniki: Patriarchal Institute for Patristic Studies, 1973.

Kysar, Robert. "The Fourth Gospel: A Report on Recent Research." *ANRW* 2.25.3 (1985): 2389–2480.

Lambrecht, Jan. *Die Redaktion der Markus-Apokalypse: Literarische Analyse und Strukturuntersuchung.* AnBib 28. Rome: Pontifical Institute, 1967.

Landry, David, and Ben May. "Honor Restored: New Light on the Parable of the Prudent Steward (Luke 16:1–8a)." *JBL* 119 (2000): 287–309.

Lausberg, Heinrich. *Handbook of Literary Rhetoric: A Foundation for Literary Study.* Edited by David E. Orton and R. Dean Anderson. Translated by Matthew T. Bliss, Annemiek Jansen, and David E. Orton. Leiden, Boston, and Cologne: E. J. Brill, 1998.

———. "Der Johannes-Prolog: Rhetorische Befunde zu Form und Sinn des Textes." Pages 191–279 (= No. 5) in the series Nachrichten der Akademie der Wissenschaften in Göttingen, I, Philologisch-Historisch Klasse, 1984. Göttingen: Vandenhoeck & Ruprecht, 1984.

Leon, Judah Messer. *The Book of the Honeycomb's Flow.* Ithaca, NY, and London: Cornell University Press, 1982.

Lerner, Alan Jay, and Frederick Loewe. *My Fair Lady: A Musical Play in Two Acts Based on "Pygmalion" by Bernard Shaw.* New York: Coward–McCann, 1956.

Lestang, François. "À la louange de dieu inconnu: Analyse rhétorique de Ac 17.22–31." *NTS* 52 (2006): 394–408.

Levine, Amy-Jill. *The Social and Ethnic Dimensions of Matthean Salvation History.* Lewistown, NY; Queenston, ON; and Lampeter: Edwin Mellen Press, 1988.

Levine, Lee I. *Ancient Jewish Synagogues: The First Thousand Years.* New Haven, CT: Yale University Press, 2000.

Lienhard, Joseph T., Earl C. Muller, and Roland J. Teske, eds. *Augustine: Presbyter Factus Sum.* Collectanea Augustiniana: New York: Peter Lang, 1993.

Lieu, Judith M. *The Theology of the Johannine Epistles.* NTT. Cambridge and New York: Cambridge University Press, 1991.

Lightfoot, R. H. *The Gospel Message of St. Mark.* Oxford: Clarendon Press, 1950.

Lischer, Richard. "The Limits of Story." *Int* 38 (1984): 26–38.

———. *A Theology of Preaching: The Dynamics of the Gospel.* Nashville: Abingdon Press, 1981.

Long, Thomas G. *Preaching and the Literary Forms of the Bible.* Philadelphia: Fortress Press, 1989.

———. *The Witness of Preaching.* Louisville, KY: Westminster John Knox Press, 1989.

Longenecker, Bruce W. "Evil at Odds with Itself (Matthew 12:22–29): Demonising Rhetoric and Deconstructive Potential in the Matthean Narrative." *BibInt* 11 (2003): 503–14.

———. "Lukan Aversion to Humps and Hollows: The Case of Acts 11:27–12:25." *NTS* 50 (2004): 185–204.

Louw, J. P. "On Johannine Style." *Neot* 20 (1986): 5–12.

Lowry, Eugene L. *The Homiletical Plot: The Sermon as Narrative Art Form.* Expanded ed. Louisville, KY: Westminster John Knox Press, 2001.

———. *How to Preach a Parable: Design for Narrative Sermons.* Nashville: Abingdon Press, 1989.

Lund, Nils W. *Chiasmus in the New Testament: A Study in Formgeschichte.* Chapel Hill: University of North Carolina Press, 1942. Repr. Peabody, MA: Hendrickson Publishers, 1992.

Luz, Ulrich. "Die Jünger im Matthausevangelium." *ZNW* 62 (1971): 141–71.

———. *The Theology of the Gospel of Matthew.* NTT. Cambridge: Cambridge University Press, 1995.

MacIntyre, Alasdair. *After Virtue: A Study in Moral Theory.* 2nd ed. Notre Dame, IN: University of Notre Dame Press, 1984.

Mack, Burton L., and Vernon K. Robbins. *Patterns of Persuasion in the Gospels.* Sonoma, CA: Polebridge Press, 1989.

Malbon, Elizabeth Struthers, and Adele Berlin, eds. *Characterization in Biblical Literature.* SemeiaSt 63. Atlanta: Scholars Press, 1993.

Marcus, Joel. "The Jewish War and the *Sitz im Leben* of Mark." *JBL* 111 (1992): 441–62.
———. *The Mystery of the Kingdom of God.* SBLDS 90. Atlanta: Scholars Press, 1986.
Marrou, H. I. *A History of Education in Antiquity.* London and New York: Sheed & Ward, 1956.
Marshall, I. Howard. *The Gospel of Luke: A Commentary on the Greek Text.* NIGTC. Grand Rapids: Wm. B. Eerdmans Publishing Co., 1978.
Martin, Michael W. *Judas and the Rhetoric of Comparison in the Fourth Gospel.* Sheffield: Phoenix, 2010.
Martin, Wallace. *Recent Theories of Narrative.* Ithaca, NY, and London: Cornell University Press, 1986.
Marxsen, Willi. *Der Evangelist Markus: Studien zur Redaktionsgeschichte des Evangeliums.* Göttingen: Vandenhoeck & Ruprecht, 1956.
Maxwell, Kathy Reiko. "The Role of the Audience in Ancient Narrative: Acts as a Case Study." *ResQ* 48 (2006): 171–80.
McCracken, David. "Character in the Boundary: Bakhtin's Interdividuality in Biblical Narratives." *Sem* 63 (1993): 29–42.
Meer, Frederik van der. *Augustine the Bishop: The Life and Work of a Father of the Church.* London and New York: Sheed & Ward, 1961.
Meier, John P. *The Vision of Matthew: Christ, Church, and Morality in the First Gospel.* New York; Ramsey, NJ; and Toronto: Paulist, 1979.
Menoud, P. H., and Oscar Cullman, eds. *Aux sources de la tradition chrétienne: Mélanges offerts à M. Maurice Goguel.* Neuchâtel: Delachaux & Niestlé, 1950.
Metzger, Bruce M. *A Textual Commentary on the Greek New Testament.* 2nd ed. Stuttgart: Deutsche Bibelgesellschaft / United Bible Societies, 1994.
Meyendorff, John. *St. Gregory Palamas and Orthodox Spirituality.* Crestwood, NY: St. Vladimir's Seminary Press, 1974.
Meyer, Paul W. Review of Hans Dieter Betz, *Galatians: A Commentary on Paul's Letter to the Churches in Galatia. RelSRev* 7 (1981): 318–23.
———. "The This-Worldliness of the New Testament." *PSB* 2 (1979): 219–31.
Miller, Ed. L., ed. *Good News in History: Essays in Honor of Bo Reicke* [†]. Atlanta: Scholars Press, 1993.
Miller, Joseph M., Michael H. Proser, and Thomas W. Benson, eds. *Readings in Medieval Rhetoric.* Bloomington and London: Indiana University Press, 1973.
Millett, Paul. *Theophrastus and His World.* CCJSV 33. Cambridge: Cambridge Philological Society, 2007.
Minear, Paul S. "The Disciples and the Crowds in the Gospel of Matthew." *AThR* Supplement 3 (1974): 28–44.
Mitchell, Margaret M. *The Heavenly Trumpet: John Chrysostom and the Art of Pauline Interpretation.* Louisville, KY: Westminster John Knox Press, 2002.
———. *Paul and the Rhetoric of Reconciliation: An Exegetical Investigation of the Language and Composition of 1 Corinthians.* Louisville, KY: Westminster/John Knox Press, 1991.
Moule, C. F. D. *An Idiom Book of New Testament Greek.* 2nd ed. Cambridge: Cambridge University Press, 1959.
Moulton, James Hope. *Prolegomena.* Vol. 1 of *A Grammar of New Testament Greek.* 3rd ed. Edinburgh: T&T Clark, 1957.
Moulton, James Hope, and Wilbert Francis Howard. *Accidence and Word Formation.* Vol. 2 of *A Grammar of New Testament Greek.* 3rd ed. Edinburgh: T&T Clark, 1929.
Moxnes, Halvor. *The Economy of the Kingdom: Social Conflict and Economic Relations in Luke's Gospel.* OBT. Philadelphia: Fortress Press, 1988.
Mrázek, Jiří, and Jan Roskovec, eds. *Testimony and Interpretation: Early Christology in Its Judaeo-Hellenistic Milieu; Studies in Honour of Petr Pokorný.* London and New York: T&T Clark International, 2004.

Muilenburg, James. "The Book of Isaiah, Chapters 40–66: Introduction and Exegesis." Pages 381–773 in vol. 5 of *IB*. New York: Abingdon Press, 1956.

———. "Form Criticism and Beyond." *JBL* 88 (1969): 1–18.

Munck, Johannes. "Discours d'adieu dans le Nouveau Testament et dans la littérature biblique." Pages 155–70 in *Aux sources de la tradition chrétienne: Mélanges offerts à M. Maurice Goguel*. Edited by P. H. Menoud and Oscar Cullman. Neuchâtel: Delachaux & Niestlé, 1950.

Murphy, James J. *Rhetoric in the Middle Ages: A History of Rhetorical Theory from St. Augustine to the Renaissance*. Berkeley, Los Angeles, and London: University of California Press, 1974.

Nadeau, Raymond, ed. and trans. "Hermogenes, *On Stases*: A Translation with an Introduction and Notes." *SM* 31 (1964): 361–424.

Nineham, Dennis E. *The Gospel of St. Mark*. PGC. Baltimore: Penguin Books, 1963.

Norden, Eduard. *Agnostos Theos: Untersuchungen zur Formgeschichte religiöser Rede*. Leipzig: Teubner, 1913.

———. *Die antike Kunstprosa vom VI. Jahrhunderts vor Christus in die Zeit der Renaissance*. Leipzig: Teubner, 1909.

O'Brien, Kelli S. "Written That You May Believe: John 20 and Narrative Rhetoric." *CBQ* 67 (2005): 284–302.

Okure, Teresa. *The Johannine Approach to Mission: A Contextual Study of John 4:1–42*. WUNT 2, no. 31. Tübingen: Mohr (Siebeck), 1988.

Olbricht, Thomas H., and Anders Eriksson, eds. *Rhetoric, Ethic, and Moral Persuasion in Biblical Discourse: Essays from the 2002 Heidelberg Conference*. New York: T&T Clark, 2005.

Olson, Elder. *Tragedy and the Theory of Drama*. Detroit: Wayne State University Press, 1961.

Oporto, Santiago Guijarro. "La articulación literaria del Libro de los Hechos." *EstBíb* 62 (2004): 185–204.

Osborn, Ronald E. *Folly of God: The Rise of Christian Preaching*. HCP 1. St. Louis: Chalice, 1999.

Palamas, Gregory. *The Triads*. Edited by John Meyendorff. Translated by Nicholas Gendle. CWS. Mahwah, NJ: Paulist Press, 1983.

Parker, Pierson. "The Authorship of the Second Gospel." *PRSt* 5 (1978): 4–9.

Parsenios, George L. *Departure and Consolation: The Johannine Farewell Discourses in Light of Greco-Roman Literature*. NovTSup 117. Leiden and Boston: E. J. Brill, 2005.

Parsons, Mikeal C., and Richard I. Pervo. *Rethinking the Unity of Luke and Acts*. Minneapolis: Fortress Press, 1993.

Paul, G. J. *St. John's Gospel: A Commentary*. Madras: Christian Literature Society, 1965.

Pedersen, Sigfred, ed. *New Directions in Biblical Theology: Papers of the Aarhus [Århus] Conference, 16–19 September 1992*. NovTSup 76. Leiden, New York, and Cologne: E. J. Brill, 1994.

Pelikan, Jaroslav. *Divine Rhetoric: The Sermon on the Mount as Message and as Model in Augustine, Chrysostom, and Luther*. Crestwood, NY: St. Vladimir's Seminary Press, 2001.

Penner, Todd C. *In Praise of Christian Origins: Stephen and the Hellenists in Lukan Apologetic History*. New York and London: T&T Clark / Continuum, 2004.

———. "Reconfiguring the Rhetorical Study of Acts: Reflections on the Method in and Learning of a Progymnastic Poetics." *PRSt* 30 (2003): 425–39.

Perelman, Chaïm. *The Realm of Rhetoric*. Translated by William Kluback. Notre Dame, IN, and London: University of Notre Dame Press, 1982.

Perelman, Chaïm, and Lucie Olbrechts-Tyteca. *The New Rhetoric: A Treatise on Argumentation*. Notre Dame, IN: University of Notre Dame Press, 1969.

Perkins, Pheme. *The Johannine Letters*. NTM 21. Wilmington, DE: Michael Glazier, 1979.

Pervo, Richard I. *Acts: A Commentary*. Edited by Harold W. Attridge. Hermeneia. Minneapolis: Fortress Press, 2009.

Pesch, Rudolf. *Das Markusevangelium*. 2nd ed. 2 vols. HTKNT. Freiberg, Basel, and Wien: Herder, 1980.

———. *Naherwartungen: Tradition und Redaktion in Mk 13*. KBANT. Düsseldorf: Patmos, 1968.

Phillips, Thomas. "Subtlety as a Literary Technique in Luke's Characterization of Jews and Judaism." Pages 313–26 in *Literary Studies in Luke–Acts: Essays in Honor of Joseph B. Tyson*. Edited by Richard P. Thompson and Thomas E. Phillips. Macon, GA: Mercer University Press, 1998.

Pilgaard, Aage. "Apokalyptik als bibeltheologisches Thema: Dargestellt an Dan 9 und Mark 13." Pages 180–200 in *New Directions in Biblical Theology: Papers of the Aarhus [Århus] Conference, 16–19 September 1992*. Edited by Sigfred Pedersen. NovTSup 76. Leiden, New York, and Cologne: E. J. Brill, 1994.

Popp, Thomas. *Grammatik des Geists: Literarische Kunst und theologische Konzeption in Johannes 3 and 6*. ABG 3. Leipzig: Evangelische Verlagsanstalt, 2001.

Porter, Stanley, ed. *Handbook of Classical Rhetoric in the Hellenistic Period, 330 B.C.–A.D. 400*. Leiden, New York, and Cologne: E. J. Brill, 1997.

———, ed. *Paul's World*. PS 4. Leiden and Boston: E. J. Brill, 2008.

Porter, Stanley, and Thomas H. Olbricht, eds. *Rhetoric and the New Testament: Essays from the 1992 Heidelberg Conference*. JSNTSup 90. Sheffield: Sheffield Academic Press, 1993.

———. *Rhetoric, Scripture and Theology: Essays from the 1994 Pretoria Conference*. JSNTSup 131. Sheffield: Sheffield Academic Press, 1996.

———. *The Rhetorical Analysis of Scripture: Essays from the 1995 London Conference*. JSNTSup 146. Sheffield: Sheffield Academic Press, 1997.

Porter, Stanley E., and Dennis L. Stamps, eds. *The Rhetorical Interpretation of Scripture: Essays from the 1996 Malibu Conference*. JSNTSup 180. Sheffield: Sheffield Academic Press, 1999.

Pregeant, Russell. "The Wisdom Passages in Matthew's Story." Pages 197–232 in *Treasures New and Old: Recent Contributions to Matthean Studies*. Edited by David R. Bauer and Mark Allan Powell. SBLSymS 1. Atlanta: Scholars Press, 1996.

Price, Martin. *Forms of Life: Character and Moral Imagination in the Novel*. New Haven, CT, and London: Yale University Press, 1983.

Rabe, Hugo, ed. *Hermogenes: Opera*. Leipzig: Teubner, 1913.

Reagan, Charles E., and David Stewart, eds. *The Philosophy of Paul Ricoeur: An Anthology of His Work*. Boston: Beacon Press, 1978.

Rhoads, David, and Donald Michie. *Mark as Story: An Introduction to the Narrative of a Gospel*. Philadelphia: Fortress Press, 1982. 2nd ed., coauthored with Joanna Dewey. Minneapolis: Fortress Press, 1999.

Riches, John, and David Sim, eds. *Matthew in Its Roman Imperial Context*. London: T&T Clark, 2005.

Ricoeur, Paul. "Listening to the Parables of Jesus." Pages 239–45 in *The Philosophy of Paul Ricoeur: An Anthology of His Work*. Edited by Charles E. Reagan and David Stewart. Boston: Beacon Press, 1978.

Robbins, Vernon K. *Exploring the Texture of Texts: A Guide to Socio-Rhetorical Interpretation*. Valley Forge, PA: Trinity Press International, 1996.

———. "From Heidelberg to Heidelberg: Rhetorical Interpretation of the Bible at Seven 'Pepperdine' Conferences from 1991–2002." Pages 335–77 in *Rhetoric, Ethic, and Moral Persuasion in Biblical Discourse: Essays from the 2002 Heidelberg Conference*. Edited by Thomas H. Olbricht and Anders Eriksson. New York: T&T Clark, 2005.

———. *Jesus the Teacher: A Socio-Rhetorical Interpretation of Mark*. Philadelphia: Fortress Press, 1984. Repr. with a new introduction, Minneapolis: Fortress Press, 1992.

————. *New Boundaries in Old Territory: Form and Social Rhetoric in Mark*. Edited by David B. Gowler. New York: Peter Lang, 1994.

————. *The Tapestry of Early Christian Discourse: Rhetoric, Society, and Ideology*. London: Routledge, 1996.

Robertson, D. W., Jr., trans. *Augustine: On Christian Doctrine*. LLA 80. New York: Liberal Arts Press, 1958.

Rorty, Amélie Oksenberg, ed. *Essays on Aristotle's Rhetoric*. Berkeley, Los Angeles, and London: University of California Press, 1996.

Rosen, Charles. Letter to *The New York Review of Books* 39 (April 9, 1992): 54.

Rotelle, John E., ed. *Saint Augustine: The Trinity*. Translated by Edmund Hill. WSA 1.11. Brooklyn, NY: New City Press, 1991. Repr. Hyde Park, NY: New City Press, 1996, 2007.

Rowland, Christopher. *The Open Heaven: A Study of Apocalyptic in Judaism and Early Christianity*. New York: Crossroad Publishing Co., 1982.

Russell, Donald A. *Criticism in Antiquity*. Berkeley and Los Angeles: University of California Press, 1981.

————, ed. *"Longinus": On the Sublime*. Oxford: Clarendon Press, 1964.

Russell, Donald A., and Nigel G. Wilson, eds. *Menander Rhetor*. Oxford: Clarendon Press, 1981.

Russell, Donald A., and Michael Winterbottom, eds. *Ancient Literary Criticism: The Principal Texts in New Translations*. Oxford and New York: Oxford University Press / Clarendon Press, 1972.

————. *Classical Literary Criticism*. Rev. ed. OWC. Oxford and New York: Oxford University Press, 1989.

Sanders, Jack T. *The Jews in Luke–Acts*. Philadelphia: Fortress Press, 1987.

Schipper, Jeremy. *Parables and Conflict in the Hebrew Bible*. New York: Cambridge University Press, 2009.

Schnackenburg, Rudolf. *The Gospel according to St. John*. Vol. 1. New York: Crossroad Publishing Co., 1982.

————. *The Johannine Epistles: Introduction and Commentary*. New York: Crossroad Publishing Co., 1992.

Schneiders, Sandra M. *The Revelatory Text: Interpreting the New Testament as Sacred Scripture*. San Francisco: HarperCollins, 1991.

Scholes, Robert, and Robert Kellogg. *The Nature of Narrative*. London: Oxford University Press, 1966.

Schüssler Fiorenza, Elisabeth. "Challenging the Rhetorical Half-Turn: Feminist and Rhetorical Biblical Criticism." Pages 28–53 in *Rhetoric, Scripture and Theology: Essays from the 1994 Pretoria Conference*. Edited by Stanley E. Porter and Thomas H. Olbricht. JSNTSup 131. Sheffield: Sheffield Academic Press, 1996.

————. "The Ethics of Interpretation: De-Centering Biblical Scholarship." *JBL* 107 (1988): 3–17.

————. "The Phenomenon of Early Christian Apocalyptic: Some Reflections on Method." Pages 295–316 in *Apocalypticism in the Mediterranean World and the Near East*. Edited by David Hellholm. 2nd ed. Tübingen: Mohr (Siebeck), 1989.

————. "Rhetorical Situation and Historical Reconstruction in 1 Corinthians." *NTS* 33 (1987): 386–403.

————. *Rhetoric and Ethic: The Politics of Biblical Studies*. Minneapolis: Augsburg Fortress, 1999.

Schweizer, Eduard. "Concerning the Speeches in Acts." Pages 208–16 in *Studies in Luke–Acts: Essays Presented in Honor of Paul Schubert*. Edited by Leander E. Keck and J. Louis Martyn. Nashville: Abingdon Press, 1966.

————. *Egō Eimi: Die religionsgeschtliche Herkunft und theologische Bedeutung der johanneischen Bildreden, zugleich ein Beitrag zur Quellenfrage des vierten Evangeliums*. FRLANT, NF 38. Göttingen: Vandenhoeck & Ruprecht, 1939. 2nd ed. 1965.

————. "What about the Johannine 'Parables'?" Pages 208–19 in *Exploring the Gospel of John in Honor of D. Moody Smith*. Edited by R. Alan Culpepper and C. Clifton Black. Louisville, KY: Westminster John Knox Press, 1996.

Scott, Bernard Brandon. *Hear Then the Parable: A Commentary on the Parables of Jesus*. Minneapolis: Fortress Press, 1989.

Segbroeck, F., C. M. Tuckett, G. van Belle, and J. Verheyden, eds. *The Four Gospels, 1992: Festschrift Frans Neirynck*. Vol. 2. BETL 100. Leuven: Leuven University Press / Peeters, 1992.

Segovia, Fernando F., ed. *Discipleship in the New Testament*. Philadelphia: Fortress Press, 1985.

————. *The Farewell of the Word: The Johannine Call to Abide*. Minneapolis: Fortress Press, 1991.

Sensing, Timothy R. "Imitating the Genre of Parable in Today's Pulpit." *ResQ* 33 (1991): 193–207.

Shiner, Whitney. *Proclaiming the Gospel: First-Century Performance of Mark*. Harrisburg, London, and New York: Trinity Press International, 2003.

Sider, Ronald Dick. *Ancient Rhetoric and the Art of Tertullian*. Oxford: Oxford University Press, 1971.

Siegert, Folker. *Argumentation bei Paulus: Gezeigt an Rom. 9–11*. WUNT 34. Tübingen: Mohr (Siebeck), 1985.

————. "Homily and Panegyrical Sermon." Pages 421–43 in *Handbook of Classical Rhetoric in the Hellenistic Period, 330 B.C.–A.D. 400*. Edited by Stanley E. Porter. Boston and Leiden: E. J. Brill, 2001.

Simmonds, Andrew R. "'Woe to You . . . Hypocrites!' Re-reading Matthew 23:13–36." *BSac* 166 (2009): 336–49.

Smith, Daniel Lynwood. *The Rhetoric of Interruption: Speech-Making, Turn-Taking, and Rule-Breaking in Luke–Acts and Ancient Greek Narrative*. BZNW 193. Berlin and Boston: W. de Gruyter, 2012.

Smith, D. Moody. *First, Second, and Third John*. IBC. Louisville, KY: John Knox Press, 1991.

————. *Johannine Christianity: Essays on Its Setting, Sources, and Theology*. Columbia: University of South Carolina Press, 1984.

————. *John*. 2nd ed. PC. Philadelphia: Fortress Press, 1986.

————. *The Theology of the Gospel of John*. NTT. Cambridge: Cambridge University Press, 1995.

Sondheim, Stephen. *Finishing the Hat: Collected Lyrics (1954–1981) with Attendant Comments, Principles, Heresies, Grudges, Whines and Anecdotes*. New York: Knopf, 2010.

Spencer, F. Scott. *Acts*. Readings. Sheffield: Sheffield Academic Press, 1997.

Spilka, Mark. "Character as a Lost Cause." *Novel: A Forum on Fiction* 11 (1978): 197–217.

Springer, Mary Doyle. *A Rhetoric of Literary Character: Some Women of Henry James*. Chicago and London: University of Chicago Press, 1978.

Staley, Jeffrey Lloyd. *The Print's First Kiss: A Rhetorical Investigation of the Implied Reader in the Fourth Gospel*. SBLDS 82. Atlanta: Scholars Press, 1988.

Stamps, Dennis L. "Rhetorical Criticism and the Rhetoric of New Testament Criticism." *JLT* 6 (1992): 268–79.

Standaert, B. H. M. G. M. *L'Évangile selon Marc: Composition et genre litteraire*. Nijmegen: Stichting Studentenpers, 1978.

Stanton, Graham N. *A Gospel for a New People: Studies in Matthew*. Edinburgh: T&T Clark; Louisville, KY: Westminster/John Knox Press, 1992.

————. "The Origin and Purpose of Matthew's Gospel: Matthean Scholarship from 1945 to 1980." *ANRW* 2.25.3 (1985): 1889–1951.

Stauffer, Ethelbert. "Abschiedsreden." *RAC* 1 (1950): 29–35.

Steiner, George. *Real Presences*. Chicago: University of Chicago Press, 1989.

Stemberger, Günter. "Response [to Folker Siegert]." Pages 45–48 in *Preaching in Judaism and Christianity: Encounters and Developments from Biblical Times to Modernity*. Edited by Alexander Deed, Walter Homolka, and Heinz-Günther Schöttler. Berlin: W. de Gruyter, 2008.

Stern, David. "The Rabbinic Parable and the Narrative of Interpretation." Pages 78–95 in *The Midrashic Imagination: Jewish Exegesis, Thought, and History*. Edited by Michael Fishbane. New York: State University of New York Press, 1993.

Sternberg, Meir. *The Poetics of Biblical Narrative: Ideological Literature and the Drama of Reading*. Bloomington: Indiana University Press, 1985.

Stevenson, J., ed. *A New Eusebius: Documents Illustrating the History of the Church to AD 337*. Revised by W. H. C. Frend. London: SPCK, 1987.

Stewart-Sykes, Alistair. *From Prophecy to Preaching: A Search for the Origins of the Christian Homily*. VCSup 59. Leiden, Boston, Cologne: E. J. Brill, 2001.

Stibbe, Mark W. G. "The Elusive Christ: A New Reading of the Fourth Gospel." Pages 231–47 in *The Gospel of John as Literature: An Anthology of Twentieth-Century Perspectives*. Edited by Mark W. G. Stibbe. NTTS 17. Leiden and New York: E. J. Brill, 1993.

———, ed. *The Gospel of John as Literature: An Anthology of Twentieth-Century Perspectives*. NTTS 17. Leiden and New York: E. J. Brill, 1993.

Stockhausen, Annette von. "Christian Perception of Jewish Preaching in Early Christianity?" Pages 49–70 in *Preaching in Judaism and Christianity: Encounters and Developments from Biblical Times to Modernity*. Edited by Alexander Deed, Walter Homolka, and Heinz-Günther Schöttler. Berlin: W. de Gruyter, 2008.

Stowers, Stanley K. *The Diatribe and Paul's Letter to the Romans*. SBLDS 57. Missoula, MT: Scholars Press, 1981.

Stube, John Carlson. *A Greco-Roman Rhetorical Reading of the Farewell Discourse*. LNTS 309. London and New York: T&T Clark, 2006.

Swearingen, C. Jan. "*Ethos*: Imitation, Impersonation, and Voice." Pages 115–48 in *Ethos: New Essays in Rhetorical and Critical Theory*. Edited by James S. Baumlin and Tita French Baumlin. Dallas: Southern Methodist University Press, 1994.

Swete, Henry Barclay. *The Gospel according to St Mark*. 3rd ed. London: Macmillan, 1927.

Syreeni, Kari. "*Incarnatus est?* Christ and Community in the Johannine Farewell Discourse." Pages 247–64 in *Testimony and Interpretation: Early Christology in Its Judaeo-Hellenistic Milieu; Studies in Honour of Petr Pokorný*. Edited by Jiří Mrázek and Jan Roskovec. London and New York: T&T Clark, 2004.

Talbert, Charles H. *Reading John: A Literary and Theological Commentary on the Fourth Gospel and the Johannine Epistles*. New York: Crossroad Publishing Co., 1992.

———. *Reading Luke: A Literary and Theological Commentary on the Third Gospel*. New York: Crossroad Publishing Co., 1982.

Tannehill, Robert C. *The Acts of the Apostles*. Vol. 2 of *The Narrative Unity of Luke–Acts: A Literary Interpretation*. Minneapolis: Fortress Press, 1990.

———. "The Disciples in Mark: The Function of a Narrative Role." *JR* 57 (1977): 386–405.

———. "Israel in Luke–Acts: A Tragic Story." *JBL* 104 (1985): 69–85.

———. *Luke*. ANTC. Nashville: Abingdon Press, 1996.

Taylor, Barbara Brown. *The Preaching Life*. Cambridge, MA: Cowley Publications, 1993.

Taylor, Robert O. P. "The Ministry of Mark." *ExpTim* 54 (1942–43): 136–38.

Taylor, Vincent. *The Formation of the Gospel Tradition*. 2nd ed. London and New York: Macmillan, 1935.

———. *The Gospel according to St. Mark: The Greek Text with Introduction, Notes, and Indexes*. 2nd ed. New York: Macmillan, 1966.

Telford, William. R. *The Barren Temple and the Withered Tree*. JSNTSup 1. Sheffield: JSOT, 1980.

Thatcher, Tom. "John's Memory Theater: The Fourth Gospel and Ancient Mnemo-rhetoric." *CBQ* 69 (2007): 487–505.

Theissen, Gerd, and Annette Merz. *The Historical Jesus: A Comprehensive Guide*. Minneapolis: Fortress Press, 1998.

Thielicke, Helmut. *The Waiting Father*. New York: Harper & Row, 1959.

Thielman, Frank. "The Style of the Fourth Gospel and Ancient Literary Critical Concepts of Religious Discourse." Pages 169–83 in *Persuasive Artistry: Studies in New Testament Rhetoric in Honor of George A. Kennedy*. Edited by Duane F. Watson. JSNTSup 50. Sheffield: Sheffield Academic Press, 1991.

Thompson, Marianne Meye. "'God's Voice You Have Never Heard, God's Form You Have Never Seen': The Characterization of God in the Gospel of John." *Sem* 63 (1993): 177–208.

Thompson, Richard P. "Believers and Religious Leaders in Jerusalem: Contrasting Portraits of Jews in Acts 1–7." Pages 327–44 in *Literary Studies in Luke–Acts: Essays in Honor of Joseph B. Tyson*. Edited by Richard P. Thompson and Thomas E. Phillips. Macon, GA: Mercer University Press, 1998.

Thompson, Richard P., and Thomas E. Phillips, eds. *Literary Studies in Luke–Acts: Essays in Honor of Joseph B. Tyson*. Macon, GA: Mercer University Press, 1998.

Thurber, James. *The Thurber Carnival*. Modern Library. New York Random House, 1957.

Thurén, Lauri. *The Rhetorical Strategy of 1 Peter, with Special Regard to Ambiguous Expressions*. Åbo: Åbo Akademis Förlag, 1990.

Thyen, Hartwig. *Der Stil der jüdisch-hellenistischen Homilie*. FRLANT 65 = NF 47. Göttingen: Vandenhoeck & Ruprecht, 1955.

Tilborg, Sjef van. *The Jewish Leaders in Matthew*. Leiden: E. J. Brill, 1972.

Tolbert, Mary Ann. *Sowing the Gospel: Mark's World in Literary-Historical Perspective*. Minneapolis: Fortress Press, 1989.

Toohey, Peter. "Epic and Rhetoric." Pages 153–73 in *Persuasion: Greek Rhetoric in Action*. Edited by Ian Worthington. London and New York; Routledge, 1994.

Trible, Phyllis. *Rhetorical Criticism: Context, Method, and the Book of Jonah*. GBSOT. Minneapolis: Fortress Press, 1994.

Tyson, Joseph B. *Images of Judaism in Luke–Acts*. Columbia: University of South Carolina Press, 1992.

————, ed. *Luke–Acts and the Jewish People: Eight Critical Perspectives*. Minneapolis: Augsburg Publishing House, 1988.

Vanhoozer, Kevin J. *Is There a Meaning in This Text? The Bible, the Reader, and the Morality of Literary Knowledge*. Grand Rapids: Zondervan Publishing House, 1998.

Vatz, Richard E. "The Myth of the Rhetorical Situation." *PR* 6 (1973): 154–61.

Via, Dan O., Jr. *Self-Deception and Wholeness in Paul and Matthew*. Minneapolis: Fortress Press, 1990.

Vickers, Brian. *In Defence of Rhetoric*. Oxford: Clarendon Press, 1988.

Wahlde, Urban C. von. *The Gospels and Letters of John*. 3 vols. ECC. Grand Rapids: Wm. B. Eerdmans Publishing Co., 2010.

————. *The Johannine Commandments: 1 John and the Struggle for the Johannine Tradition*. New York and Mahwah, NJ: Paulist Press, 1990.

Wailes, Stephen L. *Medieval Allegories of Jesus' Parables*. Berkeley: University of California Press, 1987.

Wainwright, Geoffrey. "Towards an Ecumenical Hermeneutic: How Can All Christians Read the Scriptures Together?" *Greg* 76 (1995): 639–62.

Walcutt, Charles Child. *Man's Changing Masks: Modes and Metaphors of Characterization in Fiction*. Minneapolis: University of Minnesota Press, 1966.

Wansbrough, Henry, ed. *Jesus and the Oral Gospel Tradition.* JSNTSup 64. Sheffield: Sheffield Academic Press, 1991.

Watson, Duane F. "Amplification Techniques in 1 John: The Interaction of Rhetorical Style and Invention." *JSNT* 51 (1993): 99–123.

———. *Invention, Arrangement, and Style: Rhetorical Criticism of Jude and 2 Peter.* SBLDS 104. Atlanta: Scholars Press, 1988.

———, ed. *Persuasive Artistry: Studies in New Testament Rhetoric in Honor of George A. Kennedy.* JSNTSup 50. Sheffield: Sheffield Academic Press, 1991.

———. *The Rhetoric of the New Testament: A Bibliographic Survey.* TBS 8. Blandford Forum: Deo, 2006.

Watson, Duane F., and Alan J. Hauser. *Rhetorical Criticism of the Bible: A Comprehensive Bibliography with Notes on History and Method.* Biblical Interpretation Series 4. Leiden, New York, and Cologne: E. J. Brill, 1994.

Watt, Jan Gabriel van der. "Johannine Style: Some Initial Remarks on the Functional Use of Repetition in the Gospel according to John." *In die Skriflig / In Luce Verbi* 42 (2008): 75–99.

Weaver, Dorothy Jean. "'Thus You Will Know Them by Their Fruits': The Roman Characters of the Gospel of Matthew." Pages 107–27 in *Matthew in Its Roman Imperial Context.* Edited by John Riches and David Sim. London: T&T Clark, 2005.

Webb, Joseph M. *Preaching without Notes.* Nashville: Abingdon Press, 2001.

Weeden, Theodore J., Sr. *Mark—Traditions in Conflict.* Philadelphia: Fortress Press, 1971.

Weems, Mason Locke. *The Life and Memorable Actions of George Washington, General and Commander of the Armies of America.* New ed., corrected. Fredericktown, MD: printed by M. Bartgis, 1801.

Westermann, Claus. *The Parables of Jesus in the Light of the Old Testament.* Minneapolis: Fortress Press, 1990.

Wilckens, Ulrich. "ὑποκρίνομαι." *TDNT* 8 (1972): 566–68.

Wilder, Amos N. *Early Christian Rhetoric: The Language of the Gospel.* Cambridge, MA: Harvard University Press, 1964.

———. *Jesus' Parables and the War of Myths: Essays on Imagination in the Scriptures.* Edited by James Breech. Philadelphia: Fortress Press, 1982.

———. *The New Voice: Religion, Literature, Hermeneutics.* New York: Herder & Herder, 1969.

———. "Scholars, Theologians, and Ancient Rhetoric." *JBL* 75 (1956): 1–11.

Wiles, Maurice. *The Spiritual Gospel: The Interpretation of the Fourth Gospel in the Early Church.* Cambridge: Cambridge University Press, 1960.

Wills, Gary. *Lincoln at Gettysburg: The Words That Remade America.* New York: Simon & Schuster, 1992.

Wills, Lawrence M. "The Depiction of the Jews in Acts." *JBL* 110 (1991): 631–54.

———. "The Form of the Sermon in Hellenistic Judaism and Early Christianity." *HTR* 77 (1984): 277–99.

Wilson, Paul Scott. *The Practice of Preaching.* Nashville: Abingdon Press, 1995.

Wilson, Rawdon. "The Bright Chimera: Character as a Literary Term." *CritInq* 5 (1979): 725–49.

Wire, Antoinette Clark. *The Case for Mark Composed in Performance.* BPC. Eugene, OR: Cascade Books, 2011.

———. *The Corinthian Women Prophets: A Reconstruction through Paul's Rhetoric.* Minneapolis: Fortress Press, 1990.

Witten, Marsha G. *All Is Forgiven: The Secular Message in American Protestantism.* Princeton: Princeton University Press, 1993.

Woods, James. *How Fiction Works.* New York: Farrar, Straus & Giroux, 2008.

Wooten, Cecil W. *Hermogenes' On Types of Style*. Chapel Hill and London: University of North Carolina Press, 1987.

Worthington, Ian, ed. *Persuasion: Greek Rhetoric in Action*. London and New York: Routledge, 1994.

Wright, William M., IV. "Greco-Roman Character Typing and the Presentation of Judas in the Fourth Gospel." *CBQ* 71 (2009): 544–59.

Wudel, B. Diane. "Enticements to Community: Formal, Agonistic and Destabilizing Rhetoric in the Sermon on the Mount." *SR* 29 (2000): 275–85.

Wuellner, Wilhelm. "Biblical Exegesis in the Light of the History and Historicity of Rhetoric and the Nature of the Rhetoric of Religion." Pages 492–513 in *Rhetoric and the New Testament: Essays from the 1992 Heidelberg Conference*. Edited by Stanley E. Porter and Thomas H. Olbricht. JSNTSup 90. Sheffield: Sheffield Academic Press, 1993.

———. "Hermeneutics and Rhetorics: From 'Truth and Method' to 'Truth and Power.'" Special issue, *Scriptura* 3 (1989): 1–54.

———. "Where Is Rhetorical Criticism Taking Us?" *CBQ* 49 (1987): 448–63.

Yeago, David S. "The New Testament and the Nicene Dogma: A Contribution to the Recovery of Theological Exegesis." Pages 87–100 in *The Theological Interpretation of Scripture: Classic and Contemporary Texts*. Edited by Stephen E. Fowl. Malden, MA, and Oxford: Blackwell, 1997.

Young, Frances M. *Biblical Exegesis and the Formation of Christian Culture*. Cambridge: Cambridge University Press, 1997.

Zimmermann, Ruben. "Die Ethico-Ästhetik der Gleichnisse Jesu: Ethik durch literarische Ästhetik am Beispiel der Parabeln im Matthäus-Evangelium." Pages 235–65 in vol. 1 of *Jenseits von Indikativ und Imperativ: Kontexte und Normen neutestamentlicher Ethik*. Edited by Friedrich Wilhelm Horn and Ruben Zimmermann. Tübingen: Mohr Siebeck, 2009.

Index of Scripture
and Other Ancient Sources

Index of Ancient Terms

Index of Modern Authors and Subjects

CPSIA information can be obtained at www.ICGtesting.com
Printed in the USA
LVOW06s0020290713

345047LV00002B/8/P